Colección Támesis
SERIE A: MONOGRAFÍAS, 166

LOVE POETRY OF THE LITERARY ACADEMIES
IN THE REIGNS OF PHILIP IV AND CHARLES II

JEREMY ROBBINS

LOVE POETRY OF THE LITERARY ACADEMIES
IN THE REIGNS OF PHILIP IV AND CHARLES II

TAMESIS

© Jeremy Robbins 1997

All Rights Reserved. Except as permitted under current legislation no part of this work may be photocopied, stored in a retrieval system, published, performed in public, adapted, broadcast, transmitted, recorded or reproduced in any form or by any means, without the prior permission of the copyright owner

First published 1997 by Tamesis, London

ISBN 1 85566 049 0

Tamesis is an imprint of Boydell & Brewer Ltd
PO Box 9, Woodbridge, Suffolk IP12 3DF, UK
and of Boydell & Brewer Inc.
PO Box 41026, Rochester, NY 14604–4126, USA

A catalogue record for this book is available
from the British Library

Library of Congress Cataloging-in-Publication Data
Robbins, Jeremy, 1965–
  Love poetry of the literary academies in the reigns of Philip IV and Charles II / Jeremy Robbins.
      p.   cm. – (Colección Támesis. Serie A, Monografías ; 166)
  Includes bibliographical references and index.
  ISBN 1–85566–049–0 (hc : alk. paper)
  1. Spanish poetry – Classical period, 1500–1700 – History and criticism. 2. Love poetry, Spanish – History and criticism.
  3. Spanish literature – Societies, etc. – Influence. 4. Spanish literature – Societies, etc. – History – 17th century. I. Title.
  PQ6066.R59   1997
  861'.309354 – dc20   96–42253

This publication is printed on acid-free paper

Printed in Great Britain by
St Edmundsbury Press Ltd, Bury St Edmunds, Suffolk

CONTENTS

Preface vii

Abbreviations viii

Introduction 1

1. "El seminario de los entendidos, el taller de los bien hablados, el colegio de los discretos": the academy and seventeenth-century Spain 7

2. The academy and the *justa poetica* 47

3. Academy topics and seventeenth-century love poetry 59
   - In praise of the specific 62
   - Anecdote and melodrama: the amatory scenario and academy topics 72
   - The casuistry of love: paradoxes, dilemmas and conundrums 86
   - Conclusion 96

4. From lyricism to performance: the poetic persona in academy love poetry 101

5. Unity and diversity: academy poetry and the disintegration of form 135

Works consulted 173

Index 193

PREFACE

I would like to thank the staff of the following libraries for their assistance: the Biblioteca Nacional, Madrid, the British Library, the Bodleian and Taylorian Institute, Oxford, the University of Edinburgh Library and, above all, the National Library of Scotland, without whose outstanding collection of Golden Age material this study would not have been possible. I am also grateful to the Carnegie Trust for the Universities of Scotland and the University of Edinburgh for grants in aid of publication. Various people have helped in numerous ways with this study. My thanks to Professor Trevor Dadson for discussing this work at its inception and for sending me academy material; to Professor John Varey for his careful comments on the work; to Dr Huw Lewis for obtaining microfilms from Madrid at short notice; and to Ms. Carmen Santos Maldonado, Dr Nicholas Hammond, Dr Robert Pring-Mill and Dr Colin Thompson who, in various ways and at various times, offered encouragement and advice. Above all I am indebted to David Ingham. This book is for him.

ABBREVIATIONS

AB	*Art Bulletin*
AEF	*Anuario de Estudios Filológicos*
BBMP	*Boletín de la Biblioteca Menéndez Pelayo*
BCom	*Bulletin of the Comediantes*
BH	*Bulletin Hispanique*
BHS	*Bulletin of Hispanic Studies*
BRAE	*Boletín de la Real Academia Española*
BSRS	*Bulletin of the Society for Renaissance Studies*
CSIC	*Consejo Superior de Investigaciones Científicas*
EHQ	*European History Quarterly*
HR	*Hispanic Review*
JHP	*Journal of Hispanic Philology*
JIRS	*Journal of the Institute of Romance Studies*
JWCI	*Journal of the Warburg and Courtauld Institutes*
MLN	*Modern Language Notes*
MLR	*Modern Language Review*
NLS	*National Library of Scotland*
NRFH	*Nueva Revista de Filología Hispánica*
PMLA	*Publications of the Modern Language Association of America*
RAE	*Real Academia Española*
RBAM	*Revista de la Biblioteca, Archivo y Museo*
RF	*Romanische Forschungen*
RFE	*Revista de Filología Española*
RH	*Revue Hispanique*
RHM	*Revista Hispánica Moderna*
RL	*Revista de Literatura*
RN	*Romance Notes*
RQ	*Romance Quarterly*
RR	*Romanic Review*

INTRODUCTION

Literary academies were one of the most prominent features of literary life in seventeenth-century Spain. All major cities and towns hosted them and all writers attended them, frequently on a regular basis. They provided the ideal meeting place for writers and nobles, becoming a centre for those seeking patronage. In their organization and atmosphere they developed and exploited the seventeenth-century love of theatre and public display: in many ways, they turned poetry into a dramatic performance and an entertaining spectacle. Their importance lies not only in the central role they played in the lives of seventeenth-century writers, but also in the profound effect they had on the direction taken by poetry over the course of the century. The majority of academy poems were love poems, and to neglect them means disregarding the last major development in amatory verse in the Golden Age.

Despite their prominence modern critics have either disregarded or dismissed literary academies, relegating them, when mentioned at all, to footnotes in biographical studies of individual writers. Only two book length studies written over thirty years ago treat the academy, and neither of these consider the poetry that was produced for them or the wider effects they had on poetry in the seventeenth century.[1] In recent years there has been a renewal of critical interest but this has tended to focus on profiling individual academies or on analysing academies in particular regions. Such studies are invaluable in providing historical, social, biographical and bibliographical information, and have made possible a study such as this. Surprisingly, though, there is still no detailed study of the academy as an institution expressly dedicated to the writing and enjoyment of poetry. My purpose is therefore twofold: to situate the poetry produced by academies within the institution which created it, in the belief that once we understand the expectations of those attending such events and hence their priorities in writing

---

[1] See José Sánchez, *Academias literarias del Siglo de Oro español* (Madrid: Gredos, 1961); and Willard F. King, *Prosa novelística y academias literarias del Siglo de Oro español* (Madrid: RAE, 1963). Sánchez's book is a study of individual academies across Spain, but is plagued with factual errors, and is thus often inaccurate and unreliable. Many of these errors are rectified by King, and her work remains indispensable. Her still valuable bibliography is supplemented by Julia Barella, "Bibliografía: Academias literarias", and Juan Delgado, "Bibliografía sobre justas poéticas" in *Edad de Oro*, 7 (1988), 189–95, 197–207.

poetry we are better placed to appreciate and evaluate that poetry; and to offer a detailed analysis of academy love poetry, considering especially those features, both stylistic and thematic, which are a direct result of being composed to meet the demands of a specific occasion.

The subject matter of all the poems discussed is, in the broadest sense, love, but the ways in which this subject is conceived, the treatment it receives and the attitudes adopted towards it by poets and their audiences are what makes love poetry in the academies distinctive to the point, I will argue, of constituting a discrete genre: academy love poetry. The present study aims to define this genre and to relate it to the broader trends in the practice of love poetry in the seventeenth century. Throughout I make no generic distinction between "serious" love poetry, and satirical, burlesque or parodic love poetry, treating all as equal manifestations of the academy poetic despite the obvious fact that each genre can be viewed as working according to its own, largely autonomous, established practices, poetic licence, and imitative models. Whilst I am aware that contemporary audiences/readers, much like modern critics, would have been aware of such generic differences and categories in their classification of poetry, it is part of my purpose to argue that the academy format itself serves to obscure such distinctions, with the result that the clear demarcation between genres which is expected in printed texts, and which, as a consequence, necessarily effects and shapes a reader's expectations and critical reception and evaluation of such poems, is seriously compromised by both the orality and the all-inclusive nature of a literary academy. In other words, whilst generic distinctions would have been noted, the fact that at one meeting poems were performed which ranged from serious Petrarchan subjects, through satire and scatological verse to eulogies on the royal family breaks down the evaluative and aesthetic hierarchy, the exclusivity which categories and genres serve to establish and enforce. I shall argue that the effects of this mixing of generically distinct poems, placed side by side in a single academy session, alters both implicitly and explicitly the fundamental nature and purpose of the Petrarchan project by a process of contamination and exposure. All genres and topics, however much they play with the rhetorical notions of authorial sincerity and however much they internally project a vision of the ideal receptive audience and, thereby, try to control the responses and interpretations of that audience, are ultimately reduced to the same level by the very catholicity of the academy as it developed in seventeenth-century Spain. Because of their compositional basis in an academy, poems are unavoidably revealed to be the products of necessity and artifice, however much they protest and proclaim the opposite.

As I have just indicated, literary academies did not simply compose love poetry. Whilst amatory verse predominated, it was common practice for academies to set a handful of topics on more elevated subject matters. To take an example: one academy in 1678, despite a preponderance of topics connected with love, also included poems on Hannibal poisoning himself, and on the qualities of the sun most necessary for a monarch to possess.[2] This said, academies devoted themselves in a more vigorous and sustained manner to the composition of amatory verse than to any other type of poetry. In a very real sense, therefore, academy poetry is synonymous with love poetry, albeit love poetry of a very particular and distinctive type.

Broadly speaking love poetry written for academies runs along a continuum from the openly jocular or satirical, through the trivial to the conventionally Petrarchan. A clear cut division between these three categories is rarely possible. The majority of compositions fall within the middle category, poems which treat mundane objects and incidents connected with or involving the lover and his lady. Although many such poems employ, recall and play with Petrarchan commonplaces, the location of such concepts and images in consummately trivial scenarios alters the high intent of the Petrarchan discourse as employed by generations of sixteenth- and seventeenth-century Spanish love poets, even though the poem in question may not be in the slightest bit humorous or parodic. The sheer triteness of subject matter means that these poems lack all gravity and consequently their impact tends to be somewhat comparable to that of the more overtly humorous poems. In part, then, the academies debased the Petrarchan discourse in so far as they take even further the practice which was wide spread in Europe at this time of deflecting Petrarchan idealism into the realm of mundane "reality". This debasement often brings to mind the way in which parody and burlesque also destroy the Petrarchan enterprise by revealing the gulf between theory and practice, amatory discourse and bodily passions. The result is that this middle ground on the academy spectrum, coming between openly burlesque poetry and traditional Petrarchan compositions, is very difficult to rigidly classify, for the same composition can veer between the two depending on how far it takes the particular topic into the realm of the novel, far-fetched and bizarre.

In line with this generic "confusion" is the fact that Italian and Spanish verse-forms are used indiscriminately. No one verse-form has a monopoly on a particular style or type of subject matter. The marked popularity of the *romance* arises because of the native tradition of using the verse-form for rapid narration, rather than lyrical description: it is the ideal form therefore in which to compose witty, quibbling poems, being unrestricted in length and hence capable of encompassing as many or as few of the poet's witticisms and conceits as he is capable of producing.[3] Equally the sonnet is popular precisely because of its brevity: in an institution setting such a premium on ready

---

[2] See *Real Aduana*, pp. 60–63, 46–51. All titles of academy volumes will be cited in abbreviated format, the forms used being given in the list of Works Consulted.

[3] Throughout this study I employ the masculine pronoun when referring to poets writing for academies since there is a marked absence of women composing for them, despite the fact that women attended and that they regularly submitted verse to the more public *justas poéticas*.

verbosity, the restrictions and limitations of the sonnet both test the poet and spare the audience. (The same can be said of the *décima* – with limited expansion being often restricted by the secretary stipulating precisely how many, or how few, stanzas to compose – and the *glosa*, normally a four line stanza thus automatically dictating the length of the ensuing gloss.)

One of the central concerns of the study is to place academy poetry within the wider context of seventeenth-century amatory verse. Time and again I shall have occasion to argue that academy poetry is not so much different in kind as in degree, the difference amounting primarily to one of emphasis and subtlety. Thus features which define academy poetry – its predatory sexuality, its dramatization of the trivial and the far-fetched, its excessive conceit spinning and its emphatic self-referentiality – are features which are by no means unique to poetry composed within this institutional context. In each instance, however, the thematic or stylistic trait is far more explicit, and hence far less simply the product of ingenious critical exegesis, than in non-academy verse. It is this degree of explicitness which leads me to describe academy poetry's essential quality as an absence of subtlety. This may seem surprising in an age which supposedly set so much store on subtlety as a crucial aesthetic quality, but, as we shall see, to judge or to characterize an entire century's verse by the example of Góngora or Quevedo is seriously to misrepresent both "normal" practice and, more importantly, contemporary taste – including Gracián's, whose *Agudeza y arte de ingenio* is always cited as the ultimate arbiter in matters of wit. However in no way am I claiming that academy verse is worthy of the same degree of attention as the verse of poets of the first rank like Góngora, Quevedo and Lope de Vega, or even of the second like Villamediana, Salinas, Bocángel or Hurtado de Mendoza. Academy poetry is worthy of attention not only in the interests of critical and literary accuracy and completeness but also as a means of beginning to recover a poetic, and hence a taste, which found its ultimate expression, for all the century's obeisance to Góngora's example, in the phenomenon of the literary academy. Familiarity with academy poetry is also valuable precisely because its own lack of subtlety lays bare the themes, stylistic mechanisms and organizational principles which are often occluded by a greater degree of poetic finesse, indirection, skill and artistry in seventeenth-century verse. This said, despite its aesthetic shortcomings and its obvious ephemerality, academy verse can be entertaining, ingenious, amusing and, occasionally, highly lyrical.

I have paid specific attention to regional academies, in particular those in Valencia, from the *Academia de los Nocturnos* at the close of the sixteenth century to the more theatrical academies held under the auspices of the viceroys at the close of the seventeenth. This broader context establishes, contrary to current critical opinion, both that the academy was not predominantly a Madrid-based phenomenon and that it did flourish in the second half of the century. The study also thereby offers an in-depth consideration of poetry across the Peninsula during the reign of Charles II, a forty year period entirely ignored in critical studies. The picture that emerges is of an academy style uniform across the country, albeit one that became increasingly theatrical and far-fetched in its subject matter as the century progressed. The academy emerges as an institution whose format and ethos exercised a powerful force which worked against poetic individuality and regional difference.

Two final points need to be made regarding the examples cited within the text. First, the spelling and punctuation of all quotations of academy verse have been modernized; printing errors have been silently corrected, but when the Spanish has been altered to make sense of a line this has been noted. Second, I have drawn on the accounts of some thirty literary academies, and I have considered the verse of over sixty poets to cite both identifiable academy poems and those which seem in all probability to have been composed for such occasions. However, within the body of the text I have tended to cite poems from a restricted number of these sources. The decision to do so is deliberate; given that it is one of the primary arguments of the book that the entire occasion – the full range of subjects, styles and registers – effected the reception of the individual poetic contributions, it seemed possible by partially restricting the range of sources from which complete poems were cited to gain a better impression of the nature or tone of specific individual academies and thereby to enable readers to gauge over the course of the study the prevailing atmosphere of an academy.

1

"EL SEMINARIO DE LOS ENTENDIDOS, EL TALLER DE LOS BIEN HABLADOS, EL COLEGIO DE LOS DISCRETOS": THE ACADEMY AND SEVENTEENTH-CENTURY SPAIN

It is impossible to understand academy poetry if it is divorced from the context which gave it its distinctive character. This is poetry shaped by a specific type of event and its poets never tire of telling us this. I shall therefore begin this chapter by outlining the format of the academy and drawing attention to its salient features. This descriptive function will highlight how the distinctive thematic and stylistic characteristics of academy poetry are the direct result of adapting and developing contemporary practice to the demands of the occasion. Furthermore it will convey an impression of the entertaining and diverting atmosphere of an academy, something which it is often all too difficult to appreciate when we read poems which were actually written to be recited, or performed, in front of an often boisterous and lively gathering. To assess academy poetry without attempting to recuperate and appreciate this important performative dimension is to ignore one of the key elements which differentiates it from other seventeenth-century poetry, since it ignores what actually makes such poetry academy poetry. We seriously misrepresent such poetry if we fail to treat it as essentially orally-delivered dramatic verse.

Literary academies were ubiquitous in seventeenth-century Spain: wherever two or three poets were gathered together, up sprang a literary academy. Madrid, Valencia, Zaragoza, Salamanca, Seville, Badajoz, Cadiz, Cordoba, Ciudad Real, Granada, Murcia, Toledo, and, in Spanish territories in Italy, Naples and Milan: all hosted literary academies. Seventeenth-century literary academies in Spain differed radically from their predecessors in Italy, from where the fashion came. Fifteenth-century Italian academies such as that instituted by Cosimo de' Medici and Marsilio Ficino were devoted primarily to serious intellectual discussion, as were their counterparts in sixteenth-century France.[1] By the seventeenth century, however, the academy in Spain

---

[1] For an overview of Italian academies see King, *Prosa*, 11–17; Sánchez, *Academias*, pp. 11–12; Eric Cochrane, "The Renaissance Academies in their Italian and European Setting", and Martin Lowry, "The Proving Ground: Venetian Academies of the Fifteenth and Sixteenth Centuries", both in *The Fairest Flower: The Emergence of Linguistic*

had become a purely literary phenomenon, in the sense that as an institution it existed solely for the pursuit and enjoyment of prose and poetry, and moreover poetry which was usually frivolous, light and superficial. Literary academies had existed in Spain in the sixteenth century, but only in the seventeenth century did they became a universal feature of the literary life of the country. One of the most prominent Renaissance academies was that held in Seville during the last quarter of the sixteenth century and presided over, in succession, by Juan de Mal Lara, Fernando de Herrera, Francisco de Medina and the two Francisco Pachecos (the older Pacheco, canon of Seville cathedral, was the uncle of the younger, the painter and theorist). This academy offers an interesting point of contrast with the academies of the next century since it differed from them in so far as its pursuits, whilst primarily literary, were also serious and intellectual. Testimony to the fundamentally intellectual nature of this group in Seville during its long history is provided by the fact that various important theoretical works published by its members, such as Herrera's *Anotaciones* (Seville, 1580) on the poetry of Garcilaso de la Vega and Francisco Pacheco's *Arte de la pintura* (published posthumously, Seville, 1649), are best seen, as Jonathan Brown has argued, as the products of the intellectual exchange characteristic of the academy.[2] In sharp contrast, seventeenth-century academies differed noticeably in their interests, usually cultivating wit rather than the intellect. Occasionally attempts were made to institute more intellectual academies, but these never seriously took off. Thus detailed proposals drafted around 1621 by Sebastián Francisco de Medrano, at this time also the organizer of the most famous seventeenth-century literary academy, the *Academia de Madrid*, to form an *Academia peregrina* never went further than the planning stages, possibly because its proposed format, dedicating each daily session to one of the seven liberal arts, was simply too rigorous and too distinct from the normal established pattern for such groups.[3]

National Consciousness in Renaissance Europe (Florence: Presso l'Accademia, 1985), pp. 21–39, 41–51; and François Quiviger, "The Italian Academies of the Sixteenth Century", *BSRS*, 12 (1995), 13–19. Also see Eric Cochrane, *Tradition and Enlightenment in the Tuscan Academies 1690–1800* (Rome: Edizioni di Storia e Letteratura, 1961); and James Hankins, "The Myth of the Platonic Academy of Florence", *RQ*, 44 (1991), 429–75. The basic work on French academies remains Frances A. Yates, *The French Academies of the Sixteenth Century* (London: Warburg Institute, 1947).

[2] For the cultural importance of this academy see Jonathan Brown, *Images and Ideas in Seventeenth-Century Spanish Painting* (Princeton: Princeton University Press, 1978), pp. 21–43. For a further discussion of Pacheco's academy, see Francisco Pacheco, *El arte de la pintura*, ed. by Bonaventura Bassegoda i Hugas (Madrid: Cátedra, 1990), Introduction, pp. 20–32. Also see José Sánchez, *Academias*, pp. 199–209. On Sevillian academies in general, see Joaquín Hazañas y la Rúa, *Noticias de las academias literarias, artísticas y científicas de Sevilla en los siglos XVII y XVIII* (Seville: C. de Torre, 1888).

[3] For the proposal, see Jaime Suárez Alvarez, "Los inéditos estatutos de 'La Peregrina', academia fundada y presidida por el Doctor Don Sebastián Francisco Medrano", *RBAM*, 16 (1947), 91–110. On this academy see Sánchez, *Academias*, pp. 113–16; and

Only at the start of the eighteenth century did the literary academies begin to evolve into what we now generally understand by this term, groups dedicated to the serious study of specific literary, scientific or artistic subjects.[4]

Once established as a permanent feature of the seventeenth-century literary scene, the form taken by academy meetings invariably followed the same pattern; only in the final decades of the century did the format alter significantly with the introduction of dancing and scripted dialogue between the session's organizers, creating thereby what one critic has referred to as "academias 'azarzueladas' ".[5] For the best part of a century, then, the academy was presided over by three nominated officials, a president, a secretary and a "fiscal", with the last two roles being the most important in terms of organizing the occasion. The President opened the proceedings with an oration, sometimes in prose but usually in verse, whose principle function was laudatory: the art of poetry in general and the individual academy in particular would be eulogized.[6] Such an oration was often the most serious or "academic" element of the entire event, with writers keen to show off not only their eloquence but also their learning.[7] (An example of such an oration, one delivered by José de Pellicer in 1635 to the *Academia de Madrid*, will be discussed below.) The oration was sometimes followed by the secretary reading out *cedulillas*, humorous petitions from fictional poets, or *pragmáticas*, a series of humorous rules and regulations – against *culterano* vocabulary, for example – which the participants were, in theory at least, supposed to follow

---

King, *Prosa*, pp. 55–57. The format, with its division into seven sections each with their own president, recalls the Valencian academy established towards the close of the century with various sections devoted to politics, mathematics, poetry, music and dance. See *Poética festiva*, pp. 11–14.

[4] The seventeenth century, broadly speaking, thus forms something of an interlude between the more serious pursuits of such bodies in the sixteenth and eighteenth centuries. For the transition from the Baroque to the Neoclassical academies, see Aurora Egido, "De las academias a la Academia", in *The Fairest Flower: The Emergence of Linguistic National Consciousness in Renaissance Europe* (Florence: Presso l'Accademia, 1985), pp. 85–94.

[5] See Pasqual Mas i Usó, "Academias ficticias valencianas durante el Barroco", *Criticón*, 61 (1994), 47–56 (p. 47). I shall discuss the role of theatricality in the academy in Chapter 4.

[6] For a recent consideration of this part of the academy, see Esther Lacadena y Calero, "El discurso oral en las academias del Siglo de Oro", *Criticón*, 41 (1988), 87–102.

[7] The prose *discursos* of a group such as the *Academia de los Nocturnos* (1591–94) reveal the academy's humanistic tendency to exhibit encyclopedic knowledge at the expense of either originality or scientific objectivity. The desire is to impress with accumulated references to established authorities, usually classical. On this point see Evangelina Rodríguez Cuadros, "Del saber cenacular a la Ilustración: el borrador enciclopédico de la Academia de los Nocturnos", in Rodríguez Cuadros (ed.), *De las academias a la enciclopedia: el discurso del saber en la modernidad* (Valencia: Institució Valenciana d'Estudis i Investigació, 1993), pp. 29–68 (p. 57). The academy does not preclude seriousness, therefore, though it is clear that the emphasis is on effect rather than intellectual investigation.

in their poetic submissions. Next came the poems composed on the topics and in the metres set at the previous meeting. From novelistic accounts of literary academies it seems that these were usually delivered by their authors, although sometimes the secretary himself might read them out, usually if the piece had been submitted anonymously or by a woman. On some occasions topics were given to specific poets, on others – those that more closely resembled the public poetry competitions, or *justas poéticas* – poets chose which topics they were going to write on, with the result that several pieces on the same theme might be submitted. The former was rapidly established as the standard procedure with specific topics being given to specific poets. This was presumably a source of heightened amusement and entertainment, not only fitting the topic to an individual's talents, but also challenging those talents by making the topic as abstruse as possible, or by choosing subjects to contrast with, or act as a mute commentary upon, poets' own lives, personalities and foibles. After the poetry the *fiscal* finally closed the meeting with a satirical *vejamen*.

The *vejamen* was an integral part of any academy session and its satirical nature is indicative of the tone and atmosphere of the entire occasion. The *vejamen* was a prose piece in which the *fiscal* – as his name implies – satirized and ridiculed each member of the academy in turn. The normal format taken by the *vejamen*, as Carrasco Urgoiti has indicated, was the dream or vision in which the *fiscal* meets, or is introduced to, the academy members.[8] This format provides him with a narrative rationale for producing what usually amounts to nothing more than a series of unconnected thumb-nail sketches of every poet, each sketch normally being rounded off with a short satirical stanza summarizing their literary or, more normally, their physical characteristics. Much of this prose is either pedestrian or, for modern readers, incomprehensible due to its topical but oblique allusions to poets whose biographic and/or bibliographic details are largely unknown to us. However, the *vejamen*, unique to the academy, is an important sub-genre of satirical prose: in the words of Carrasco Urgoiti, "el arte de la caricatura halla su clima más propicio en el salón literario".[9]

The overall light-hearted, humorous and satirical character of an academy meeting was thus intensified and encapsulated in miniature in the *vejamen*. A meeting which ended with a satirical portrayal of those attending could hardly hope to foster and sustain an atmosphere of seriousness. Indeed at times the

---

[8] The satirical narrative thread is usually provided by a journey ("al trasmundo" or to the moon), or by a guide who leads the *fiscal* on his satirical quest. For examples of the former see Pantaleón, *Obras*, ed. by Rafael de Balbín Lucas, 2 vols (Madrid: CSIC, 1944), II, pp. 11–44; and *Real Aduana*, 16 unfoliated pages at the close of the volume; and of the latter, see *Pascua de Reyes*, fols 44r–60v (corrected foliation). On the narrative situations used to justify the satirical accounts, see María Soledad Carrasco Urgoiti, "La oralidad del vejamen de academia", *Edad de Oro* 7 (1988), 49–57 (p. 54).

[9] See Carrasco Urgoiti, "Notas sobre el vejamen de academia en la segunda mitad del siglo XVII", *RHM*, 31 (1965), 97–111 (p. 98).

satirical tone overtook the entire occasion with poets delivering burlesque orations instead of the more normal hyperbolic encomia.[10] This is not to imply that all academy poetry is of a satirical or burlesque nature, simply that the formal embodiment of satire as an integral component of the academy format tended to set the tone of the entire proceedings. This tone was further compounded, of course, by the very competitiveness of the occasion. When several poems were submitted in a particular category they were often judged and graded, and prizes occasionally awarded. Even when this practice abated in the second half of the century, poems were still read out to an audience of fellow poets who were not necessarily sympathetic towards other academicians. The combination of competitiveness and satire could at times create a volatile situation, which could lead to violence. Francisco de Rojas Zorrilla's *vejamen* for the academy held in the Buen Retiro in February 1638, for example, caused such outrage that an assassination attempt on the poet later in the same year was attributed directly to the offence this had caused.[11] Similarly the academy presided over by the Count of Saldaña at the start of the century in Madrid broke up after a violent row between Pedro Soto de Rojas and Luis Vélez de Guevara split its members into two opposing factions.[12] Whilst such disturbances were the exception rather than the norm, they do indicate how the *vejamen* was often close to the bone and, given the egos of many of the poets in an age obsessed with reputation, the *fiscal* had to tread a thin line between satire and outright offence.

One aspect of an academy which it is impossible now to recuperate is the role which music played in the overall proceedings. The opening oration was often preceded by, and interspersed with, music and/or song. An account of an academy held in Ciudad Real in 1678, for example, begins with the following poem set to music:

> Cortesanos, oid los primores,
> en quien resplandece el ingenio sutil,
> y veréis que de Apolo en el templo
> se juntan los genios hoy a competir.
> Venid, venid,
> corred, volad, porque en esta lid
> el que mejor discurre

---

[10] See, for example, Jerónimo Cáncer y Velasco's oration, in *Obras varias poéticas* (Madrid: Manuel Martín, 1761), pp. 90–95.

[11] See Hannah E. Bergman, "A Court Entertainment of 1638", *HR*, 42 (1974), 67–81 (pp. 71–73); and "El «Juicio final de todos los poetas españoles muertos y vivos» (MS inédito) y el Certamen poético de 1638", *BRAE*, 55 (1975), 551–610 (pp. 567–68). The *vejamen* is printed as an appendix to Luis Vélez de Guevara, *El diablo cojuelo*, ed. by Adolfo Bonilla y San Martín (Vigo: Eugenio Krapf, 1902), pp. 262–71.

[12] See King, "The Academies and Seventeenth-Century Spanish Literature", *PMLA*, 75 (1960), 367–76 (p. 368); and Romera-Navarro, "Querellas y rivalidades en las academias del siglo XVII", *HR*, 9 (1941), 494–99 (p. 498).

> es quien el premio merece feliz.
> Volad, volad,
> suspended y parad,
> oiréis en dulces acentos
> el métrico son del entendimiento.[13]

Often there were musical interludes between compositions, as in the academy held under the auspices of the Marquis of Jamaica to celebrate the birthday of the Queen Regent in 1672.[14] Furthermore if novelistic accounts such as that given by Vélez de Guevara in his *El diablo cojuelo* (1641) or Castillo Solórzano in his *El tiempo de regocijo y carnestolendas de Madrid* (1627) are taken as accurate portrayals of literary academies, then meetings could also include verse set to music sung by academy members: in *El diablo*, three women, one playing the guitar, sing a *romance* by Antonio Hurtado de Mendoza;[15] whilst in *Tiempo* a humorous poem is sung by one of the participants.[16] The literary academy thus mobilized prose, poetry and music, but the essential element of these formalized occasions remained the performance of verse. This, then, is one of the central ways in which the academy is the product of a culture in which the theatrical, the performative, plays a central – indeed, I shall argue, a defining – role. Not only are topics clearly selected for their dramatic potential, but the fact that they are encountered orally together with their dramatic "performance" by their composers adds a dimension to academy verse entirely lost when it is encountered on the page.[17] The immediate and primary result of this emphasis on theatricality and performance in academy production is that, as in the theatre proper, poets aim to write so as to produce an immediate impact: academy verse is as it is primarily because it was necessarily a poetry of immediacy.

On occasion this element of theatricality threatened to overwhelm the entire event. For a *certamen* held in the Buen Retiro in 1638 the Italian theatrical designer Cosme Lotti had constructed a special stage upon which

---

[13] See *Ciudad Real*, fol. 1r.

[14] See *Jamaica*, passim.

[15] See *El diablo cojuelo*, ed. by Angel R. Fernández and Ignacio Arellano (Madrid: Castalia, 1988), pp. 214–15. All quotations are taken from this edition. Compare Gareth A. Davies, *A Poet at Court. Antonio Hurtado de Mendoza (1586–1644)* (Oxford: The Dolphin Book Co., 1971), pp. 200–01.

[16] See *"Las harpías en Madrid" y "Tiempo de regocijo"*, ed. by Emilio Cotarelo y Mori (Madrid: Librería de los Bibliófilos Españoles, 1907), pp. 363–65, on "un casado que comía y triunfaba sin tener renta alguna en la Corte" (p. 363). In *Las harpías* he similarly portrays an academy in the capital which is attended by "poetas, músicos, los mayores señores de la Corte". See *Las harpías en Madrid*, ed. by Pablo Jauralde Pou (Madrid: Castalia, 1985), p. 138. All future references are to this edition.

[17] Compare Carrasco Urgoiti who talks of the *vejamen* as a script performed by the *fiscal* and who comments on the probability that the *fiscal* would act out the physical characteristics of individual poets satirized in the *vejamen*. See "La oralidad", pp. 52–53.

the academy was performed as if it were literally a theatrical performance. On the stage a curtain was drawn back to reveal the forest of Diana; in the middle distance was the temple of Jupiter (decorated with paintings of the labours of Hercules, recalling the iconography of the Hall of Realms of the new palace with its paintings by Zurbarán); whilst beyond this was Parnassus:

> Y creciendo la admiración en tercero lugar, apareció el monte Parnaso tan expresado y delineado y de la manera que los poetas antiguos y modernos le dibujan y describen en sus poemas, presidiendo en él Apolo, que con su lira o cítara en la mano cantó con gran suavidad y melodía unos versos [. . .] Estuvieron los poetas laureados y haciendo su reverencia a la majestad de Apolo, refirieron los versos, que en conformidad del certamen habían escrito [. . .] Y para fiesta tan grande se desencajaron los planetas de sus orbes, y entraron en sus carros tan luminosos y arrogantes que bien se echó de ver en su grandeza y esplendor ser de los cielos.[18]

The setting for this academy, recalling the elaborate machine plays growing in popularity at Court in the 1630s, formalizes the innate theatricality of the academy format itself, but in so doing the poetry and *vejámenes* ran the real danger of being very much of secondary importance: the Jesuit newsletter which describes this *certamen* says next to nothing about the poetry – the supposed *raison d'être* of the whole occasion – and comments at great length on the wonder of the staging itself. Such overt theatricalization of the academy was not the norm, however, in seventeenth-century Spain. Only at the turn of the century in Valencia were academies regularly theatrical in conception, reaching their apogee in 1705 when the stage represented Arcadia and the members dressed as shepherds.[19]

For a fuller and more descriptive account of academy meetings we must turn from published and manuscript records of specific academy sessions which, given their nature, fail to give any real sense of the local colour and of the boisterous and entertaining atmosphere, to novelistic portrayals. In so far as these necessarily describe the occasion they enable a more rounded and accurate impression of what attending an actual academy session was really like. Appreciating the academy's format and its atmosphere helps us to understand its immense and enduring popularity. It also helps to explain why it practised and disseminated the type of poetry it did, since it seems clear that the context for which academy poetry was written and in which it was performed was one of the most decisive factors in shaping it, both stylistically and thematically.

---

[18] See Hannah E. Bergman, "El «Juicio final»", pp. 555–56. Gareth Davies takes this as an account of the 1637 *Academia burlesca* also held in the Retiro (*Poet at Court*, p. 62), but Bergman correctly argues that it describes a *certamen* held in the Retiro in 1638 ("El «Juicio final»", pp. 553–57).
[19] See *Señoras*, pp. 26–27.

Given the ubiquity of academies in seventeenth-century Spain and their immense popularity it is hardly surprising that they became a popular feature in many contemporary novels. These provide useful information on their character and atmosphere, thereby supplementing, by dramatizing, both the information we can glean from contemporary critics' assessments of them and the actual accounts of real academies which, by reducing the event to print, necessarily exclude the more ephemeral aspects of their setting, tone and theatrical format, all of which arguably contribute as much as – if not more than – the poetry itself. The accounts of academy sessions in such works as Alonso de Castillo Solórzano's *El tiempo de regocijo y carnestolendas de Madrid* (Madrid, 1627) and *Las harpías en Madrid, y coche de las estafas* (Barcelona, 1631), Gabriel de Corral's *La Cintia de Aranjuez* (Madrid, 1629), Diego Duque de Estrada's *Comentarios del desengañado de sí mismo*, Salvador Jacinto Polo de Medina's *Academias del jardín* (Madrid, 1630), Luis Vélez de Guevara's *El diablo cojuelo* (Madrid, 1641), Antonio Enríquez Gómez's *El siglo pitagórico* (Rouen, 1644), and José Camerino's *La dama beata* (Madrid, 1655), novels which describe meetings in places as diverse as Toledo, Madrid, Murcia, Seville and Naples, give the impression that seventeenth-century academies were lively and vigorous affairs which required of their members a keen mind, a high degree of mental agility, and a sharp and ready wit.[20] Duque de Estrada, for example, describes an academy meeting in Naples presided over by the Count of Lemos at which members were permitted to speak only in verse – any infringement of this rule being punished with a fine.[21] Moreover, the spontaneity and theatricality of an academy's proceedings are formalized in the Neapolitan session described by Duque de Estrada when the members decide to perform a "comedia de repente". This highlights the need for great acuity of mind as well as a flare for flamboyance and ostentation: in Dadson's words, "las academias alentaron un tipo de agudeza mental que obligó al poeta a pensar y contestar rápidamente ante la mirada crítica y sardónica de sus compañeros; el que tuviese esta facultad aseguraba su fama, al subrayar tan públicamente su ingenio".[22]

---

[20] In her *Prosa novelística* Willard King has convincingly argued that the form and content of much seventeenth-century prose was deeply influenced by the literary academy. She discusses in detail all these novels mentioned here. The academy as an institution is also parodied as early as 1605 in the first part of *Don Quijote* which closes with verses submitted to the "Academia de la Argamasilla, lugar de la Mancha" in praise of the life and deeds of the eponymous hero. See *El ingenioso hidalgo don Quijote de la Mancha*, ed. by Luis Andrés Murillo, 2 vols, 5th edn (Madrid: Castalia, 1987), I, pp. 605–08. Francisco Márquez Villanueva has recently argued that the *Viaje del Parnaso* is a "sorna monumental de las pretensiones pompas académicas". See "El retorno del Parnaso", *NRFH*, 38 (1990), 693–732 (p. 699).

[21] See Diego Duque de Estrada, *Comentarios del desengañado de sí mismo. Vida del mismo autor*, ed. by Henry Ettinghausen (Madrid: Castalia, 1982), p. 194.

[22] See Gabriel Bocángel, *La lira de las musas*, ed. by Trevor J. Dadson (Madrid: Cátedra, 1985), p. 80.

Some academy accounts such as Vélez de Guevara's in *El diablo cojuelo* have the members attend under pseudonyms, following – according to the novelist – Italian practice.[23] This was certainly the custom in a number of academies such as the famous Valencian *Academia de los Nocturnos* and the *Academia de Madrid*. In the former, picturesque names such as Silencio (Bernardo Catalán), Sombra (Gaspar Aguilar), Tristeza (Jaime Orts), Relámpago (Gaspar Mercader, Count of Buñol), and Cometa (Hernando de Balda) were adopted by the participants.[24] (The names used in the *Academia de Huesca* in 1610–12 were apparently adopted on the basis of them describing attributes of the writers concerned.[25]) In the *Academia de Madrid* the members used more prosaic and humorously nonsensical pseudonyms – some actual or partial anagrams – such as Lucido Intervalo (Alonso de Oviedo), Carinemo (José Camerino), Lisofeo Zeligerpio (José Pellicer), Coriandro (Gabriel de Corral), and Gelcambo (Gabriel Bocángel).[26] Again, this aspect is one that rarely enters into the published proceedings of individual meetings, except sometimes in the *vejamen*, and in the second half of the century rarely even there, such that it is difficult to know whether the practice fell into disuse or whether it was simply deemed inappropriate in published accounts. The sharp increase in the number of such accounts after 1650 suggests that this public (printed) exposure mitigated against concealing a poet's identity if he wished to take advantage of an opportunity to gain a reputation beyond the immediate circle of fellow academy members – as it appears many poets did. Certainly the use of pseudonyms is a further indication of the playful and, in a very real sense, performative nature of academy attendance. As well as such jocularity, of course, the use of assumed names adds to the academy's sense of

---

[23] Don Cleofás, the student hero, takes the name "el Engañado", whilst the limping devil calls himself "el Engañador". See *El diablo cojuelo*, p. 214.

[24] See *Academia de los Nocturnos*, I, pp. 55–57; and Pasqual Mas i Usó, "Poetas bajo nombres de pastores en *El Prado de Valencia* de Gaspar Mercader", *RL*, 197 (1992), 283–334. Compare the types of name which the Argamasilla academy adopted: El Monicongo, El Paniagudo, El Caprichoso, etc. See *Don Quijote*, I, pp. 605–06.

[25] See Sánchez, *Academias*, p. 262; King, *Prosa*, pp. 67–70.

[26] These are the names as printed by Pellicer in his edition of Pantaleón de Ribera's verse, and are taken from one of the latter's *vejámenes*. The real figures whose "dignity" is thus concealed by Pellicer are revealed in a manuscript of the same *vejamen*. See Pantaleón, *Obras*, II, pp. 11–44; and Kenneth Brown, *Anastasio Pantaleón de Ribera (1600–1629). Ingenioso miembro de la república literaria española* (Madrid: José Porrúa Turanzas, 1980), pp. 283–303. Although pseudonyms are here adopted to conceal the identity of the real writers, the fact that the same names often appear in different works – Pedro Méndez de Loyola, for example, appears as Gerardo in Corral's *La Cintia* and Castillo Solórzano's *Jornadas alegres*, and as Gerardico in Pantaleón's *vejamen* – suggests that they must, in part at least, have arisen from and been used in the *Academia de Madrid*. On the identification of these names, from where I have taken the example of Méndez de Loyola, see Ruth L. Kennedy, "Pantaleón de Ribera, 'Sirene', Castillo Solórzano, and the Academia de Madrid in Early 1625", in *Homage to John M. Hill. In Memoriam*, ed. by Walter Poesse (Bloomington: Indiana University Press, 1968), pp. 189–200 (pp. 190–91).

exclusivity, automatically creating a distinction between members and non-members and helping to foster a cliquish atmosphere.

A further point of interest to emerge from novelistic accounts of academies is that they are usually attended by both sexes: "damas tapadas" and "damas encubiertas" are an integral part of the occasion. Their reasons for attending are similar to those evinced by contemporary critics, namely to show their social refinement: in the Madrid academy depicted in *Las harpías en Madrid*, for example, there are "algunas damas que de embozo quisieron gozar de aquel buen rato por acreditarse de buenos gustos".[27] Only rarely, however, does a woman's verse get included in published accounts, which would suggest that women attended primarily as silent spectators, the audience in front of whom the male poets performed.[28] Their silent and effectively decorative presence is apparent from a *vejamen* by Luis Nieto presented at one of Fonseca de Almeida's academies, the various accounts of which carry no compositions by female poets, in which the scene of the meeting is described in the following terms: "Llegamos pues a la casa dispuesta, entramos en una sala, aunque pequeña, de mucha capacidad, brillante de luces, poblada de ingenios, adornada de ocultas deidades, y toda hecha un motivo de admiraciones".[29] Similarly Sebastián Francisco de Medrano in his address to an *Academia para un certamen de Carnestolendas* alludes to its members in an analogous way:

> ... príncipes magnánimos;
> señoras, cuanto hermosas, discretísimas;
> cultos poetas, claros, doctos, críticos;
> auditorio florido y celebérrimo.[30]

This division of roles according to gender, with the men being marked by their wit and the women by their beauty, is further emphasized in the account of an academy held in Valencia in 1658 in which the content of Francisco de la Torre y Sevil's opening introduction is described as follows: "Cíñense todos los asuntos en una inventiva, y por los mismos se celebra la agudeza de los poetas y se pinta la hermosura de las damas."[31] In part, of course, this is presumably a clichéd courtly compliment; yet the almost total lack of verse by

---

[27] See Castillo Solórzano, *Las harpías en Madrid*, p. 138.

[28] Thus, for example, a *romance* on the following topic, "Pide una dama confites y danla azar confitado", was written and read out by a "dama incógnita", later revealed to be a Sebastiana Cruzate, at the 1674 *Pascua de Reyes*, fols 40r–41r (corrected foliation). When Lucinda in one episode in Camerino's *La dama beata* acts as the president of an academy this is very much the exception rather than the rule. See *La dama beata* (Madrid: Pablo de Val, 1655), pp. 93–94.

[29] See *Fonseca April 1662*, fol. 52v.

[30] See *Favores de las musas* (Milan: Juan Baptista Malatesta, 1631), p. 182.

[31] See *Sol de academias*, p. 1. Compare Bocángel's academy oration, probably for the *Academia de Madrid* in the 1620s or 30s, transcribed in Trevor J. Dadson, "Dos

women in printed academy accounts is a strong indication that their participation was essentially passive and decorative, which contrasts sharply with their active participation in the many *justas poéticas* held over the course of the century. It is important to bear this "silent" female audience in mind when reading academy verse not only because it is a further link between academy and theatre but because the more misogynous, scurrilous and scatological verse obviously gains a certain edge if one imagines it being read out in the presence of various "damas tapadas", veiled precisely to protect their modesty and maintain decorum. With this type of topic the skill, as well as the humour and enjoyment, must have consisted largely in fully exploiting the risqué potential whilst keeping the composition within the bounds of good taste, the presence of women presumably adding a certain edge to the task. Interestingly, in contrast to the female audience, male academicians were expected to be active contributors, as can be gauged from a satirical academy poem by Castillo Solórzano addressed to "los mirones de academia" in which he suggests that those who "sólo para mirar / se han venido tras nosotros" should not continue to attend the academy.[32]

The comments, both favourable and unfavourable, of many contemporary writers suggest a variety of reasons for attending an academy. These contemporary assessments provide valuable insights into the academy as a social phenomenon and hence into its function within seventeenth-century literary life. They thus enable the literary concerns of academies to be placed in a broader perspective, and in so doing suggest that for poets and writers the academy's function was in fact more social than literary. This may in part, but only in part, explain the paradox of why a supposedly literary phenomenon whilst producing poetry which is often noticeably inferior to non-academy verse nevertheless remained a constant and popular part of seventeenth-century culture. A consideration of such critiques leads us towards two broader and closely related questions raised by the phenomenal success of literary academies in Spain: who actually attended them, and why?

José de Pellicer, an academy habitué, offers a generally highly favourable critique of the academy. In an oration delivered to the *Academia de Madrid* in 1635 Pellicer, not surprisingly given the occasion, offers an uncritical eulogy in hyperbolic terms of the academy he is addressing:

> Este es el seminario de los entendidos, el taller de los bien hablados, el colegio de los discretos. [...] No vale el embeleco superficial de la ignorancia, ni la afectación exterior de la apariencia. Sólidos son los argumentos, macizos los silogismos. La alquimia sobredorada se conociera en el peso de las razones, y en el sonido de las palabras. Traslúmbrase el azogue plateado

autógrafos desconocidos de Gabriel Bocángel", *El Crotalón. Anuario de filología española*, 2 (1985), 275–98 (p. 287).

[32] Cited in full by Alan Soons, *Alonso de Castillo Solórzano* (Boston: Twayne Publishers, 1978), p. 93.

al examen del oído, a la censura de la verdad. [...] Lucir sin ruido es fineza, aumentarse sin estruendo valentía. Barnizar de colores las afrentas es pintar, no escribir papeles.³³

What is praised here is the notion of the academy as a training ground for writers and gentlemen: the nouns "entendidos", "bien hablados" and "discretos" implying both categories. Also of note is the repeated emphasis on orality and performance; clearly the effective delivery of a poem was deemed as important as its successful composition, although undue ostentation is implicitly censured ("lucir sin ruido es fineza, aumentarse sin estruendo valentía"). The role of academies in instilling and propagating a certain literary style which is implied in the opening sentence quoted from Pellicer's oration is elaborated in his introduction to the posthumous edition (1631) of the works of Anastasio Pantaleón de Ribera, one of the most accomplished products of the academy phenomenon. Pellicer discusses Pantaleón's attendance at the *Academia de Madrid* and in so doing he emphasizes social reasons behind such participation more than literary ones:

> Resucitaron en Madrid aquellas academias de Grecia y Roma antiguas, por no tener envidia España a las de la Crusca de Italia. Y aunque en éstas no se disputaba de la aprehensión de la verdad, como en aquéllas que, comenzando en Sócrates, se fueron continuando hasta Tulio, y después hasta Favorino y Plutarco; tal vez se veían en ellas algunas luces de la escuela de Platón, de Speusipo y Xenocrates, hasta las novedades de Arcesilas Pirronio, y los argumentos de Carneades, que fue el último después de Lacides, Teleco, Euandro, y Egesino Pergameno. Fueron el tiempo que duraron estas academias un seminario de los más lucidos ingenios cortesanos, entre los cuales se descollaba Anastasio con grande admiración de todos. Fue él primero que halló méritos sin envidia, gloria sin contradición, fama sin repugnancia, adquiriendo un valimiento estrecho con los mayores señores de Castilla, una competencia modesta con los más superiores hombres de su patria, y en fin una aclamación general en nobles y plebeyos.³⁴

Setting the *Academia de Madrid* in the context of its illustrious Classical and Italian predecessors inevitably draws an unfavourable intellectual comparison, for as Pellicer recognizes Spanish academies concerned themselves neither with philosophy as did Plato's academy throughout its long eight hundred year history under thinkers such as Speusippus, Xenocrates, Arcesilaus and Carneades, nor with philology, as did the Accademia della Crusca (founded in

---

³³ See Sánchez, *Academias*, p. 81.

³⁴ See Pellicer's introduction, reprinted in Ribera, *Obras*, I, pp. 20–21. I cite Pellicer's typically pompous catalogue of Classical precedents in full since it gives a succinct, if eclectic, survey of Greek and Roman academicians; for information on these, see under "Academy" and individual entries in *The Oxford Companion to Classical Literature*, ed. by M. C. Howatson, 2nd edn (Oxford: Oxford University Press, 1993).

Florence in 1582) which published its *Vocabulario della Crusca* in 1612.³⁵ The portrayal of this Spanish academy as a poetic training ground, a view similar to that offered in Pellicer's oration, and as a meeting-place for poets and nobles, makes it appear meagre and trivial in comparison, especially as its instructional role effectively takes second place here due to Pellicer's more explicit social emphasis: "un seminario de los más lucidos ingenios cortesanos". The critique implicit in this phrase, namely that attendance at an academy is both a fitting and formative occupation for a gentleman, is then extended. Not only can a poet gain a reputation but, more importantly, a reputation amongst the people who matter most, "los mayores señores de Castilla". In this account, then, the desire for a literary reputation and a poetic education are linked with the cultivation of useful social contacts as reasons for attending an academy. (This note is struck time and again in contemporary assessments of the academy: discussing Antonio de Solís' attendance of an *Academia de Salamanca* as a young man, for example, his seventeenth-century editor comments that the young poet shone amongst "tantos y tan eminentes ingenios" and that, more importantly, he was consequently "muy mirado y muy admirado".³⁶)

It is possible then to detect in Pellicer's eulogy a slightly critical note in his statement that Madrid academies have a marked preference for entertainment, both literary and social, in comparison with those of Greece and Rome. Indeed, Pellicer immediately prior to the passage just quoted condemns Pantaleón's total dedication to poetry in his youth, accusing the poet of being attracted more by "lo deleitoso" than "lo útil" and hence of pursuing a pastime devoid of any "aprovechamiento hondo" (p. 19). This censure of the younger poet, taken with his contrast of ancient and modern academies, suggests that Pellicer, for all his hyperbole, actually regarded the academy with a degree of intellectual reserve. For Pellicer the academy is a useful social occasion affording literary pleasure and instruction but one which falls short of its illustrious Classical antecedents.

Interestingly Pellicer delivered another paper to the *Academia de Madrid* in 1635 entitled "Idea de la comedia en Castilla" which is prefaced with a eulogy which makes substantially the same points as his introduction to Pantaleón's verse, with the difference that here, actually addressing the academy in question, he states that it does as an institution fuse "lo útil o lo moral" and "lo deleitoso" like its illustrious forebears:

---

³⁵ Compare his slight reservations here with his subsequent unreserved encomium of the *Academia de Madrid* in his 1635 oration: "¿Fue mayor ninguna de las Academias de Grecia y Roma antiguas? La Crusca moderna de Partenio, ¿fue mayor? ¿Contaba de más esclarecidos sujetos el Areópago de Atenas?" (Sánchez, *Academias*, p. 81).

³⁶ See Solís, *Varias poesías sagradas y profanas*, ed. by Manuela Sánchez Regueira (Madrid: CSIC, 1968), p. 41.

> En aquellas primitivas [academias] siempre se disputaba de la aprehensión de la verdad, objeto a que miran todas las ciencias. Lo mismo contenían las de la Media Edad, y al propio cuidado parece que las de nuestros tiempos se introducen. Conócese que imita ejemplar tan venerable esta grande y numerosa academia que me escucha, esta palestra grave de Apolo, esta arena festiva de las musas, este heroico estadio de Aganipe, este solemne circo de Helicona, donde tenidos en judicioso polvo sus campiones científicos, enjugan el sudor virtuoso los céfiros del aplauso.[37]

Indeed, like all such addresses, this prescriptive discourse is itself evidence of "lo útil", for it simply continues on a theoretical level the academy's defining purpose, the composition of poetry. (In this regard, notice how all the epithets he uses to describe the academy categorically place poetry as its sole concern: "esta palestra grave de Apolo, esta arena festiva de las musas, este heroico estadio de Aganipe, este solemne circo de Helicona".) A discourse on the *comedia* is not out of place since Pellicer here views the *comedia* as "el poema más arduo" (p.265); in so doing he is obviously implicitly drawing a comparison between "poesía lírica" and "poesía dramática", and this Golden Age parallel between theatre and lyric is one that, as we shall see, academies generally in their own practice draw even closer by making the poetic truly performative.[38] Pellicer's criticisms of the academy, then, suggest simply that he would have preferred more theoretical rigour and less frivolous practice in the communal pursuit of poetry.

Another academy attender, Juan de Zabaleta, writing some thirty years later in his *El día de fiesta por la tarde* (Madrid, 1660), shares Pellicer's reservations and implied criticism of the frivolity of literary academies which, more severely than Pellicer, he describes as having a useful but clearly limited role to play in contemporary life. Zabaleta begins his satire by describing a poet who is struggling to compose his piece for an academy meeting:

> Toma un libro de poesía española que le ayude a cumplir con la obligación del asunto. Anda en él escogiendo las palabras por el sonido, como si escogiera cantarillas. La que no es de ruido grande, la desprecia, y como lo macizo suena poco, deja lo macizo. Su intención es hacer poesía que atruene, no poesía que hable. Porque no se repara en los ratos serenos, piensa que son mejores los ratos del torbellino. Porque la mansedumbre discreta de la poesía mueve a pocos, cree que es mejor la que turba y desasosiega a muchos.[39]

---

[37] See Federico Sánchez Escribano and Alberto Porqueras Mayo, *Preceptiva dramática española del renacimiento y el barroco*, 2nd edn (Madrid: Gredos, 1972), pp. 263–72 (p. 264).

[38] Pellicer's address obviously brings to mind Lope's *Arte nuevo de hacer comedias* written in verse for another academy in 1609. See Sánchez Escribano and Porqueras Mayo, *Preceptiva dramática*, pp. 154–65.

[39] See Juan de Zabaleta, *El día de fiesta por la mañana y por la tarde*, ed. by Cristóbal Cuevas García (Madrid: Castalia, 1983), pp. 390–91. For an astute overview of Zabaleta

The criticism here is not only that the young poet is resorting to other poet's work as a form of rhyming dictionary to compose his piece but, more significantly, that in doing so his criteria for selection are based on nothing more than wanting to create a composition which will have an immediate and striking effect when read aloud at the meeting. Clearly the desire for effect means that this pseudo-poet is failing to heed Pellicer's aesthetic criteria already cited, namely that "lucir sin ruido es fineza, aumentarse sin estruendo valentía". This poet's priorities are clear: dramatic effect matters more than subtlety and poetic decorum.

Zabaleta moves from this sarcastic pen-portrait of a desperate poet to a more general discussion of the advantages and disadvantages of the literary academy:

> No sólo no tengo por culpables los concursos de las academias de poesía, sino por muy loables. Ellas obligan a ejercitar con fatiga el ingenio, y como al hierro le hace relumbrar el uso, al ingenio le hace lucir la fatiga. En ellas se desembarazan los mozos para hablar en público, y de turbarse donde no importa sacan el no turbarse donde importa. En ellas le cogen al aplauso el sabor y se engolosinan en el aplauso. En ellas se aprende la urbanidad de no desconsolar al que obra con corto ingenio, y a tratar con humanidad discreta la humanidad defectuosa del prójimo. En ellas se aprende a chancear sin hiel y a punzar sin dolor, y en ellas, en fin, se estudia la lengua de la poesía, de donde sale sin poesía y con elegancia la prosa. (p. 392)

Here Zabaleta makes similar points to Pellicer: the academy trains a poet, practice making the *ingenio* perfect; it enables the young to practice and perfect speaking in public; it inculcates social graces – elegance and urbanity – and so educates a gentleman. (The context in which this last point is made, namely that the individual learns to give and receive criticism sensitively and judiciously, is an indication of the prevailing tone of an academy session.) Zabaleta continues his assessment by criticizing amatory topics which he declares should be outlawed completely as they are morally reprehensible and hence spiritually dangerous. This banning of amatory poems is obviously surprising given that they constituted the majority of topics set in seventeenth-century academies: to ban them would have been to alter fundamentally the nature of the academy as it had developed in Spain at this time. (I shall return to this condemnation in a subsequent chapter.) Finally, he concludes his discussion with the following paragraph which severely limits the utility of the academy:

> Luego, de las academias sale otra cosa digna de reprehensión, que es andar leyendo después a los conocidos los papeles sus dueños. Ya dije que aquellos asuntos son la espada negra del entendimiento, que habilita para cosas

---

and his career, see Nigel Griffin, review of *El día de fiesta por la mañana y por la tarde*, ed. by Cuevas García, in *MLR*, 82 (1987), 1003–06.

de importancia grande. Todos saben que en acabando de hacer ejercicio con una espada negra, se deja en un rincón de los más escondidos. Ninguno hay que, sin que le tuvieran por loco, saliera con ella a la calle. Pues en verdad que lo que se aprendió con ella suele importar la vida. No importa, que no todo lo que hace buena obra hace buena compañía. Los papeles académicos, allí y para allí son de utilidad; leídos después por ostentación, o hacen calumnia, o significan flaqueza. (p. 393)

Zabaleta here limits the function of the academy to its potential to act as a social and poetic school, but his insistence on the fact that academy verse is not suited for consumption outside an academy session indicates that, for him at least, the academy was of greater social than literary importance. The academy produces "rounded courtiers" via the communal pursuit of poetry; it does not produce poets. Poetry in the academy is thus viewed as a means to a social end, not as an end in its own right. It is interesting to note in connection with Zabaleta's strictures on not reading academy verse outside the academy session for which it was composed that by 1660, the year *El día de fiesta por la tarde* was published, the trend for publishing accounts of academy meetings and their compositions was a relatively recent phenomenon, but one which was rapidly gaining momentum.[40]

The views of Pellicer and Zabaleta are synthesized in a sonnet by García de Salcedo Coronel which purports to describe a meeting of an *Academia del Prado* and in which the notions of social contact, bad poetry, orality and satire are seen not only as the hallmarks of the occasion but as a recipe for a tedious lack of originality:

> El teatro, un jardín con varias flores,
> luz poca, en muchas velas prevenida,
> hermosura, ignorada de escondida,
> de par en par ministros y señores:
>   secretario, un poeta de menores,
> oración escuchada, no entendida,
> la gracia en un vejamen mal vestida,
> y con menos vergüenza, que primores:
>   a cuatro solamente reducidos
> los poetas, por un pedante lego,
> en su misma ignorancia disculpado:
>   muchos versos, y pocos aplaudidos,
> torpe rumor, llorar cantando un ciego,
> fue la Academia, o Lisiada, del Prado.[41]

---

[40] See the chronology of works listed, for example, in José Simón Díaz, "Primer índice de publicaciones poéticas del siglo XVII", *RL*, 27 (1965), 144–96; and Simón Díaz, *Siglos de oro: Indice de justas poéticas* (Madrid: CSIC, 1962).

[41] See *Cristales de Helicona* (Madrid: Diego Díaz de la Carrera, 1650), fol. 16v.

The context for which academy poetry was produced is paramount in the formation of a distinctive poetic, an academy poetic. The communal, competitive and satirically charged atmosphere established the writers' horizon of expectations, for in the academy poetry was a means primarily of enjoyment, not of serious reflection, lyric intensity or amatory sincerity. This said, it is clear that contemporary writers and critics felt there to be three distinct reasons underlying an individual's attendance at regular meetings of a literary academy: first, the prospect of establishing a literary reputation amongst fellow poets and consequently finding patronage; secondly, the acquisition and practice of good manners; and thirdly the opportunity to become versed in contemporary literary taste.[42] The writing of poetry itself thus appears to be only one of various reasons behind writers going to academies, and a minor one at that to judge by the little real prominence it receives in contemporary assessments. Whilst poetry remained a cohesive and defining factor, shaping and directing the writers' gatherings and giving them a purpose, if not an excuse, the academy needs equally to be viewed as a social phenomenon in which poetry is the medium for both entertainment and social interaction. Within the academies both these facets are inseparable; indeed, in many ways their prolonged success lies in having so completely fused the two.

It is this contemporary view of the academy as a social occasion structured around the composition and performance of poetry which I propose to consider in detail in the final section of this chapter, precisely because to understand the attractions of the academy to contemporary Spaniards will enable a clearer understanding of their expectations of the event and hence also of both the place of poetry within it and their priorities when they set about composing their academy pieces. The view of the academy as an important meeting-place obviously raises the question of who actually attended them. Since it is not possible here to undertake an exhaustive coverage of every academy, I shall instead concentrate upon selected academies in Madrid as a means of assessing what types of individuals were brought together at such events. In so doing I want also to consider in what ways the academy itself developed over the century, and thereby to try to speculate whether the reasons for their popularity, and thus for attending them, similarly changed over the same period. As we shall see, whilst the key note is continuity, significant differences do exist in the format and the members of academies both between the first and second halves of the century and between regional academies and those in the capital.

In his biography of the court poet Antonio Hurtado de Mendoza Gareth

---

[42] See, for example, Lupercio Leonardo de Argensola's comments on an academy in Zaragoza in 1585: "En estas juntas y conversaciones todos somos maestros y discípulos; todos mandamos y todos obedecemos, comunicando las profesiones diversas y tomando cada uno lo que ha menester para la suya". Cited by Sánchez, *Academias*, p. 17. See also King, *Prosa*, p. 28.

Davies describes how the academy acted as an indispensable point of contact between the nobility and poets:

> The growth of court life during the reigns of Philip III and Philip IV had brought about a situation in which many of the aristocracy, including titled nobility, delighted in their devotion to poetry [...] But another type of poet had multiplied too; the shiftless, feckless *ingenio* who trusted that his poetic gift would bring him the patronage he needed to keep the wolf from the door. Within the exclusiveness of court life the academies [...] provided a common meeting ground for two very different sorts, whose paths in real life might not have otherwise crossed.[43]

As we shall see, this view of the academy as a meeting ground for nobles and poets needs some modification in the light of the development of the phenomenon over the course of the seventeenth century. Despite this, it remains an accurate assessment of the social function played by such occasions in the first half of the century, particularly in Madrid. As political, social and cultural life became ever more centred on the capital and as the Count-Duke of Olivares and Philip IV enthusiastically devoted themselves to constructing a dazzling court of artists, poets, writers and playwrights – a project which led to, and culminated in, the expansion of the Buen Retiro, a purpose built "pleasure palace" in the 1630s – so the city played host to a series of literary academies attended by the literary and social elite which formed an almost unbroken continuum from the 1600s through to the late 1640s. Indeed a consideration of this series of academies shows that they forged precisely that type of "valimiento estrecho" between poet and nobility mentioned by Pellicer which enabled poets to gain access to cultural institutions such as the Buen Retiro and to the royal festivities held there which otherwise would have been inaccessible.[44] The various Madrid academies therefore acted as a kind of showcase for an individual's talent and hence facilitated access to favour and patronage. It is no coincidence that such academies flourished in Madrid during the exact period when the Duke of Lerma and, especially, the Count-Duke of Olivares were seeking to make the capital a fitting setting for their respective monarchs. Poetry was at a premium in this political-cultural exercise, since it was a relatively cheap way of creating the desired type of cultural atmosphere – one of dazzling display, intellect, wit, urbanity and refinement.

In the capital the most famous, influential and long-running academy during the reign of Philip IV was the *Academia de Madrid*; indeed, because of the quality of the writers who attended it, it is the most famous seventeenth-century Spanish academy. This academy had various predecessors in the capital but unlike them it did not prove to be short lived. Its principal

---

[43] See *Poet at Court*, p. 60.
[44] See Pellicer, Introduction to Pantaleón de Ribera, *Obras*, I, p. 21.

predecessors had been the academy held under the auspices of Diego Gómez de Sandoval y Rojas, Count of Saldaña (second son of the Duke of Lerma), between 1606 and 1612; and the *Academia Selvaje*, founded and presided over by Francisco de Silva, a brother of the Duke of Pastrana, from the spring of 1612 to the summer of 1614. Saldaña's academy, attended by writers such as Lope de Vega, Hurtado de Mendoza, Vélez de Guevara, Soto de Rojas and nobles such as the Dukes of Feria and Pastrana, had a somewhat stormy history. The academy eventually split up for good when a violent disagreement between Soto de Rojas and Vélez de Guevara split the group.[45] Pastrana's brother then established an academy, called originally "El Parnaso" but soon renamed the *Academia Selvaje* after its patron, Francisco de Silva. In many ways it was simply a continuation of Saldaña's academy; indeed, its first session was opened with a prose discourse on poetics by Soto de Rojas who in 1623 writes of the group,

> En Madrid, se abrió la Academia Selvaje, así llamada porque se hizo en casas de don Francisco de Silva, aquel lucido ingenio, aquel ánimo generoso, calidad de la casa de Pastrana, lustre de las musas, mayor trofeo de Marte [. . .] Asistieron en esta academia los mayores ingenios de España que al presente estaban en Madrid.[46]

The *Academia de Madrid* itself was first presided over by Sebastián Francisco de Medrano from 1617 until 1622 when Medrano took orders and consequently suspended the academy and its activities. So popular had it become with its members, however, that it was subsequently resurrected under the control of Francisco de Mendoza, secretary to the Count of Monterrey (Olivares' brother-in-law) from 1623 to 1637. Moreover if Willard King's suggestion that this academy is identical with an *Academia Castellana*, for which Cáncer y Velasco wrote a *vejamen* around 1649, is correct, there is a possibility that it continued to meet until at least as late as the mid-century.[47] There was, therefore, an almost unbroken chain of academies in the capital during

---

[45] As Lope writes to the Duke of Sessa: "Sólo me cuentan de las academias, donde acuden todos los señores y muchos de los poetas. [. . .] Esta última se mordieron poéticamente un licenciado Soto, granadino, y el famoso Luis Vélez; llegó la historia hasta rodeles y aguardar a la puerta; hubo príncipes de una parte y de otra, pero nunca Marte miró tan opuesto a las señoras musas". See *Cartas*, ed. by Nicolás Marín (Madrid: Castalia, 1985), p. 111. On the academy itself, see King, *Prosa*, pp. 42–47; Davies, *Poet at Court*, pp. 19–21; and Emilio Cotarelo, "Luis Vélez de Guevara y sus obras dramáticas", *BRAE*, 3 (1916), 621–52 (pp. 639–44).

[46] See Soto de Rojas, *Obras*, ed. by Antonio Gallego Morell (Granada: CSIC, 1950), pp. 268–69. For the discourse itself, see pp. 25–33. See also Antonio Chicharro Chamorro, "En torno a una oración académica de Soto de Rojas: el 'Discurso sobre la poética' ", in *Al Ave el Vuelo. Estudios sobre la obra de Soto de Rojas* (Granada: Universidad de Granada, 1984), pp. 13–31. On the academy, see King, *Prosa*, pp. 47–49; and Sánchez, *Academias*, pp. 100–12.

[47] See King, "The Academies", p. 368; and *Prosa*, p. 62, where she makes the

the first fifty years of the century, continuity being provided by the poets who attended them if not by the name of the academy itself.[48]

The central importance of this series of academies to the literary life of the capital cannot be overstated. The sheer range of writers who attended their meetings attests to their significance to the flourishing cultural life of Madrid. In his *Favores de las musas* (Milan, 1631), in an introductory letter to Alonso de Castillo Solórzano, Sebastián Francisco de Medrano cites a long list of poets, writers and playwrights who had attended meetings of the *Academia de Madrid* when it was held in his house. The names range from such luminaries as Góngora, Quevedo, Calderón, Lope de Vega, Tirso de Molina and Ruiz de Alarcón, through a long list of important "secondary" writers (Bocángel, Hurtado de Mendoza, Vélez de Guevara, the Prince of Esquilache, López de Zárate, Mira de Amescua, Pérez de Montalbán, Salas Barbadillo, Castillo Solórzano, Pellicer, Corral, Valdivieso, Benavente), down to a whole array of lesser-known writers.[49] Even given the fact that Medrano's aim here is to impress the reader with the range and quality of the members of the academy he presided over, and that some of these writers mentioned may not have been regular attenders, the list of names cited amounts to a veritable roll-call of seventeenth-century literary figures. Medrano's academy was clearly at the very centre of contemporary literary life, providing a focus for talent and a meeting place for the best and most popular writers of the day. Any session attended by such figures must have been both stimulating and intimidating and, given the competitive nature of any academy, together with the often vicious competitiveness of the literary world in general (as revealed by the intensity and ferocity of the polemic over Góngora's *Polifemo* and *Soledades* – many of whose critical protagonists are listed as attending Medrano's academy), this presumably meant that any poet choosing to submit verse to the public scrutiny of such an august and talented group must have taken great care that what was submitted was of a good quality and represented the poet at his best. With such company and in such an atmosphere it is easy to see why

---

suggestion more tentatively. For the *vejamen*, see Sánchez, *Academias*, pp. 93–97. I follow both Dadson and Sánchez in viewing Medrano's and Mendoza's academies as one, the latter simply becoming the former's successor. See Bocángel, *Lira*, p. 73; and Sánchez, *Academias*, p. 51. In contrast King regards the two as distinct entities ("The Academies", p. 368). Either way, a significant number of poets attended both academies.

[48] At least one of the poets mentioned by Cáncer, Antonio Sigler de Huerta, was a member of the *Academia de Madrid* in the mid 1620s. On this writer, see E. M. Wilson, "Calderón's Enemy: Don Antonio Sigler de Huerta", *MLN*, 81 (1966), 225–31; and Harold G. Jones, " 'El hortelano del Prado': Tirso or Don Antonio Sigler de Huerta", *BCom*, 29 (1977), 25–27.

[49] Juan de Androsilla, Felipe Bernardo del Castillo, Guillén de Castro y Bellvís, Gaspar Dávila, Diego Jiménez de Enciso, Rodrigo de Herrera, Francisco López de Aguilar, Francisco de Mendoza, Cristóbal de Mesa, Francisco de Quintana, Gabriel de Roa, Miguel de Silveira, Pedro Vargas Machuca, José de Villaizán, Diego de Villegas. See Medrano, *Favores de las musas*, fols 4v–5v.

contemporaries viewed the academy as an indispensable "hot house" and proving ground for poetic talent: academy verse was written to impress and to do so in Medrano's *Academia de Madrid* a poet would have to spend some time and effort to ensure such poetry accorded to current poetic taste, outshone all other submissions, and, equally importantly, was worthy of maintaining a public image and reputation.

Under the stewardship of Francisco de Mendoza the *Academia de Madrid* continued its activities with a significant number of its members having earlier been members of Medrano's academy, including Bocángel, Pellicer, Castillo Solórzano, Corral, Salas Barbadillo and Vélez de Guevara. Two *vejámenes* written in either 1625 or 1626 by Pantaleón de Ribera for this academy (and the first to have survived in writing), together with a surviving exchange of poems between members, give a vivid impression of the lively activities of the group. From these academy writings Ruth Kennedy has pieced together the brief liaison between Pantaleón and a dissolute *cortesana*, herself an attender of the academy, which caused the former to miss a session during which the latter was described as "easy" in a *vejamen* by "Coriandro", Gabriel de Corral, later published in his *La Cintia de Aranjuez*. This *cortesana*, Sirene/Lisarda, then enlists Pantaleón to achieve poetic revenge on her slanderers in a *vejamen*, the liaison itself being discussed in a poetic interchange between Pantaleón and Castillo Solórzano.[50] In this exchange Pantaleón describes the *cortesana* in frank terms such as the following:

> Por armas tiene un botín
> con una ingeniosa letra,
> que dice en lengua vulgar:
> "Alejandro de sí misma".

He expresses his fears that he may have caught some venereal disease from her:

> Dase a todos muy barata,
> aunque muy cara les cuesta;
> y si no es por lo que dan
> viene a ser por lo que llevan.

---

[50] See Kennedy, "Pantaleón de Ribera", pp. 189–200. For Pantaleón's *vejamen* referring to Corral's earlier slanderous *vejamen*, see *Obras*, II, pp. 45–53 (p. 51). This *vejamen* as printed by Pellicer omits its second half in which the academy poets are satirized in turn. The original version has been published from a manuscript source by Blecua and Brown. See José Manuel Blecua, "El vejamen segundo de Anastasio Pantaleón de Ribera", in *The Two Hesperias. Literary Studies in Honour of Joseph G. Fucilla on the Occasion of his 80th Birthday*, ed. by Américo Bugliani (Madrid: José Porrúa Turanzas, 1977), pp. 55–67; and Brown, *Pantaleón*, pp. 380–90. Kennedy takes Corral's piece to be the one printed in his academic novel: see Gabriel de Corral, *La Cintia de Aranjuez*, ed. by Joaquín de Entrambasaguas (Madrid: CSIC, 1945), pp. 173–98.

>   . . .
>   Esta noche no he dormido,
>   llorando mis desdichas,
>   pensando en lo que pasó
>   y temiendo lo que queda.
>   Rogad, amigo, a los cielos,
>   si os oyen sus luces bellas,
>   que mi temor sea por bien,
>   o por menos mal siquiera;
>   y que de tan grave culpa
>   se me dé la penitencia,
>   ya que pecó la carne,
>   sin que los huesos lo sientan.[51]

I mention this incident, and its repercussions in the *Academia de Madrid*, to illustrate just what a tight-knit coterie the academy could be in the early seventeenth century. The academy, and the prose and poetry which it gives rise to, are seen here as primarily means of social interaction; the writers involved in this incident reveal in other words that the academy was more to do with entertainment than with literature.

The success of the *Academia de Madrid* under both Medrano and Mendoza as a means of facilitating access to the aristocracy and nobility can be gauged by the number of poets from them who attended and contributed to the Buen Retiro festivities in 1637. The *Academia burlesca*, held as an integral part of the festivities (the most lavish ever seen in Madrid, according to J. H. Elliott) to celebrate the election of Ferdinand, King of Hungary, as King of the Romans, was evidence of the official and very public royal approval of the academy as a form of entertainment.[52] The range and quality of the writers participating in these royal celebrations is probably as much to do with the desire of the organizers to make the event as spectacularly impressive as possible and with – in some instances – the high literary reputations of certain participants as it is with any contacts formed between writers and nobles in the meetings of the *Academia de Madrid*. Nevertheless, a significant proportion of those attending – Luis de Benavente, Gaspar Dávila, Vélez de Guevara, Esquilache, Hurtado de Mendoza, Calderón, Pellicer, Sigler de Huerta, Pedro Méndez de Loyola and Juan Mexía – were also regular members of this academy. If nothing else, this indicates that the academy was in the vanguard of the literary scene.

This said the aristocracy – that is the upper echelons of the nobility (*títulos* and grandees) – were indeed assiduous attenders of academies. According to Sánchez, Saldaña's academy was attended by as many nobles as poets and

---

[51] See Soons, *Castillo Solórzano*, pp. 112–13.
[52] See Elliott, *The Count-Duke of Olivares. The Statesman in an Age of Decline*, 2nd edn (New Haven and London: Yale University Press, 1988), p. 522.

writers, including figures such as the Duke of Medinaceli and the Counts of Lemos and Olivares.⁵³ The *Academia de Madrid* was attended by such luminaries as the Dukes of Lerma and Híjar, the Marquis of Velada and the Count of Salinas, whilst Philip IV himself attended a meeting of the *Academia de Madrid*, under the auspices of Medrano, in the spring of 1622, a visit which may well have been behind the original inspiration for the royal academies which formed such a significant feature of court life in the 1630s.⁵⁴ The relationship between nobility and poets was presumably symbiotic. In an age in which poetry was still considered a necessary pursuit for a gentleman, a nobleman's status was enhanced by the quality not only of his own verse but also, and principally, by the entourage of writers supported by him in his role as a patron.

The patronage of nobles was central to the academy as an institution across Spain and throughout the century. Their participation and sponsorship confirmed poetry as a noble and elite pastime, that is to say, one that gave prestige to both noble and poet alike. Such participation was not restricted to the court in Madrid. In viceregal courts such as those in Aragon, Valencia and Naples, the nobility were active patrons of the literary activities of the academies. To some extent such patronage can be viewed as the result of the provincial nobility reflecting the tastes and fashions of the Court, although noble patronage does obviously predate the official sponsorship of academy activities by Philip IV and the Count-Duke in the 1620s and 30s. Thus when the Count of Lemos, Pedro Fernández de Castro, left Spain to become Viceroy of Naples in 1610, for example, he was courted by poets and writers, including Góngora and Cervantes, eager to fill one of the secretary's posts of his "literary court", as Otis Green calls it.⁵⁵ Once in Naples he established the *Accademia degli Oziosi* in 1611 which was attended by poets such as Lupercio and Bartolomé Leonardo de Argensola and the Count of Villamediana. By the mid-century noble sponsorship of academies in the peninsula's various viceregal centres had largely overtaken such sponsorship in the capital. Thus, although the academy continued in popularity in Madrid, provincial academies surpassed them in terms of continued official support. This means that post 1650, the initial pattern is reversed, with Zaragoza and Valencia, for example, cultivating academy activities as assiduously as Madrid had previously done in the 1620s and 30s. In Zaragoza throughout the 1640s, 50s and 60s, the viceroys actively supported academies. Both the Count of Lemos (son of Pedro Fernández de Castro, mentioned above) and his own eldest son, the Count of

---

⁵³ Sánchez, *Academias*, p. 45.
⁵⁴ See Sánchez, *Academias*, p. 53.
⁵⁵ See Otis Green, "The Literary Court of the Conde de Lemos at Naples, 1610–1616", *HR*, 1 (1933), 290–308; and Sánchez, *Academias*, pp. 304–12. For a biography of the count, see Alfonso Pardo Manuel de Villena, *Un mecenas español del siglo XVII. El Conde de Lemos* (Madrid: J. Ratés Martín, 1911).

Andrade, patronized active literary academies whose members include Juan de Moncayo, José Navarro, Francisco de la Torre y Sevil, Andrés de Uztarroz and Alberto Díez y Foncalda, and nobles such as the Duke of Híjar and the Marquises of Torres and Cañizares; whilst the Prince of Esquilache similarly sponsored an academy during his period as viceroy.[56] (Other Aragonese academies under noble patronage include those of the Count of Aranda[57] and the Marquis of Ossera.[58]) In the second half of the century academies began to flourish in Valencia as nowhere else in the country. This resurgence of interest may have been due to the direct influence of the Aragonese example: it is significant that Francisco de la Torre y Sevil, active in so many Aragonese academies, also played a fundamental role in the 1658 Valencian academy which seems to have sparked a renewal in the popularity of such academies within the Mediterranean kingdom.[59] With the active and continuing support of the viceroys, or of nobles such as the Marquis of Villatorcas, the academy developed in Valencia along ever more dramatic and performative lines, such that by the 1690s its format, whilst still broadly similar to that of academies at the start of the century, nevertheless had developed their innate sense of the theatrical beyond all recognition: music, dance and scripted interchanges between the academy officials were now as integral to the occasion as the recital of poetry on pre-ordained topics.[60] Furthermore, its status as an integral part of official celebrations is evident from the fact that in the last half of the

[56] On these academies, see Aurora Egido's introduction to her edition of Moncayo, *Rimas* (Madrid: Espasa-Calpe, 1976), pp. xxv–xxvi (and pp. 112–24, 154–59, 177–81 for various presidential addresses given by Moncayo at the Lemos academy); Sánchez, *Academias*, pp. 267–79, 283–85; and King, *Prosa*, pp. 70–73 who corrects Sánchez on important points of fact. For various academy pieces (*vejámenes* and an oration) given by Navarro to the Count of Lemos' academy, see *Poesías varias* (Zaragoza: Miguel de Luna, 1654), pp. 53–68, 141–57, 157–67. See also Ricardo del Arco y Garay, *La erudición española en el siglo XVII y el cronista de Aragón Andrés de Uztarroz*, 2 vols (Madrid: CSIC, 1950), I, pp. 54–59; and the various studies by Egido fundamental to any work on Aragonese poetry in this period: "Los modelos en las justas poéticas aragonesas del siglo XVII", *RFE*, 60 (1978–80), 159–71; *"Retratos de los reyes de Aragón" de Andrés Uztarroz y otros poemas de academia* (Zaragoza: Institución Fernando el Católico, 1983); "Certámenes poéticas y arte efímero en la Universidad de Zaragoza (Siglos XVI y XVII)", in *Cinco estudios humanísticos para la Universidad de Zaragoza en su centenario IV*, ed. by Aurora Egido et al. (Zaragoza: Caja de Ahorros de la Inmaculada, 1983), pp. 9–78; and "Las academias literarias de Zaragoza en el siglo XVII", in *La literatura en Aragón*, ed. by M. Alvar (Zaragoza: Caja de Ahorros y Monte de Piedad de Zaragoza, Aragón y Rioja, 1984), pp. 101–28.
[57] See Sánchez, *Academias*, pp. 282–83.
[58] See the *octavas* by Moncayo praising this academy in *Rimas*, pp. 168–70 (and Egido's brief comments in her introduction, p. xxiv).
[59] See his Introduction in *Sol de academias*, pp. 1–28.
[60] For an excellent discussion of the history and practice of Valencian academies as they evolved from the *Academia de los Nocturnos* to the first decades of the eighteenth century, see the various studies in Rodríguez Cuadros (ed.), *De las academias a la enciclopedia*.

century it was an institutionalized form of celebrating the king's birthday, often under the aegis of the viceroy and frequently in his palace. Indeed, the popularity of the academy as an institution in Valencia negates Willard King's assertion that "seventeenth-century Spain had two chief centres of academic activity – Madrid and the viceroyalty of Aragon, particularly Zaragoza".[61]

As with the desire of nobles to become patrons of academies, the broader appeal of these literary circles in the provinces was consciously linked to a desire to emulate the capital.[62] In an increasingly centralized state, the capital and its court became the focus of cultural attention: to hold an academy was to emulate the literary mode of both the capital and the Court itself, with its penchant for academies. Whilst academies had been held in the sixteenth century in various cities across Spain, indicating that the phenomenon was not initially associated with either the capital or the court, but simply with literary and cultural life in general, by the mid seventeenth century, as a result of Philip IV's creation of a vibrant and spectacular cultural centre around his Madrid court, it was increasingly seen as the artistic mode of the Castilian capital *par excellence*. This view of the academy comes across in a *vejamen* given in 1658 in Valencia by Antonio de Cardona, who in the usual dream *topos* imagines the following scenario:

> [S]oñé que estaba en la raya donde se juntan este reino y el de Castilla. Allí había un hombre como atalaya, a quien movido de curiosidad, le pregunté qué esperaba. Díjome, "Sabrá V.M. que en Valencia solía haber muy lucidas academias. Estas empezaron a adolecer del achaque de la pereza, del cual murieron, porque la pereza es uno de los siete achaques mortales. Viendo acabada esta útil congregación de ingenios, trataron en Castilla de venir a fundar, aspirando a la gloria de adquirir este patronazgo. Sabiendo esto algunos poetas valencianos, descendientes por línea recta de aquellas academias antiguas, han resuelto oponerse a esta instrucción ofreciendo premios grandes a cualquiera de la Corona de Aragón, que por ensalmo, o empíricamente, se atreviere a dar nueva vida a las academias valencianas; y

---

[61] See "Academies", p. 367. For the academies held under the aegis of Villatorcas, see Sánchez, *Academias*, p. 230. For Valencian academies in this period, see *Señoras*, Introduction, pp. 1–2. Of course, academies took place in other towns under the patronage of nobles: to take a single example, the Count of Fuensalida held an academy in Toledo in the first years of the seventeenth century. See José María Blecua, "La academia poética del Conde de Fuensalida", in *Sobre la poesía de la Edad de Oro. (Ensayos y notas eruditas)* (Madrid: Gredos, 1970), pp. 203–08. See also Joaquín de Entrambasaguas, "Lope de Vega en las justas poéticas toledanas de 1605 y de 1608", *RL*, 32 (1967), 5–104, and 33 (1968), 5–52.

[62] The authority of the capital as a cultural centre and model was profound, and influenced the development of other types of poetry, such as that offering advice to the aspiring courtier. On the latter, see *Avisos a un cortesano. An Anthology of Seventeenth-Century Moral-Political Poetry*, ed. by Trevor J. Dadson (Exeter: University of Exeter, 1985), pp. xvi–xix.

> entretanto que esto se logra, se han emboscado en este sitio para impedir el paso a cualquier poeta castellano, fortificándose y atrincherándose en aquella eminencia.[63]

Here, despite acknowledging the existence of previous Valencian academies such as the famous *Academia de los Nocturnos* as prestigious models and predecessors, Cardona sees Valencian academy life under threat from Castilian hegemony, and imagines the native poets actively resisting the cultural dominance of Castile in matters poetic and academic.[64] The writer acknowledges, implicitly, that the academy as an institution has flourished in Castile and not suffered the decline he claims it has undergone in Valencia; this may be taken as recognition that the academy was viewed by mid-century as a predominantly Castilian, and in particular Madrid-based, phenomenon and, perhaps more significantly, that the regional political and cultural centres used the academy model popularized by the capital as a means of resisting its literary dominance by encouraging local poetic "talent".[65] The lament voiced here over the decline of the institution and the desire expressed to revitalize them marks a resurgence in their popularity in Valencia as they became a fashionable and frequent phenomenon and one which enjoyed the stamp of official approval and support: after this academy in 1658, the number of academies held until the end of the century was double those in the first half.[66] Whether this increase in academy activity can be partially attributed to the specific nature of the nobility in the Crown of Aragon who, as I. A. A. Thompson notes, were defined far more by wealth, culture and civility (the "public demonstration of rank") than by innate racial characteristics like their more numerous Castilian counterparts, is uncertain;[67] but such a resurgence is clear evidence of a heightened literary and social self-awareness and self-presentation (as Cardona's *vejamen* makes explicit) which indicates that the Valencian nobility were making a sustained effort to participate in the cultural activities which had long been pursued in Madrid and Zaragoza, Valencia's more dynamic cultural equivalents.

---

[63] See *Sol de academias*, p. 53.

[64] For an overview of both the *Academia de los Nocturnos* and Valencian academies in general (the latter not exhaustive), see the excellent introduction in *Academia de los Nocturnos*, I, pp. 13–47.

[65] Such academies also, to a very minor extent, fostered poetry in Catalan. See, for example, the poems by Marco Antonio Ortí included in *Sol de academias* (pp. 32–33) and *Repetida carrera* (pp. 32–34).

[66] See the comments by Mas i Usó in *Señoras*, p. 1.

[67] See Thompson, "The Nobility in Spain, 1600–1800", in *The European Nobilities in the Seventeenth and Eighteenth Centuries*, ed. by H. M. Scott, 2 vols (London: Longman, 1995), I, pp. 174–236 (pp. 175–85). This might explain, too, their continued popularity and "official" support in Zaragoza. For a history of Valencia, see James Casey, *The Kingdom of Valencia in the Seventeenth Century* (Cambridge: Cambridge University Press, 1979).

Despite the success of the academy elsewhere in Spain, the *Academia de Madrid* is nevertheless exceptional both for the quality and the quantity of the poets and nobles who attended its sessions. The expansion and development of court life and culture which played such a central part in the plans of the Count-Duke for the education and glorification of the young monarch Philip IV meant that not only the court but the entire capital became a cultural focal point of great significance in seventeenth-century Spain: both political and cultural centralism drew writers and would be writers to Madrid, the concentration of power and wealth proving an irresistible magnet. Consequently, the level of literary ability within academies during the 1620s and 30s when this cultural "programme" was inaugurated and reached its peak was consistently high, simply because the pool of writers from which to draw was so large and diverse. This academy provided the ideal showcase for these writers, bringing art and power, poets and nobles together. So impressive was the *Academia de Madrid* in terms of the quality of its members and its longevity that Willard King has argued that it was the last major seventeenth-century academy.[68] As a qualitative assessment, it is difficult to refute King. However, in terms of literary history it is possible to accept this evaluation only if one ignores the phenomenal success of the academy in cities such as Valencia and if one discounts the very many academies which continued to meet in the capital, albeit in a different form in so far as they, like Saldaña's academy and the *Academia Selvaje* in the first two decades of the century, had a much shorter life-span. After the *Academia de Madrid*, in other words, academies in Spain are marked by their discontinuity rather than by their continuity and longevity.

This said, academies continued to play a dominant, and arguably the predominant, role in the literary life of the country. The academy held in Madrid under the auspices of the Portuguese gentleman and man of letters, Melchor de Fonseca de Almeida, is a case in point. This academy published six separate accounts of its meetings between 1661 and 1663. In addition to these Fonseca de Almeida also published an anthology volume of academy verse entitled *Jardín de Apolo. Academia celebrada por diferentes ingenios*. Published in 1655 this would seem to indicate that Fonseca was an inveterate academy attender and that he hosted, or at least attended, other meetings prior to the six academy sessions recorded in the early 1660s. Fonseca de Almeida's academy is worth detailed consideration as an example of the phenomenon of the academy in the latter half of the century for it exemplifies the ways in which the academy as an institution had evolved, and would continue to evolve, from the types of academies popular in the capital in the first decades of the century. His academy marks the end of the practice of using the academy itself as a means of constituting and defining a group of writers and their literary activities over an extended period of time. Its regular members

---

[68] See "Academies", p. 368.

are now largely unknown literary figures in contrast to many of the writers who attended the *Academia de Madrid*. It is precisely for this reason that I have chosen Fonseca de Almeida's academy to consider in depth, for the very anonymity of its members is precisely what makes them representative. With various important differences, the social make-up of Fonseca's academy is representative of the backgrounds of the majority of writers who attended academies in the seventeenth century. Consequently a biographical analysis of its various members provides a picture of the academy in Madrid at precisely the time when it was developing the more sporadic or occasional format which defined it as a popular institution in the second half of the century.[69]

Very little is known about Fonseca de Almeida, the probable author of the satirical poem the *Sueño político*.[70] It has been suggested that he was of Jewish origin and that he might have been related to the Portuguese banker Manuel de Cortizos de Villasante.[71] (An influential banker in the service of Philip IV, Cortizos himself attended the *Academia burlesca* in the Buen Retiro, being mentioned by several poets during the course of the event.[72]) What is certain is that he must have been relatively wealthy and have had a real penchant for literary academies to judge by the six volumes of proceed-

---

[69] Unless otherwise stated, in the pages that follow general biographical information is taken from the following sources: the *Enciclopedia Universal Ilustrada*; Cayetano Alberto de la Barrera y Leirado, *Catálogo bibliográfico y biográfico del teatro antiguo español desde sus orígenes hasta mediados del siglo XVIII* (London: Tamesis, 1968; facsimile of Madrid 1860 edn); José Simón Díaz, *Bibliografía de la literatura hispánica*, vol. 1– (Madrid: CSIC, 1950–); "Censo de escritores al servicio de los Austrias", in *Censo de escritores al servicio de los Austrias y otros estudios bibliográficos* (Madrid: CSIC, 1983), pp. 7–32; Carlos Ramírez de Arellano y Gutiérrez de Salamanca, *Ensayo de un catálogo biográfico-bibliográfico de los escritores que han sido individuos de las cuatro órdenes militares de España*, in *Colección de documentos inéditos para la historia de España*, vol. 109 (Vaduz: Kraus Reprint Ltd, 1966; reprint of Madrid 1898 edn); and Ann L. Mackenzie, *La escuela de Calderón. Estudio e investigación* (Liverpool: Liverpool University Press, 1993). Carrasco Urgoiti provides useful data on some individual members of this group, although she is little concerned with their wider literary and academy activities: see "Notas", pp. 105–07.

[70] For a modern edition of the *Sueño político*, see Miguel Avilés, ed., *Sueños ficticios y lucha ideológica en el siglo de oro* (Madrid: Editora Nacional, 1981), pp. 271–338. Although the *Sueño* is more often attributed to Fonseca than to any other writer in the many seventeenth-century manuscripts which contain this work, there is still some doubt over Fonseca's authorship (Avilés, pp. 243–49). Antonio Porqueras Mayo has recently published a seventeenth-century manuscript of an "oración apologética en favor de la poesía" given by Fonseca: see *La teoría poética en el manierismo y barroco españoles* (Barcelona: Puvill Libros, 1989), pp. 319–29.

[71] See Carrasco Urgoiti, "Notas", p. 105; and also "La oralidad", p. 50. For Cortizos, see Jonathan Brown and J. H. Elliott, *A Palace for a King. The Buen Retiro and the Court of Philip IV* (New Haven and London: Yale University Press, 1980), pp. 100–01, 202; Elliott, *Count-Duke*, p. 303; R. A. Stradling, *Philip IV and the Government of Spain, 1621–1665* (Cambridge: Cambridge University Press, 1988), pp. 224–30.

[72] See *Academia burlesca*, pp. 636, 667.

ings he published. These give a fascinating picture of an academy "in action".[73] In the *vejamen* to one of the sessions, the *fiscal* Alonso de Zárate y la Hoz has Fonseca himself give a description of the group, based on a sustained comparison of the academy with a woman, which suggests something of Fonseca's proprietorial attitude:

> Dijome que la academia era su dama, y que vivía dentro de su casa, por excusar costa y estar con más comodidad; que no la dejaba tan a sus anchas, como ella quisiera, porque después que corría por su cuenta, vivía con gran recogimiento. Y comenzómela a pintar, diciendo, que tenía muy lindos cabellos, porque eran grandes pensamientos; la frente espaciosa, porque tenía mucha capacidad; las cejas arqueadas, por ser cosa de admiración; y muy lindos ojos, porque eran muy de notar; la nariz, claro está, que teniendo tanto de águila, había de ser aguileña, aunque por sus muchas gracias podía ser Roma; sus mejillas rojas, por estar siempre con el furor poético encendidas; y la boca la mejor del mundo, porque habla siempre muy bien; sus dientes famosos, porque siendo en ella cada uno el mejor, son todos iguales; que sólo la garganta no era buena, porque no lo pasa todo. . . .[74]

From the evidence of the poems published, each meeting was attended, on average, by some eighteen members, though this figure takes no account of the unspecified number of female spectators mentioned by Luis Nieto in the *vejamen* cited earlier.[75] Normally the academy devoted itself to the usual range of amatory and humorous topics, but one entire session was dedicated to a poetic celebration of the birth of the future Charles II.[76] (In this Fonseca's group follows the growing trend in the latter half of the century to use the academy to celebrate royal events, a development which will be discussed in detail in the next chapter.) Although only three individuals attended all six meetings (Fonseca himself, Francisco Pinel y Monroy and Vicente Suárez de Deza y Avila), a nucleus of regular attenders is clearly discernible: Zárate y la Hoz attended five of the sessions recorded; Juan Alonso Guillén de la Carrera, Bernardo de Monleón y Cortés, Luis Nieto, Juan José Porter y Casanate and Sebastián Ventura de Vergara Salcedo attended four sessions; and Diego de Enciso y Velasco, José de Ledesma, Juan de Montenegro y Neira, Román Montero de Espinosa, Juan de Olivenza, Luis Antonio de Oviedo y Herrera,

---

[73] I have taken information regarding one of these accounts from Simón Díaz, *Bibliografía de la literatura hispánica*, IV (1955), pp. 373–74, who lists the writers attending and all topics given. The session in question is: *Academia que se celebró en siete de Enero, en casa de Don Melchor de Fonseca de Almeida, siendo Presidente Don José Porter y Casanate, Secretario D. Luis de Oviedo y Fiscal D. Juan de Montenegro y Neira* (Madrid: Francisco Nieto, 1663).
[74] See *Fonseca Jan 1662*, pp. 107–08. Compare *Fonseca April 1662*, fol. 42v.
[75] See *Fonseca April 1662*, fol. 52v.
[76] See *Fonseca Jan 1662*. The volume is dated Madrid, 1652 – an obvious error for 1662, for Mariana of Austria bore no other children called Charles (born Nov. 6 1661).

José Reinalte, Pedro de Oviedo y Herrera and Diego de Sotomayor three. Most of these individuals who formed the core of the academy are now just names, yet what can be learnt of them suggests that they formed a relatively coherent social and literary group, sharing similar educational, class and professional backgrounds: the majority were minor courtiers and officials, many of them were also playwrights, and a number of them attended a variety of literary academies besides Fonseca's.

To start with the group's literary activities. Seven of the academy's regulars had also published verse in Fonseca's 1655 *Jardín de Apolo* volume: Fonseca himself, Jerónimo de Cuéllar, Antonio de Espinosa, Sebastián de Olivares Vadillo, Olivenza, Reinalte and Sotomayor. Several other members, besides those just mentioned who must have attended whatever academy or academies the *Jardín de Apolo* records from the early 1650s, clearly shared Fonseca's fondness for literary academies. One member, Román Montero de Espinosa, took part in the 1637 *Academia burlesca* held in the Buen Retiro, submitting a *romance* on the ever popular academy subject of doctors causing illness rather than disease.[77] Another four, Juan Alonso Guillén de la Carrera, Pinel y Monroy, Fermín de Sarasa y Arce and Diego de Sotomayor later took part in the *Academia que se celebró en día de Pascua de Reyes* held in Madrid in 1674, whilst Luis Nieto and Sarasa y Arce attended the academy held in 1678 in the *Real Aduana*.[78] Finally various members of Fonseca's academy also presided over their own: Matías Diego de Villanueva and Juan José Porter y Casanate both held academies in 1661 at which they acted as president;[79] whilst José Reinalte, a knight of Santiago, held an academy in his own house some time before 1651, the year in which López de Zárate printed the following sonnet to the academy:

> Ceda Atenas y Roma, ceda Egipto,
> con fábricas soberbias opulento;
> que éste vanos asombros prestó al viento,
> en ellas fue lo idólatra delicto.
> Aquí sí, que se trata lo infinito,
> pues las ciencias están en su elemento,
> apurado de Apolo el sacro aliento,

---

[77] See *Academia burlesca*, pp. 654–55. On this writer, see Frédéric Serralta, "Román Montero de Espinosa, escritor del XVII: apostillas biográficas", *Criticón*, 28 (1984), 119–35.

[78] Carrasco Urgoiti suggests that Luis Nieto may have been related to the palace functionary depicted in the open doorway in the background of Velázquez's *Las meninas*, José Nieto ("Notas", p. 104). On the latter, see Jonathan Brown, *Velázquez. Painter and Courtier* (New Haven and London: Yale University Press, 1986), pp. 176, 256–67.

[79] See Agustín Palau Claveras, *Addenda & corrigenda o volumen complementario del tomo primero del "Manual del librero hispanoamericano" de Antonio Palau y Dulcet* (Empuries Palacete Palau y Dulcet, 1990), p. 41, nos 1614, 1615 II. At Porter y Casanate's academy, the secretary was Juan Pellicer de Tovar, another member of Fonseca's group.

y mejorado con cristiano rito.
Cuanto allá presumieron de grandeza,
aquí eleva perfecto en breve espacio:
que la virtud consiste en su fineza.
El dilatado término es cansancio,
por grande, no es mayor la forteleza,
corto templo es mayor que gran palacio.[80]

What emerges from this, then, is a picture of a group of individuals committed to the attendance of various academias as a regular and integral part of their social and literary life. It should be added here, therefore, that although in Spain no one group post 1650 enjoyed the longevity of the *Academia de Madrid*, the fact that the same group of writers would regularly turn up at distinct, one-off academias obviously lent these occasions a degree of continuity and unity which they otherwise appear to us to lack.

Also of interest is the fact that several of the group's members had literary interests and pretensions beyond writing academy poetry: Cuéllar, Montero de Espinosa, Oviedo y Herrera, Suárez de Deza y Avila, Vergara Salcedo and Olivares Vadillo also wrote for the theatre (*loas*, *entremeses*, *mojigangas*, or full *comedias*). This is an indication of how omnipresent the theatre was in seventeenth-century literary life and also, perhaps, one of the possible explanations for the theatricality and melodramatic nature of love poetry produced by both this and other academias. However as well as academy poetry and various writings for the stage, members of the group also published other types of literature. These range from Vergara Salcedo's literary compendium, entitled *Ideas de Apolo y dignas tareas del ocio cortesano* (Madrid, 1663), to eulogistic journalese and also devotional pieces. Nieto, for example, published a "descripción panegírica" of the military successes of Diego de Ibarra;[81] whilst Oviedo y Herrera wrote a life of Santa Rosa de Lima.[82] Montero de Espinosa seems to have been the most prolific of the group both in terms of

---

[80] See Francisco López de Zárate, *Obras varias*, ed. by José Simón Díaz, 2 vols (Madrid: CSIC, 1947), II, p. 85. Sánchez (*Academias*, p. 161) reproduces this sonnet with substantial differences which render it incomprehensible. For a discussion of Zárate's involvement with literary academias, which included the *Academia de Madrid*, see María Teresa González de Garay Fernández, *Introducción a la obra poética de Francisco López de Zárate* (Logroño: CSIC, 1981), pp. 73–78.

[81] See *Descripción panegírica en los progresos militares del segundo viaje que hizo ... Diego de Ibarra ... en el cual conquistó el Castillo de las Verlangas* (Cadiz: Juan Lorenzo, 1668).

[82] See *Vida de la esclarecida virgen Santa Rosa de Santa María, natural del Lima, y patrona de Perú* (Madrid: Juan García Infanzón, 1711). See also Olivares Vadillo, *Descripción de la real festividad que hizo Felipe IV el grande a la virgen santísima N. Señora, implorando su auxilio por medio de su antiquísima imagen de Atocha* (Madrid: María de Quiñones, 1643); and *Colocación de Nuestra Señora del Buen Alumbramiento en el religiosísimo convento de la Merced de ... Segovia, invocando el feliz oriente del V Sol de Austria, Felipe Próspero q.D.g.* (Madrid: Diego Díaz de la Carrera, 1658).

his theatrical pieces and his prose works, which range from a dialogue account of military events in Flanders to verse glosses on Santa Teresa's meditations on the Lord's prayer, a work which went through five editions.[83]

In terms of their background Fonseca's academy formed a relatively homogeneous group, consisting primarily of court officials and bureaucrats with few individuals of real social distinction. They were typical *caballeros*, a group which increasingly dominated seventeenth-century life since, as I. A. A. Thompson notes, they came to constitute "almost the entirety of the middle and much of the upper cadres of the central administration, the judiciary, the army and the Church, the royal governors of the cities (the *corregidores*), the king's secretaries, councillors, and so on".[84] Fonseca's group boasted various knights of Santiago (Cuéllar, Oviedo y Herrera, Sotomayor, Nieto Reinalte and Guillén de la Carrera), one knight of Alcántara (Montero de Espinosa), one of the Order of San Esteban (Zárate y la Hoz), and a Comendador of the Order of Avís (Freire de Andrade). Several poets in Fonseca's circle served, or would go on to serve, the royal family in some capacity or other: Cuéllar was a royal secretary ("de los Reales Descargos", "de Cámara del Consejo de Cruzada" and "de las Ordenes") and was in the king's entourage in 1660 when the court went to the French frontier to hand over his daughter María Teresa to his nephew Louis XIV; Porter y Casanate was eventually appointed chronicler to Charles II;[85] Zárate y la Hoz served the same monarch as a gentleman-in-waiting; Suárez de Deza y Avila was a royal usher; whilst Vergara Salcedo, appointed *alcalde* of Nájara by its Duke, was chosen by Philip IV to write a verse account of Felipe Próspero's baptism. Other members served the nobility: Pinel y Monroy, for example, as well as being "regidor perpetuo de Toro" was also tutor to the eldest son of the Duke of Medina-Sidonia; Sarasa y Arce, a stage-censor, served the Dukes

---

[83] See *Diálogos militares y políticos discurridos por Eráclito y Demócrito sobre las campañas y ejércitos de Flandes* (Brussels: Humberto Antonio Velpio, 1654); and *Siete meditaciones sobre la oración del Padre nuestro, escritas por la seráfica Madre Santa Teresa de Jesús; glosadas en verso* (Antwerp: Balthasar Moreto, 1654). The latter was reprinted in 1656, 1658, 1659 and 1668.

[84] See "Nobility in Spain", p. 190. As Thompson also states: "the *caballeros* were almost exclusively an urban elite, sharing a common role in local power, and, in the seventeenth century as mercantile backgrounds receded and *letrado* values began to be absorbed into the cabalerresque, a common lifestyle, common attitudes to consumption, family and culture" (p. 190). I shall argue here that the academy played a central role in this process of group definition (both social and cultural).

[85] Aurora Egido incorrectly identifies this Porter y Casanate with Pedro Porter y Casanate (1611–1662), the Aragonese admiral who discovered the Gulf of California. See "Literatura efímera: oralidad y escritura en los certámenes y academias", in *Fronteras de la poesía en el barroco* (Barcelona: Editorial Crítica, 1990), 138–63 (p. 160). The two were in fact brothers. For a brief consideration of the involvement of Pedro in literary academias, see Egido, "Descubrimientos y humanismo: el almirante aragonés don Pedro Porter y Casanate", *Edad de Oro*, 10 (1991), 71–86 (pp. 73, 77).

of Medinaceli;[86] whilst Montero de Espinosa served the Admiral of Castile.[87] The latter, veteran of the 1637 Buen Retiro academy, had accompanied Queen Christina on her journey from Brussels to Rome, recording the occasion in an account published in 1656.[88] At least three academy regulars had fought in the Spanish army in Flanders, Montero de Espinosa, Zárate y la Hoz and Oviedo y Herrera, the latter being eventually made Conde de la Granja and governor of Potosí, dying in Peru in 1717.

Although there are differences between academies in the two halves of the century – the primary one being the decline in the longevity of individual groups – Fonseca de Almeida's academy is a reminder of their essential continuity of purpose, format and character. Indeed, after the end of the *Academia de Madrid* in the 1640s – and following that bleak decade which marked the most severe crisis in seventeenth-century Habsburg power, when both civil and international wars, together with the deaths of the queen (1644) and the heir apparent (1646), profoundly shook the monarchy, provoking a sense of crisis and catastrophe which, indirectly, may have been instrumental in putting an end to the academy's frivolous poetic activities during a period of national mourning and emergency[89] – Fonseca de Almeida's group sees the re-emergence of the academy as a cultural force within the capital, a force which, if in a slightly revised form, continued throughout Charles II's reign. Like the *Academia de Madrid* in the 1620s, Fonseca's academy is formed from a small nucleus of individuals meeting on a regular basis to read and write poetry and, perhaps more importantly, to be seen to do so. The primary difference is that Fonseca's academy is made up of individuals who clearly did not have the same, or the same degree of, literary pretensions as the writers in Mendoza's *Academia de Madrid*. The members of Fonseca's academic circle all come from the same respectable if largely undistinguished social background, the gentleman soldiers, financiers, bureaucrats, university graduates and court officials who swarmed around the court in Madrid. Although they are indeed united by their pursuit and practice of literature this is

---

[86] On his function as censor, see E. M. Wilson, "Calderón and the Stage-Censor in the Seventeenth-Century. A Provisional Study", *Symposium*, 15 (1961), 165–84.

[87] See Serralta, "Román Montero de Espinosa", pp. 120–21.

[88] See *Epílogo del viaje que hizo desde Bruselas a Roma la Majestad de Cristina Alejandra de Suecia* (Rome: Emprenta del Reu. Cam. Apost., 1656).

[89] For an overview of the effects of the 1640s on Aragon, Valencia and Castile, see Xavier Gil, " 'Conservación' y 'defensa' como factores de estabilidad en tiempos de crisis: Aragón y Valencia en la década de 1640", and J. H. Elliott, "Una sociedad no revolucionaria: Castilla en la década de 1640", in *1640: La monarquía hispánica en crisis* (Barcelona: Editorial Crítica, 1992), pp. 44–101, 102–22. For the impact of these royal deaths on the theatre, see J. E. Varey and N. D. Shergold, "Datos históricos sobre los primeros teatros de Madrid: prohibiciones de autos y comedias y sus consecuencias (1644–1651)", *BH*, 62 (1960), 286–324.

secondary to their professional status and activities; in this the entire membership of Fonseca's academy is representative of the "average", fundamentally untalented, individual who attended an academy during the century. Whilst regulars at the *Academia de Madrid* such as Bocángel, Pellicer, Castillo Solórzano, Salas Barbadillo and Vélez de Guevara were also, to a greater or lesser extent, "literary courtiers", dependent on obtaining posts and privileges from those in power to exist, their professional status and self-perception as writers is more pronounced, for not only did they publish complete works and collections but their literary activities were not simply confined to, and therefore restricted by, the academy as were many of the members of Fonseca's group. It would be a mistake, though, to take Fonseca's circle of literarily undistinguished professionals as entirely representative of the level of poetic ability and talent within academies generally in the second half of the century, for writers of the distinction of Juan de Matos Fragoso,[90] Francisco de la Torre y Sevil,[91] Antonio Solís y Rivadenyra[92] and Francisco Bances Candamo[93] were regular attendants at academies during this period. Indeed it is worth stating that it is the difference in quality between writers who attended academies in the first and second halves of the century which has contributed to the erroneous view that they declined in popularity over the course of the century. Whilst we may now, with justification perhaps, relegate these writers of the last decades of the century to oblivion, individuals such as Juan Vélez de Guevara,[94] Antonio de Zamora,[95] Agustín de Salazar y

---

[90] See Elsa Leonor di Santo, "Noticias sobre la vida de Juan de Matos Fragoso", *Segismundo*, 14 (1978–80), 217–31.

[91] See Torre y Sevil, *Entretenimiento de las musas*, ed. by Manuel Alvar (Valencia: Universitat de València, 1987), pp. 3–9, 65–73. All future references will be to this edition. See also Manuel Alvar, "Dos notas sobre don Francisco de la Torre y Sevil", in *Teatro del Siglo de Oro. Homenaje a Alberto Navarro González* (Kassel: Reichenberger, 1990), pp. 1–3; and Trevor Dadson, "Dos autógrafos desconocidos de Gabriel Bocángel", *El Crotalón*, 2 (1985), 275–98.

[92] See Frédéric Serralta, "Nueva biografía de Antonio de Solís y Rivadenyra", *Criticón*, 34 (1986), 51–157.

[93] See the Introduction to Francisco Bances Candamo, *Theatro de los theatros de los passados y presentes siglos*, ed. by Duncan W. Moir (London: Tamesis, 1970), pp. xvii–xxxvii.

[94] See the Introduction to Juan Vélez de Guevara, *Los celos hacen estrellas*, ed. by J. E. Varey and N. D. Shergold (London: Tamesis, 1970), pp. xvii–xxxvi. A sonnet and a *romance* by the writer are published in Fonseca's *Jardín de Apolo*. See *Jardín*, foliated in two parts, I, fol. 33; II, fols 33r–34v.

[95] See John Dowling, "La farsa al servicio del naciente siglo de las luces: *El hechizado por fuerza* (1697), de Antonio de Zamora", in *El teatro español a fines del siglo XVII. Historia, cultura y teatro en la España de Carlos II*, 3 vols, vol. 2, *Dramaturgos y géneros de las postrimerías*, ed. by Javier Huerta Calvo, Harm den Boer, Fermín Sierra Martínez (Amsterdam, Atlanta: Rodopi, 1989), pp. 275–86.

Torres,[96] Diego and José de Figueroa y Córdoba,[97] Pedro Ignacio de Arce y Tofiño,[98] Francisco de Avellaneda,[99] along with Matos Fragoso and the other writers just mentioned, were important and prominent writers and literati of their day. Regardless of literary merit, therefore, it is clear that the academy continued as a prominent part of the life of a writer. Furthermore, whilst Fonseca's academy itself had no writers of great literary merit, its members would certainly have had regular contact with writers of a higher "literary profile" via the other academies and *justas* they attended. To take but one example, for the *Certamen angélico* held in 1656 to celebrate the dedication of a new church to Thomas Aquinas a significant number of Fonseca's members submitted poetry together with writers such as Bocángel and Cubillo de Aragón.[100] It would appear that whilst more established poets did not join the newer academies, perhaps because their status and reputation were already established, they did join the fray in composing verse for the occasion when an important civic event was celebrated.

A further important difference between the *Academia de Madrid* and Fonseca's academy is the absence of titled nobility in the latter in comparison with the active involvement of a whole host of nobles and aristocrats in the

---

[96] See Vern G. Williamson, *The Minor Dramatists of Seventeenth-Century Spain* (Boston: Twayne, 1982), pp. 107–14; and Thomas Austin O'Connor, "A Bibliographical Note on Salazar y Torres' *Cytara de Apolo*", *RN*, 15 (1973), 129–31; "Don Agustín de Salazar y Torres: a Bibliography of Primary Sources", *Bulletin of Bibliography and Magazine Notes*, 32 (1975), 158–61, 167–80; "On Dating the *comedias* of Agustín de Salazar y Torres: A Provisional Study", *Hispanófila*, 23 (1979), 158–61.

[97] See Emilio Cotarelo y Mori, "Los hermanos Figueroa y Córdoba", *BRAE*, 6 (1919), 149–91. Both have compositions in Fonseca, *Jardín*, I, fols 1r–5r, 23v–25r, 26v–28r.

[98] See D. W. Cruickshank, "A Contemporary of Calderón", *MLR*, 63 (1968), 864–68; and John E. Varey, "An Additional Note on Pedro de Arce", *Iberoromania*, 23 (1986), 204–09.

[99] See Wilson, "Calderón and the Stage-Censor", pp. 163–164; and Cotarelo y Mori, "Los hermanos Figueroa y Córdoba", pp. 165–66.

[100] See José de Miranda y la Cotera, *Certamen angélico en la grande celebridad de la dedicación del nuevo y magnífico templo que su grave convento de religiosos de la esclarecida Orden de Predicadores consagró a Santo Tomás de Aquino, Dotor de la Iglesia, el octubre de M.DC.LVI* (Madrid: Diego Díaz de la Carrera, 1657). The members from Fonseca's academy include Nieto, Vélez de Guevara, Oviedo, Suárez, Ledesma, Antonio de Espinosa, Juan de Zamora and Lorenzo Guerra. The editor of the volume, Miranda y la Cotera, had himself contributed a *romance* to Fonseca, *Jardín*, II, fols 17r–19v. See also Miranda y la Cotera, *Días festivos del círculo del año que componen corona gloriosa a la fe viva que profesa, con demostraciones piadosas, y ostenta en aras públicas la Congregación de los indignos Esclavos del SS. Sacramento, siempre reconocida esclava de Dios, en todo dedicada a su gusto y servicios generosos humilde y noblemente religiosa. Renuévase su clara luz dándose a la estampa las virtuosas acciones y que en sus horas se exercitan* (Madrid: Diego Díaz de la Carrera, 1654), in which compositions by Olivares Vadillo and Zárate y la Hoz, together with Francisco de Avellaneda and Bocángel are published.

former over the course of its long existence. In this instance, Fonseca's academy would appear not to have facilitated socially useful communication between the upper and lower echelons of the nobility.[101] However in its absence of titled nobility Fonseca's group is again atypical of post 1650 academies for as I have already mentioned many academies held in the second half of the century still testify to the fact that nobles regularly hosted and attended them.[102] Far more representative are its roots in the educated, professional sector of the noble class. Carrasco Urgoiti has suggested that the attraction of the academy as an institution to this predominantly "middle-class" group (as she anachronistically terms them) during the reign of Charles II lay in them exploiting poetry, the courtly art form *par excellence*, as a means of making up for the "demérito de un linaje oscuro o comprometido".[103] Linking the popularity of the academy to a lack of social pedigree is certainly suggestive especially when one recalls how intensely conscious of status seventeenth-century society was, yet it obviously fails as a universally applicable explanation for the appeal of the academy. More generally, though, it seems valid to argue that the professional classes, the *caballeros*, utilized the academy as a means of consolidating and bolstering their social (or group) identity by conspicuously participating in what was still regarded as the most "noble" and urbane art form, for the academies made the gentlemanly pursuit of poetry more accessible whilst at the same time still conferring upon it a sense of elitism due to the closed nature of the format (in contrast, say, to the *justa poética*). Even in the first half of the century the social advantages to be gained from attending academies were repeatedly stressed by writers such as Pellicer. However to judge from the members of academies held in the latter half of the century it would seem that, as the practice of holding them took root and became an integral part of contemporary literary life, so the ever present emphasis on them as a social phenomenon came to predominate, such that, as in Fonseca's group, they were even more markedly the preserve of gentleman poetasters than of poets. The difference between the *Academia de Madrid* and Fonseca's academy is perhaps simply that social utility for a group such as Fonseca's has less to do with

---

[101] In the dedication of the 1662 academy held to celebrate the future Charles II's birth Fonseca holds it an extraordinary honour to have the participation of the Duke of Aveiro and the Count of Linares (to whom the volume is dedicated), thereby confirming that titled nobility were normally absent at his academies. See *Fonseca Jan 1662*, Dedication.

[102] Indeed, the conjunction of nobility and poets is often referred to in the title of the printed account: the printed version of a 1658 Valencian academy, for example, plays both implicitly and explicitly with the notion of illustrious participants in its title, *Sol de academias o academia de soles, en los lucidos ingenios de Valencia que la celebraron y en la hermosura y nobleza que la asistieron*.

[103] See "La oralidad", p. 51. Carrasco calls the post 1650 academy a "medio burgués", and also states that the nobility rarely attended (p. 51), which as we have seen is inaccurate.

establishing useful contacts than with using the academy as a means of identifying with the (cultural) values associated with the dominant social elite, and hence of declaring one's social status and allegiance. Via the academy the *caballeros* could begin to behave both culturally – and thereby socially – like their superiors. These are groups then which did not necessarily need or seek patronage, but which still wished to be seen to adhere to the cultural activities of the titled nobility.

Nevertheless despite whatever reservations we may have as to the quality of its poetry the academy continued to play an undeniably central part in any seventeenth-century poet's bid for literary *reputación*, for involvement in an academy was essential for any individual with literary pretensions and, consequently, the work produced for academies was a strategic element in a poet's attempt to secure a literary reputation. Academy poetry, together with that written for *justas poéticas*, presents the official or public face of the Baroque poet; that is, it represents the poet as he was, and as he wished to be, seen by contemporaries. Similarly for the gentleman-poet with literary pretensions the academy was not only a means of expressing his active involvement with a "noble" occupation, and hence a statement of his social pretensions, but was also a very real public forum in which to practise the art of poetry, and in which the success (or otherwise) of that practice would be judged.

This should remind us that for all its potential social caché, the academy was still explicitly defined by its concern with poetry. Indeed the attraction of the academy's relative exclusivity has also an important literary dimension. Various critics have considered the effects on literature of the polarization of contemporary readers/theatre goers into two distinct groups, the *vulgo* and the *discretos*.[104] At the end of the sixteenth and well into the seventeenth century Golden Age critics warned of the negative effects on literature and theatre of the *vulgo*, characterized by Frenk (in a manner that echoes contemporary evaluations) as "la gran masa amorfa de los que no pertenecen ni a la aristocracia, ni al alto clero ni a los círculos literarios, artísticos y científicos".[105] The popularity of the theatre produced a huge audience for whom illiteracy was no bar to enjoyment and cultural consumption; whilst a revolution in education, brought about by the need to create civil servants for the ever-expanding government bureaucracy, led to an increase in literacy, and

---

[104] See Keith Whinnom, "The Problem of the 'Best-Seller' in Spanish Golden Age Literature", *BHS*, 57 (1980), 189–98 (p. 195); and Margit Frenk, " 'Lectores y oidores'. La difusión oral de la literatura en el siglo de oro", in *Actas del séptimo congreso de la Asociación Internacional de Hispanistas*, ed. by Giuseppe Bellini, 2 vols (Rome: Bulzoni Editore, 1981), I, pp. 101–23 (pp. 117–18). See also Margit Frenk, "La ortografía elocuente. (Testimonios de lectura oral en el Siglo de Oro)", in *Actas del VIII congreso de la Asociación Internacional de Hispanistas*, ed. by A. David Kossoff, José Amor y Vázquez, Ruth H. Kossoff and Geoffrey W. Ribbans, 3 vols (Madrid: Ediciones Istmo, 1986), I, pp. 549–56.

[105] See " 'Lectores y oidores' ", p. 118.

hence to the development of a larger potential reading public.[106] The effects of this were varied. In general terms, Cruickshank has persuasively argued that the book trade was increasingly economically geared over the course of the seventeenth century to this mass public, producing large amounts of "ephemera" (such as *pliegos*, *relaciones de sucesos* and *comedias sueltas*) whose price and content appealed to this group, with the result that the quality of literature steadily declined over the century.[107] Moreover writers were faced with the dilemma of whether to produce commercially popular works or, rather, ones that, appealing to the elite, aimed at classic status.[108] More specifically, the almost hysterical polarization of readers into two camps, the highly educated elite and the "barely literate" masses, in the earlier decades of the seventeenth century can be viewed as one of the reasons behind the development in poetry of an elitist aesthetic, exemplified by Carrillo y Sotomayor and Góngora, marked by its cultivation of lexical and conceptual difficulties. Similarly the academies by their very format enabled the establishment of a kind of "cordon sanitaire" around poetry, less perhaps as a means of continuing and protecting poetry's elite status in an age when the "common reader" was repeatedly vilified and viewed as negatively affecting literature, than as a means of distinguishing and elevating the very practitioners of such a "noble" art. It is no coincidence that as the theatre and novel become ever more popular, in the sense of appealing to, and consequently being shaped by, the *vulgo*, poetry, the "aristocratic" genre, is increasingly practised in closed coterie worlds to which access is restricted. Moreover, as I have already mentioned, the burgeoning strata of society which made up the bulk of members in such academies as Fonseca de Almeida's – the *caballeros* – found in the academy one means of constituting themselves as a discrete social and cultural unit. In this way an important sector of contemporary society was able to use the academy to express its aspirations by identifying itself visibly and, perhaps paradoxically, in a semi-public way with the values and ideals of the social elite. The academy is a ready-made mechanism to

---

[106] See D. W. Cruickshank, " 'Literature' and the Book Trade in Golden Age Spain", *MLR*, 73 (1978), 799–824 (pp. 809–12). The popularity of the academy itself is also linked to the growing number of university-educated individuals in seventeenth-century Spain, particularly in the capital. Such a literate group not only supplied the Habsburg bureaucracy with its officials and functionaries but also provided the academies with their basic membership. On this point, see Elias L. Rivers, "La poesía culta y sus lectores", *Edad de Oro*, 12 (1993), 267–79 (pp. 273–74). On universities and their role in providing bureaucrats, see Richard L. Kagan, *Students and Society in Early Modern Spain* (Baltimore: The Johns Hopkins University Press, 1974), Chapters 3–6.

[107] See " 'Literature' and the Book Trade", pp. 818–22. Also see Whinnom's comments on this argument, "The Problem of the 'Best-Seller' ", p. 198 n. 22. See Chapter 3 for a consideration of the similarities between academy topics and *relaciones de sucesos*.

[108] See E. C. Riley, *Cervantes's Theory of the Novel* (Oxford: Oxford University Press, 1962), pp. 107–15 (p. 110).

express one's affiliation and allegiance to the *discretos* rather than the amorphous mass of the *vulgo*.

Significantly, however, whilst having an elite format the academies did not foster an elite aesthetic. The relative absence of a *culterano* aesthetic is due more to the nature and format of the event – and, of course, the poor quality of the poets attending – than with any desire to propagate a more accessible style.[109] If the elitism of the academy is taken to be one of the causes of its continued popularity, then paradoxically an institution, popular precisely because it was elitist and therefore excluded the demonized *vulgo*, because of its institutional format actually served to make poetry stylistically less elitist (because less rhetorically, lexically and conceptually complex) and hence more accessible: appearing to be elitist, a *discreto*, is more important than producing elitist – "quality" or "classic" – literature.

A further important reason for the century-long popularity of the academies, then, is that they offered an easily imitated style and a ready audience. The academy did not foster or facilitate the development of an individual style; instead its format and atmosphere tended to encourage an homogeneous, "in-house" style, which it institutionalized and hence made acceptable. As Clara Giménez Fernández puts it: "se aprecia una pérdida de la identidad del poeta, una 'absorción' por parte de la academia que, en algunos casos, acaba con las peculiaridades estilísticas de éste".[110] As the century progressed, and as the academy became the central feature of literary life, so this "absorption" of individuality increased. (It is significant here that compositions are generated by an external stimulus – the academy topic – rather than by the "free" choice of an individual poet's imagination.) Rather than strive to differentiate their lyric voice from poetic contemporaries and predecessors, mediocre poets could opt for the lowest common denominator, the academy style, and be assured of a modicum of success. Poets of little talent can readily conceal their poetic inadequacies behind an easily imitated style. Of course this raises the question of the academy's role in the decline of the Spanish lyric over the century. Whilst it is obviously extremely difficult, if not impossible, to ascertain to what extent a common poetic has a stultifying effect on literary and artistic development, it is certainly true that the majority of poems submitted to academies share a paucity of invention which is symptomatic of

---

[109] It is worth noting that *pliegos* often printed compositions full of what appear to us as complex wordplay and puns, a kind of "popular" *conceptismo*. On this point, see E. M. Wilson, "Quevedo para las masas", in *Entre las jarchas y Cernuda. Constantes y variables en la poesía española* (Barcelona: Editorial Ariel, 1977), pp. 275–97 (pp. 281–82). The existence and popularity of such wordplay etc. (which recalls the style of many academy pieces) perhaps indicates that a distinction between *culteranismo* and *conceptismo* is still a necessary and valid one, despite the very many similarities in practice between the two "styles".

[110] See "Poesía de academias (MSS. 1–4000)", *Manuscrt.Cao.*, 2 (1989), 47–55 (p. 52).

the decline of the Spanish lyric after the mid-seventeenth century. The role of the academy in fostering such a decline is one of the key questions to be considered over the remainder of this study.

The reasons adduced here for the continued popularity of the academy should also be seen therefore as the principal cause of the relative mediocrity of the poetry which academies existed to practice. Social prestige, and a desire for entertainment made more attractive by the occasion's elitism, brought individuals to academies; once there, both the orality of the occasion and its fundamental frivolity meant that all and sundry could turn out hackneyed verse with relative ease. In this way, the institution itself helped to lower poetic expectations, with the result that, as the century progresses, topics often become mere clichés, and exhausted ones at that, and the organization, register and rhetoric of the poems often simply crystallize into rigid formulae lacking any real spontaneity. The academy did of course continue to challenge those poets who wished to be challenged, but its very popularity was both a cause and an effect of its nurturing a poetic accessible to poetasters who, as is the case with Fonseca de Almeida's academy, gradually came to form the majority of regular members by the second half of the century.

2

THE ACADEMY AND THE *JUSTA POETICA*

The popularity of the literary academy was mirrored in the seventeenth century by another type of poetic forum, the *justa poética*, or public poetic competition. The *justa poética* was in many ways similar in format to the academy in so far as compositions were submitted on set subjects and in prescribed metres. Both were part and parcel of the same seventeenth-century phenomenon, the communal practice of poetry. The vast majority of *justas* were held to celebrate either a religious event of some significance (such as a beatification or canonization) or, in the secular arena, an occasion connected with the monarchy (typically births, deaths and marriages). In either case, the event was deemed to be of fundamental importance to the life of the community, and celebrated or commemorated as such. The rationale behind the *justas* has been succinctly expressed by Mercedes Blanco: "lo habitual es, pues, que la fiesta obedezca a la necesidad de representar de modo visible la adhesión de la sociedad a ciertos símbolos cuya autoridad acaba de ser refrendada por el poder soberano".[1] In celebrating the births of respective crown princes with *justas poéticas*, for example, as the births of Philip IV (1605), Baltasar Carlos (1629), Felipe Próspero (1657) and Charles II (1661) were celebrated by civic and university authorities, communities are officially asserting their allegiance to and supposed dependence upon the Habsburg monarchy, thereby signalling their loyalty to the regime itself. Such events also enable the local authorities in question to make the concerns of an often distant monarch appear more immediate and relevant to a particular community, whilst at the same time enhancing the monarchy itself, and all that it represents, by making it the focus of elaborate and spectacular public festivities. The existence of the social and political hierarchy, and of its ideology, is brought home to a community in an enjoyable and entertaining way. In some senses, therefore, such events can be taken as examples of the imposition of certain cultural and political values upon whole communities and hence of the utilization and manipulation of public events and festivities to serve the interests of the Habsburg regime both locally and nationally – and in both its secular and religious aspects – under the guise of apparent popular spontaneity.

As well as their public and civic aspects, the *justas* were often mobilized as

---

1   See "La oralidad en las justas poéticas", *Edad de Oro*, 7 (1988), 33–47 (p. 35).

a means of promoting certain poetic styles. This use of the *justa* as a weapon of literary propaganda occurred especially during the intense debate over Góngora's innovations in the 1610s and 1620s. The most notorious example of this occurred during the Madrid poetic festivities organized by Lope de Vega in 1620 and 1622 to celebrate respectively the beatification and canonization of San Isidro. Lope used the occasion both to promote his friends amongst the poets who entered the competitions and, in his published accounts of the events, to promote his own poetic.[2] Not surprisingly these competitions attracted the same writers who regularly attended academies: at the 1622 *justa*, for example, prizes went to many of the poets who formed the core of the *Academia de Madrid* at the time, such as Guillén de Castro, Mira de Amescua, Francisco de Quintana, Diego de Villegas and Sebastián Francisco de Medrano.[3]

The format of a *justa poética* invariably followed the same pattern. The obsequies held by the University of Oviedo to mark the death of Philip IV in September 1665 included a poetry competition celebrated on 19 November, at three o'clock in the afternoon, which is typical in every respect of such events.[4] The University, having decided to hold the usual poetry competition, ordered one Manuel Serrano de la Paz to draw up the rules and various sections of the competition. This he did, putting up notices in all public places in the city, including the cathedral and the main lecture theatre.[5] The competition consisted of ten sections: the first three for poetry in Latin, followed by sections for the sonnet, the *canción real*, the *glosa, octavas, décimas,*

---

[2] For Lope's prose accounts of the two *justas*, which are interspersed with critical comments on the poems submitted which promote his own aesthetic position, see *Obras escogidas*, 2 vols, vol. 2, *Poesías líricas. Poemas. Prosas. Novelas*, ed. by Federico Carlos Sainz de Robles (Madrid: Aguilar, 1946), pp. 1572–76, 1589–1601. On Lope's involvement, see Emilio Orozco Díaz, *Lope y Góngora frente a frente* (Madrid: Gredos, 1973), pp. 312–54; Javier Portus Pérez, "La intervención de Lope de Vega y de Gómez de Mora en las fiestas de canonización de San Isidro", *Villa de Madrid*, 26 (1981), 30–41.

[3] See *Obras escogidas*, p. 1585.

[4] For an account of the final illness and death of Philip IV, see Pedro Rodríguez de Monforte, *Descripción de las honras que se hicieron a la católica majestad de don Felipe cuarto, rey de las Españas y del nuevo mundo en el Real Convento de la Encarnación, que de orden de la reina nuestra señora como superintendente de las Reales Obras dispuso D. Baltasar Barroso de Ribera, Marqués de Malpica* (Madrid: Francisco Nieto, 1666).

[5] See *Relación de las exequias que en la muerte del rey nuestro señor don Felipe Cuarto el Grande, rey de Españas, y emperador de las Indias hizo la Universidad de Oviedo en el Principado de Asturias. Ofrécela en la real mano de la reina nuestra señora doña María Ana de Austria* (Madrid: Pablo de Val, 1666), pp. 94–95. Compare the account of the obsequies organized by the University of Salamanca given by Francisco de Roys, *Pira real, que erigió la mayor Atenas a la mayor majestad; la Universidad de Salamanca, a las inmortales cenizas, a la gloriosa memoria de su rey y señor don Felipe el Grande* (Salamanca: Melchor Estevez, 1666). On the subject of royal exequies, see Steven N. Orso, *Art and Death at the Spanish Habsburg Court: The Royal Exequies for Philip IV* (Columbia: University of Missouri Press, 1989).

epigrams, and finally the *romance* (pp. 97–104). Prizes were given to the winning poem in each category: those for the sonnet section, for example, were a silver-gilt salt-cellar; for the runner-up, a small silver bowl; and for third place, a coconut with silver decorations (p. 100).

The *justa*, then, was a celebration of a public event in public. Its major difference from the academy was that the competition was normally advertised and hence open to all. As a result an immense number of people composed competition poetry; as Cristóbal Suárez de Figueroa commented in his novel *El Pasajero* (Madrid, 1617) "apenas tiene el mar tantas arenas cuantos poetas se descubren [en las justas poéticas]".[6] As with literary academies, the *justas* also had the allure of granting the successful poets very public recognition; given that many *justas poéticas* were held under the auspices of a university or a town council, the audience was likely to include the most influential and important members of a given community. In one sense, therefore, the *justa poética* provided the means of gaining a wider public reputation than the literary academy. Of course, against this must be set the fact that the very public nature of the *justa* would probably mitigate against it: power and patronage were more likely to be courted and found at an academy, precisely because its private and regular nature provided an intimate atmosphere more conducive to gaining contacts and friendships. This said, outside the large cities, especially those with royal or vicegeral courts, the *justa* was an important means of gaining a reputation.

Over the course of the seventeenth century, as the academy became an established and increasingly dominant element of literary life, the initial distinction between *justas* and academies – one a public celebration of a "national" event, the other a private meeting devoted to amatory and burlesque topics – became progressively blurred, both in the capital and beyond. The academy began in a minor way to appropriate the *justa*'s more public orientated subject matter, setting the occasional poem on a "public" subject. More significantly, it appropriated the *justa*'s rationale by holding sessions to mark significant events. From the start of the century academies had set laudatory topics on the royal family, such as the *romance* composed in 1623 for the *Academia de Madrid* by Pantaleón de Ribera on the birth of the princess María Margarita Catalina.[7] However as the century progressed academies began to centre entire one-off sessions, rather than just the occasional poem, around the celebration of a particular event. This point is worth emphasizing as it is an indication of how the academy developed in part by encroaching upon an initially distinct poetic phenomenon. From an examination of the bibliographic details of seventeenth-century printed poetry volumes it is clear that 1650 marked the turning point when academies began to celebrate public

---

[6] See Cristóbal Suárez de Figueroa, *El pasajero*, ed. by María Isabel López Bascuñana, 2 vols (Barcelona: PPU, 1988), I, p. 236.
[7] See *Obras*, I, pp. 137–44.

events, and when there was a marked increase in the published proceedings of literary academies.[8] After this date the *justas* still continued, but were now primarily – though not exclusively – concerned with religious events and celebrations. During the last four decades of the century, then, the academy became a standard way for poets, nobles and commoners to mark important public events and dates in the king's life.

Two academies held to celebrate the birth of the future Charles II in 1661 are indicative of the broadening of the academy's thematic range to encompass subject matters once held to be the preserve of the *justa poética*. The first of these was held in Granada and the second in Madrid under the auspices of Fonseca de Almeida.[9] In the case of Fonseca's academy, this meeting is clearly a continuation of the group's normal poetic activities, with the same poets attending, the only difference being that their compositions are based around the birth of Charles and the death of the previous heir, Felipe Próspero, rather than the amatory subjects which were standard in the academy. In contrast, the academy meeting in Granada was, according to José Sánchez, a one-off occasion.[10] To all intents and purposes, therefore, it functioned as a *justa poética*. This illustrates the close affinity between the two phenomena as well as the expansion in meaning of "academia" noted by Willard King which meant that by the mid-century the term was increasingly applied to one-off literary meetings, as here, rather than to a literary gathering held with a degree of regularity.[11] Indeed, in a small city like Granada, poetry competitions must have had the feel of a literary academy, since the number of possible entrants must have been limited. Entrants to such competitions would thus have had the sense of writing for a coterie of known individuals, and the feel of such occasions must therefore have been similar to the cliquish atmosphere of many academies.[12]

---

[8] See Simón Díaz, "Primer índice", pp. 145–60.

[9] See *Academia que se celebró en la ciudad de Granada en ocho de diciembre al nacimiento del Príncipe Don Carlos*; and *Academia que se celebró en siete de enero al feliz nacimiento del serenísimo Príncipe D. Carlos*.

[10] See Sánchez, *Academias*, p. 291.

[11] See King, *Prosa*, p. 93. One of the sonnets from Fonseca's academy takes as its subject the fact that Charles was born just five days after the death of the existing heir, Felipe Próspero. It is preceded by the following gloss: "exórtase a España que llore, significando su gozo en el nacimiento de Carlos Leonardo, como mostró su pesar en la muerte de Felipe Próspero" (*Fonseca Jan 1662*, p. 101). Similarly, in the Granada academy one of the topics set was "ponderar la tristeza y alegría que en breve tiempo tuvo España con la muerte de uno y nacimiento de otro [heredero]" (*Granada*, fol. 9v). These two sonnets demonstrate how poetry written for different venues but on the same event nevertheless demonstrates a remarkable uniformity of subject and sentiment. Such homogeneity is typical of commemorative verse in general, and of competition poetry in particular.

[12] For an idea of the importance of *justas poéticas* to the literary life of a provincial city, and to the provincial poet in particular, see Antonio Gallego Morell, *Francisco y Juan*

The linking of private academies and public occasions most probably stems from the adoption by the court of Philip IV of the academy as an integral part of palace celebrations and fiestas, the most striking and frequently cited example of this being the academy held in the Buen Retiro in 1637. This *Academia burlesca*, in all probability an extraordinary session of the *Academia de Madrid*, is an excellent example of the extravagance with which these occasions could be celebrated at Court.[13] Held on 20 February, the competition's president was Luis Vélez de Guevara, its secretary Alfonso de Batres, and its *fiscal*, Francisco de Rojas Zorrilla; whilst the judges were a mixture of nobles and poets in the service of the regime – the Prince of Esquilache, Antonio Portocarrero de la Vega (major-domo to Isabel of Bourbon), Luis de Haro (Olivares' nephew and the future *valido*), Francisco de Rioja, Francisco de Calatayud, Gaspar Bonifaz and Antonio Hurtado de Mendoza. The poetic competition itself formed part of the celebrations which lasted from 15 to 24 February and which were held to commemorate the election of Ferdinand (Philip IV's brother-in-law and future father-in-law) as King of the Romans at Ratisbon on 22 December, 1636, as well as to honour the Princess of Carignano who had arrived in Madrid in November. As well as the academy the week-long celebrations included a succession of masques, plays, pageants, dances, bull-fights, tournaments and banquets, all held in the newly built Buen Retiro palace.[14] The academy itself formalized the prevailing atmosphere of any academy in making the entire event one of humour and burlesque. In his opening address Vélez de Guevara comments on the spectacular nature of the entire proceedings during the week's festivities: he is unable to decide whether he is awake or asleep "porque es imposible que Plaza, máscara y carros triunfales pudieran caber menos que en sueños de los siete durmientes".[15] The topics set are all humorous and the vast majority take subjects specific to the occasion, its location and participants. Many of the topics simply satirize and generally poke fun at poets and court officials taking part in the event; they thus strongly resemble the type of caricatures normally the exclusive preserve of the *vejámenes*. Thus we find topics such as an eulogy to the beauty and elegance of Alonso de Carbonel, site architect and master of works at the Retiro renowned for his ugliness (pp. 639–40);[16] or resolving the question of whether Diego de Covarrubias y Leyva, chief

---

de Trillo y Figueroa (Granada: Universidad de Granada, 1950), pp. 9–37. (The *justas* in Granada entered by Francisco de Trillo y Figueroa are discussed on pp. 21–34.) See also Aurora Egido, "Floresta de vejámenes universitarios granadinos", *BH*, 92 (1990), 309–32.

[13] See King, *Prosa*, p. 93. Also see Davies, *Poet at Court*, pp. 62–63.

[14] For an account of these festivities, see J. E. Varey, "Calderón, Cosme Lotti, Velázquez, and the Madrid Festivities of 1636–37", *Renaissance Drama*, New Series 1 (1968), 253–82; and Brown and Elliott, *Palace*, pp. 199–203.

[15] See *Academia burlesca*, p. 614. Subsequent references will be given in the text.

[16] On this individual, see Brown and Elliott, *Palace*, pp. 59, 91; Elliott, *Count-Duke*, p.

custodian of the new palace, will best defend the Buen Retiro with his vigilance or his large belly (pp. 640–42).[17] (These two individuals, together with Francisco Calero, a *guardadamas*, and José Martínez de Grimaldo, secretary to Philip IV, were the butt of another satirical topic in an academy held the following year in the Retiro, when poets were asked to compose a *romance* congratulating the four for the fact that they were no longer going to be satirized.[18]) Other topics comment on palace customs, such as the *romance* set "extirpar la herejía de llamar mondongas a las criadas de las damas, pues no hay cosa más lucida ni de más generoso nombre que servirlas; mas, y que de aquí adelante, se llamen doncellas de honor" (pp. 630–34). A minority are less specific, more run-of-the-mill subjects more normal of literary academies, such as how sick people fall ill from disease but die because of the doctor (pp. 653–55); and the *romance* asking forgiveness from an ugly woman for having loved her (pp. 647–48).

The Buen Retiro academy is an excellent example of a recurrent feature of academies held to mark a specific royal event: unlike a *justa*, the academy's relation to the event may often be extremely tenuous. When this is so, such occasions are clearly less public displays of loyalty, propagandistic court flattery or celebrations of monarchy than excuses to hold a literary academy; they become pure entertainment. Thus, whilst academies were held as occasions to mark an event, like *justas*, they did not necessarily dedicate every poem to the event in question. Furthermore, by the second half of the century the question of access to the meeting, rather than the purpose of the event, or whether it was part of a regular cycle of meetings, was one of the key differences between the academy and the *justa* or *certamen*. What makes an academy an academy, in other words, is that access to the event is relatively restricted, by invitation only, whereas the *justa* proper was a truly public open event. Thus, whilst the public domain increasingly impinged upon the private coterie world of the academy, this world itself remained resolutely closed and elitist. What occurs by mid-century, then, is less a shift in definition than an increase in the number of private academies basing meetings around public events, events associated in the first half of the century with the *justa poética*. This probably also explains the sharp increase in published accounts of

---

475; and Brown, *Velázquez*, pp. 231–32. His ugliness made him the ideal person to play the queen in a burlesque court play in 1638. See Bergman, "A Court Entertainment", p. 78.

[17] For Covarrubias' role in the administration of the Buen Retiro, see Brown and Elliott, *Palace*, p. 95. Covarrubias also edited a volume of eulogistic verse on the Retiro: see *Elogios al Palacio Real del Buen Retiro. Escritos por algunos ingenios de España. Recogidos por Diego de Covarrubias y Leyva* (Madrid: Imp. del Reino, 1635). Many of the poets contributing sonnets to this volume were also members of the *Academia de Madrid*, such as Vélez de Guevara, Pellicer de Tovar, Gaspar Dávila, Juan Francisco de la Barreda and Gabriel de Roa, whilst others, like Pedro Rosete Niño, were regulars at other Madrid-based groups.

[18] See Bergman, "El «Juicio final»", p. 560.

private academy sessions post 1650: having appropriated the organizational rationale of the *justas*, the printed word became the academy's more exclusive equivalent of the public display typical of the latter. After all, there is little point in celebrating or commemorating something if no one is aware that such celebrations have taken place.

The appropriation and adoption by the academy of the public event-orientated subject matter of the *justas* significantly altered the nature and purpose of occasional verse which, not surprisingly, was affected by its association with, and production within, the literary academy. As the question of the effects of the thematic heterogeneity on the reception of individual compositions is central to the question both of the academy's atmosphere and, more importantly, to the horizon of expectations of those attending, it is worthwhile considering the juxtaposition of celebratory verse with the more numerous amatory topics. The fact that the difference between such compositions is unambiguous, being one of theme rather than just style, allows a clear impression to be gained of the consequences of thematic heterogeneity. A consideration of this clearer type of compositional division will therefore lay the ground for a subsequent analysis of the effects of such differences on the reception of standard Petrarchan poetry when performed alongside more frivolous, salacious and flippant love poems. It also serves to highlight the influence and effect of the academy on other types of poetry apart from amatory poetry and to give a more accurate and rounded picture of the academy itself as a poetic institution.

Over the course of the century occasional verse becomes increasingly tinged with the lighter more frivolous tone of academy poetry, in stark contrast to the high seriousness of such verse in the early years of the reign of Philip IV. The very content of some occasional poems becomes lighter and less serious, but more significantly even when the content of a poem and the treatment of its subject matter remain serious such gravity is always implicitly undermined by the poem's very association with other less serious non-celebratory poems typical of an academy meeting. An example of this undermining of the earnest celebratory tone of eulogistic verse is the academy held in 1678 in Ciudad Real. In the published account, two poems "En alabanza de Carlos segundo nuestro gran monarca (que Dios guarde) deseando sus felicidades" (fols 15r–16r) are preceded by a sonnet and some *quintillas* on the subject of a lady breaking wind by accident ("a una dama que, a vista de su galán, sopló la lumbre y, alabándola su buen aliento, respiró por otra parte", fols 13v–14v).[19] What is striking here is the coexistence within one occasion of poems which belong to two rigidly distinct genres – sober and hyperbolic public poetry, and risqué, mildly scatological, burlesque

---

[19] Similar juxtapositions occur in novelistic accounts: in the *El diablo cojuelo*, for example, Don Cleofás declaims an encomiastic sonnet on Philip IV and is followed by El Cojuelo who recites a humorous one on a "gentleman" tailor. See *El diablo*, pp. 212–13.

verse. The association of one with the other, their coexistence in a single academy meeting, has the effect of minimalizing the very difference between monarch and subject, majesty and mundane reality, a difference that occasional verse and the *justa poética* normally strive both to establish and to celebrate. Majesty is here reduced to just another academy topic, becoming thus more an occasion for wit than a demonstration of loyalty.

Of course, it could readily be argued that the seventeenth century was capable of distinguishing between poems of different genres (solemn occasional poetry and burlesque), and that they would therefore readily disassociate the two. This is particularly the case in academies such as that held in Valencia in 1669 in the presence of the Count of Paredes, the new viceroy, to celebrate Charles II's birthday, in which the poetic topics were subdivided into four distinct categories, "heroic", "lyrical", "humorous" and "various".[20] However, such divisions by genre were very much the exception, and the Valencian academy in question was probably attempting to mitigate against the kind of cross-genre influence and debasement which I am discussing by categorizing its topics. Whilst contemporaries would undoubtedly have expected to evaluate poems according to distinct genre criteria, and therefore to disassociate the tone or register of one composition from another, some of the mystique normally carefully cultivated within occasional poetry written in connection with the monarchy is lost in the switch between topics and registers which is inevitable in an academy meeting.

Even those academies whose topics are entirely dedicated to a single important event reveal the negative or deflationary influence on occasional poetry of the academy ethos and atmosphere. Earlier collective volumes such as the *Anfiteatro de Felipe el grande* (1631) and *Elogios al Palacio Real del Buen Retiro* (1635), although not the products of academies, perfectly exemplify occasional poetry: both maintain a constant elevated tone and have a clear purpose, namely the celebration and exaltation of the Habsburg monarchy. Both tone and purpose are at best diminished, at worst lost, in an academy context. The most striking characteristic of the *Felipe el grande* volume, for example, is the high seriousness with which the poets record and celebrate what is clearly a minor and insignificant event – the shooting of a bull by the king – an event, moreover, hardly capable, even for the most loyal and sycophantic contemporary reader, of bearing the hyperbolic interpretations heaped upon it by court poets. The point, obviously, is that it is this very seriousness which deflects attention away from the insignificance of the event being celebrated and which thus attempts to centre the reader's attention on positive values, such as Philip's valour and prowess, rather than on mundane realities, such as Spain's military weaknesses in the European

---

[20] See *Real academia*, p. 4.

arena.²¹ In contrast, the academy meeting attended by a host of court poets some fifty years later to commemorate Charles II's "heroic" deed in giving up his carriage to a priest taking the Viaticum to a dying man shows how far the academy has actually undermined occasional verse. By its very unevenness in tone, its refusal to seek always to elevate and so dignify the event in question, the volume inevitably draws attention to the very gulf between the king's action and the poets' attempted hyperbolic interpretation of this as an act of exemplary piety and hence as a confirmation of Charles' successful embodiment of Habsburg values. Such a failure to maintain a consistent, elevated tone is directly attributable to the influence of the academy format in which the poetic celebration of this event took place, since the academy's keynote is heterogeneity, in subject matter and style. The very academy context, in other words, means that the credibility gap between the actual event and the poets' re-interpretation cannot be bridged. Thus, poetic attempts to link the king's pious deed to that of his Austrian ancestor, Rudolf, whose similar action was the subject of a painting by Rubens and Wildens which hung in the Alcázar,²² or to take Charles' action as an indication that God will reward such meritorious religious zeal with the birth of an heir,²³ are unsettled and made to appear exaggerated and overstated by their proximity to other compositions such as the *romance jocoserio* in which the Manzanares lays claim to be the best river in the world since Charles' "heroica acción" took place on its banks, or the *romance* put into the mouth of the king's carriage itself.²⁴ The following verse *vejamen*, composed by Francisco de Bustos, which the mules drawing the royal carriage address to the doctor's mule, and for which there is an academy precedent in the late sixteenth-century Valencian *Academia de los Nocturnos*,²⁵ is typical of this type of lighter celebratory verse produced by academies in the second half of the century:

> Carlos (nuestro rey) del Pardo
> a su Corte se volvía,
> y en el camino encontró
> al Rey de tejas arriba.

---

²¹ For a detailed analysis of this volume as court propaganda, see my "The Habsburgs and Hunting: Creating an Image of Philip IV", *JHP*, 17 (1993), 103–28.

²² See *Católica acción*, fols 10v–11r (corrected foliation). The "Devotion of Rudolf I" hung in Philip IV's summer bedroom. See Mary Crawford Volk, "New Light on a Seventeenth-Century Collector: The Marquis of Leganés", *AB*, 62 (1980), 256–68 (p. 262). Also see Brown, *Velázquez*, 209; and Steven Orso, *Velázquez, "Los borrachos" and Painting at the Court of Philip IV* (Cambridge: Cambridge University Press, 1993), pp. 119–120.

²³ See *Católica acción*, fol. 14r (corrected foliation).

²⁴ See *Católica acción*, fols 14v–15r (corrected foliation), 17v–18r.

²⁵ See *Academia de los Nocturnos*, II, pp. 152–56.

Apeóse de su coche,
y con reverencia digna,
se le dio, y le fue serviendo:
¡gran cosa es la cortesía!
   A visitar a un enfermo
piadosamente Dios iba,
porque el médico y el mal
entre el Réquiem le tenían.
. . .
   Adonde iban llegó el coche,
y fue grande maravilla,
que llevando el cielo a cuestas,
no se rompiese la viga.
   A la puerta del enfermo
estaba la mula misma
del doctor; lo mismo fuera
estar él (menos la silla).
   Las mulas del coche regio,
que la vieron de sardina,
la dieron este vejamen,
mientras duró la visita.
   "Dinos, esqueleto en zancas,
¿eres mula o chirimía?,
que en lo flaco y en el soplo
o te enflautas o te entiplas.
   ¿Eres clavo a la gualdrapa,
que cuelga de tus costillas?
¿O eres fiera, en que se parte
el jinete que va encima?
   Más que mula eres la vara
o la espuela que te pica;
corteza de mula vete
de Lázaro a ser tablilla.
   Sólo por el pelo engordas,
cual caballera postiza,
no sirviéndote el pellejo
más que de aforrar las tripas.
   ¿Comes cebada pobreta?
¿Susténtaste con ortigas?
¿O con tripas? Que éstas sólo
te habrán hecho longaniza.
   Del doctor eres sin duda,
y te trae para que sirvas
(por tenerte más a mano)
al enfermo como jeringa".
   Viendo que esto iba adelante,
respondió a todas muy viva;
que ser del doctor, y no

estar muerta, fue gran dicha:
"Yo soy una mula honrada,
original de Galicia,
y no sé si sus mercedes
son merced o señoría.

Mas pues la merced de Dios
traen a esta casa pajiza,
mercedes serán, sin duda,
desde la cola a la cincha.

Y así, hablando con respeto
y con toda cortesía,
no merezco que me ultrajen,
queriéndome hacer mohína.

Yo traigo al doctor mi amo
acuestas todos los días,
a ser muerte de este enfermo
algo más de medicina.

Yo no veo los que sana,
sólo, señas, querría
que lo que mata a mí
repartiera en otras vidas.

En cuanto al comer, no tengo
que quejarme (si se mira),
porque nunca de la boca
el bocado se me quita.

No me da a comer cebada
ni paja, aunque se la pida;
que por regalarme sólo
me da a comer gollorías.

Yo, agradecida de aquesto,
porque me precio de fina,
adonde quiera que va
le regalo con caídas.

La salud deste enfermo,
ya me parece precisa,
porque viendo al rey la cara
todos los males se alivian".

Dijo, y no pasó adelante,
porque a este punto salían
Dios y el Rey, dejando en todos
acción tan heroica escrita.[26]

Whilst in no way disrespectful, the poem's jocular and frivolous approach to its subject exposes the full-blown rhetoric employed by other poets eulogizing the same insignificant event. It is difficult to switch from treating something

---

[26] See *Católica acción*, fols 11v–12v (corrected foliation).

lightly to treating it with utter gravity without some loss of credibility. Such a poem totally disproves the recent assertion that academies convened to celebrate a royal event "apenas permiten la burla ni a la hora de proponer los asuntos ni en el momento de resolverlos".[27] It is the fact that academies did allow humour alongside solemnity, rather than opting either totally for the former, like the 1637 Buen Retiro academy, or for the latter, as in the *Anfiteatro de Felipe el grande* or the *Elogios al Palacio Real*, which alters the impact of occasional verse. Hence in this sphere also the academy contributed to the development of seventeenth-century poetry.

The academy's appropriation of the *justa*'s traditional subject matter is not simply a question of the broadening of academy thematics or the indiscriminate extension of the term "academia" itself, for in drawing the public sphere into its distinctive milieu occasional poetry is in turn itself altered. The diversity of topics and registers detracts from, and indeed is diametrically opposed to, the single-minded purpose and sober tone necessary to prevent bathos from undermining, by exposing, the hollowness and patent insincerity which are at the heart of occasional verse. Whether a single poem or the entire occasion is devoted to such non-amatory subject matter, the effect is still one of deflation, the potential shattering of an illusion. The same conflict between individual poems and the overall nature of the occasion will be evident when I consider the detrimental effect of the academy on any attempt to produce and sustain a credible lyric persona along Petrarchan lines. Before reaching this point, however, I shall turn to an examination of the sheer range and diversity of love poetry in the academy.

---

[27] See María José Rodríguez Sánchez de León, "La academia literaria como fiesta barroca en tres ejemplos andaluces (1661, 1664 y 1672)", *Diálogos hispánicos de Amsterdam*, 8 (1989), 2 vols, II, 915–26 (p. 917).

3

ACADEMY TOPICS AND SEVENTEENTH-CENTURY LOVE POETRY

Apart from the atmosphere and ethos of a literary academy, the single most important element in creating and maintaining a distinctive academy poetic was the fact that academy verse was composed within the dual constraints of set topics and metres. The set topic in particular radically affected the style of amatory verse composed for academies and completely altered the Petrarchan psychology of love in several ways: it directed the poetic focus away from an analysis of emotions to the description and narration of amatory scenarios; it shifted poetic interest from the ideal world of courtly and/or neoplatonic love to the voyeuristic and often banal sphere of mundane reality; and, consequently, it replaced the sustained analysis of the internal psychology of the poet-lover with the vicissitudes of the frequently melodramatic interaction between two lovers. These shifts taken together effectively constitute the last major development in amatory poetry in Golden Age Spain. Their specific effects on, and deviations from, the Petrarchan tradition will be discussed in subsequent chapters. Here I am primarily concerned with establishing the subject matter of academy love poems and with considering the relationship between academy and non-academy love poetry.

To determine whether academies were simply using existing lyric trends or if, in so doing, they were actually substantially altering and extending them, I propose to trace the origins of such topics back to both the Petrarchan and the native *cancionero* traditions and, more pertinently, to situate academy practice squarely within contemporary amatory verse. This raises two related questions. First, the degree to which academy verse is determined by non-literary or social factors; and second, the exact relationship between academy and non-academy verse: is their influence mutual and reciprocal, and does the direction of influence alter over the decades in which the academy became a firmly established facet of contemporary literary life? With regard to the first question, I shall suggest that the distinctive character of academy poetry owes as much to the social milieu in which it was composed, a milieu which in many ways is very similar to those in which its closest precedents were written, as it does to the direct and conscious influence of those precedents. To answer the second, possibly more important, question and to facilitate my evaluation of the distinctiveness of academy verse, I shall cite extensively the works of a wide range of seventeenth-century poets to provide a broader (that is, non-academy) perspective for the purposes of contrast and comparison. Setting academy poetry in its contemporary lyrical context prevents it from being viewed simply as a Baroque aberration or anomaly whilst also facilitating a more informed evaluation of its thematic originality. What emerges is that academy poetry exercised a profound, if clearly delimited, influence on the development of love poetry in general over the course of the seventeenth century by moving it in a more anecdotal direction.

In exemplifying academy poetry I have not hesitated to cite poems for which there is no explicit indication that they are academy pieces. I only cite such pieces when there is a clear thematic parallel with definite academy topics and when the poet concerned is known to have regularly attended an academy. This is obviously begging the question of influence, yet by the 1620s academy poetry, whilst having its origins in wider seventeenth-century practices, had developed its own style and dynamic. Since all the poets I cite also composed love poetry in a more Petrarchan, or less academic, style, it seems only natural to assume that those poems exhibiting all the stylistic and, more pertinently, thematic characteristics of academy poetry, and which were written once the academy had become a permanent and regular feature of literary life, are the result of the influence exerted by continuing academy practice rather than, conversely, the actual cause of, or impetus behind, that practice. The institution did not originate its distinctive amatory subject matter, but by developing it along increasingly dramatic lines it was responsible for its longevity both within and beyond its confines.

Academy topics can be divided very loosely into three broad types: praise of a specific object belonging to, or associated with, the woman, and, connected to this, praise of specific features of her face or body; the description of an amatory scenario or mini-drama which places the lovers in mundane, far-fetched or embarrassing situations; and the resolution of an amatory dilemma or paradox. The first two types have their roots primarily in Petrarchan poetry but, whilst the academies are simply following a long established Petrarchan tradition in using a particular object as the basis for a love poem, they significantly develop this tradition to the extent that they make the object part of a wider anecdote. This brings this particular category of topic closer to the second type in which the love affair itself is entirely anecdotal, with the emotions of the individual lovers being of far less importance than the melodramatic situations in which they are placed. The second type of topic, besides being the most innovatory, became the most popular; indeed, its very popularity was probably due in large part to its relative novelty in comparison with the other two types. Both categories elevate the incidental at the expense of the universal and in so doing are part of what has long been recognized as the general trend of seventeenth-century poetry towards the incorporation of the ordinary, material world into the love poem. (This trend, which is in complete contrast to the Aristotelian dictum that *poesis* should treat universal truths, is theorized in the various treatises on wit in which wit is considered to arise from the contingent and the circumstantial: phrases such as "alguna circunstancia especial" and "contingencia rara y singular", for example, which emphasize the conceit's particularity, abound in the *Agudeza y arte de ingenio*.[1]) The last category mentioned can be traced back to the native *cancionero* tradition of the fifteenth century with its cultivation of both the *pregunta/respuesta* format, which set a premium on witty repartee, and the *cuestión de amor* topics, exploring and defining the paradoxical nature of love.

The distinction between these three types of amatory topic is often far from absolute, especially by the second half of the century when all three types are more-or-less anecdotally conceived. Consequently the vast majority of academy topics typically involve a clearly delineated amatory narrative in which events, objects and, usually, emotional reactions are stipulated, or at least strongly hinted at, in the setting of the actual topic itself. Thus whilst straightforward debate topics continue to be set in an unadorned manner, such as the following taken from a 1674 academy, "Se pregunta y se decide en seis décimas si un hombre puede amar perfectamente a un objeto incapaz de correspondencia, y se intenta probar que sólo puede ser el amor perfecto, amando lo imposible", more often than not they are framed in a more contextually specific way. The presentation of the debate format within what I am calling an anecdotal frame can be seen in two other topics drawn from the same 1674 academy: "Pregúntase a un amante despreciado, en qué estación del tiempo se halla con menos tormento, en el día o en la noche" and, more specific (and humorous) still, "Duda y resuelve si un novio a quien desafían la noche de la boda debe salir o no".[2] As a result of the eventual predominance of this dramatic framing of a poem's subject, hard-and-fast divisions between types of academy poems are impossible. The distinction between the first two types of academy topic in particular – objects and scenarios – is often

---

[1] What Emilio Orozco Díaz refers to as the "irrupción de lo real" into the Baroque lyric has been commented upon by various critics. See, for example, Orozco, *Manierismo y barroco*, 4th edn (Madrid: Cátedra, 1988), p. 39; José Manuel Blecua (ed.), *Poesía de la edad de oro*, II, *Barroco* (Madrid: Castalia, 1985), pp. 11–12; and Paul Julian Smith, *Quevedo on Parnassus: Allusive Context and Literary Theory in the Love-Lyric* (London: The Modern Humanities Research Association, 1987), pp. 43–44, 162.

[2] See *Pascua de Reyes*, fols 28r–29r, 30v–31v (corrected foliation). It is worth noting that whilst in volumes publishing a single poet's work titular headings may be the work of an editor rather than the poet, in academy accounts the printed titles normally reproduce the topics as set in the academy. See, for example, the *Real academia* where there is only the slightest of disparities between the topics as set (p. 4) and the poem headings as printed. In seventeenth-century volumes which publish one poet's work the headings often indicate if a poem was written for an academy; even where they do not, a heading describing the contents in detail, as opposed to interpreting them (as happens, for example, with many of González de Salas' headings to Quevedo's poetry), can be taken as a reasonable indication that the piece originated in an academy when the poet in question was a regularly academy attendant and where similar subjects are known to have been set in an academy.

somewhat arbitrary, the second type simply exhibiting a greater thematic emphasis on a particular action and its specific and detailed contextualization than the first, which tends more towards a static and less dramatic focus on the object in question. Nevertheless, it is still possible to categorize broadly on the basis of how the set topic requires the poet to treat or conceptualize the anecdotal topic. Moreover whilst often subjective, a thematic distinction between academy topics is useful for it enables a clearer picture to emerge of the provenance of academy subjects and of how the academies took up and exploited to the full the more dynamic and dramatic topics in vogue in the early decades of the seventeenth century.

I shall begin my discussion of academy topics with a consideration of those which involve an object associated with the woman. Of all the thematic types I have distinguished this is the one most widely practised by love poets beyond academies themselves and, perhaps as a direct result of this and of their long-familiarity and consequent lack of novelty, is the least popular of all three types within academies. Nevertheless the seventeenth-century lyric's emphatic preference for concrete reality as opposed to the abstraction and (neoplatonic) idealization of a Petrarch or, in Spain, an Herrera, Villamediana or Salinas, finds its earliest, fullest and most influential expression in precisely this late sixteenth-/early seventeenth-century development in Spanish Petrarchism. Given that the academy itself becomes the definitive expression of this movement towards specificity and mundane banality, it seems appropriate to start with this category even though it receives little original or sustained treatment in the academies themselves.

IN PRAISE OF THE SPECIFIC

Poetic consideration of objects belonging to the beloved was an established part of the Petrarchan manner long before the seventeenth century; indeed, it could be traced to, and hence be sanctioned by, Petrarch's own *Canzoniere*. For example, Laura's clothes and her veil are mentioned – if briefly and in passing – together with her mirror and glove.[3] This said, in comparison with later poets, the lover portrayed in the *Canzoniere* has, in the words of one critic, a "limited active life", preferring a life of dreaming, desiring and meditating to that of active involvement with the world of the beloved.[4] Petrarch thus tends to distance himself from empirical reality, and this distinguishes his verse from seventeenth-century love poetry, and from academy poetry in particular, though as I shall argue the academy's pursuit of

---

[3] See Francesco Petrarca, *Rime*, ed. by Guido Bezzola, 2nd edn (Milan: Rizzoli Editore, 1985), pp. 130–33, no. 29; p. 148, no. 38; p. 155, no. 45; and p. 398, no. 225.

[4] See Jennifer Lorch, "Petrarch and Petrarchism in Italy", *JIRS*, 2 (1992), 87–99 (p. 91).

particularity and specificity has little or nothing to do with "realism". Leonard Forster attributes the origin of eulogizing the beloved's possessions to two of Petrarch's sonnets which are based on the painter Simone Martini's portrait (now lost) of Laura, "Per mirar Policleto a prova fiso", and "Quando giunse a Simon l'alto concetto", and cites a list of typical objects that were the subjects of love poems by Petrarch's followers and imitators: rings, necklaces, bracelets, furniture, pet dogs, birds and fleas.[5] By the late fifteenth century Italian poets had popularized this type of composition in which the poet, extemporizing on the woman's various possessions, uses them as starting points for a "virtuoso exhibition of conceit-spinning".[6] Serafino Aquilano, for example, wrote various poems in which the objects mentioned become more specific and individualized than they had been in Petrarch's verse: a present of a shirt or a pomegranate, a marble cupid, an artificial fly worn by the Duchess of Urbino.[7] Similarly in the poetry of the most famous and influential seventeenth-century Italian exponent of the Petrarchan idiom, Giambattista Marino, we find poems on the lady's dog, her serpent shaped earrings, her beauty spot and on her tears occasioned by a dead boy.[8]

This tradition continues throughout the seventeenth century and even a

---

[5] See Forster, *The Icy Fire. Five Studies in European Petrarchism* (Cambridge: Cambridge University Press, 1969), p. 10. Giuseppe Mazzotta has recently commented on Petrarch's appreciation and evaluation of this portrait: "Simone Martini's painting [. . .] places the natural objects and the phenomenal world away from their ordinary context in a transfigured space". See *The Worlds of Petrarch* (Durham and London: Duke University Press, 1993), p. 27. In other words, whilst Petrarch may initiate the poetic treatment of individual objects connected with the lady, his own emphasis is idealistic unlike subsequent poets – and those of the seventeenth century in particular – for whom this trend becomes a means both of individualizing the woman and, consequently, of more realistically portraying her and her domestic environment.

[6] See A. J. Smith, *Metaphysical Wit* (Cambridge: Cambridge University Press, 1991), p. 26. Smith (pp. 20–31) provides a valuable discussion of the influence of late fifteenth-century and early sixteenth-century Italian and English poets on the development of a witty style. See also his chapter on seventeenth-century English poetry and the "failure of love" in *The Metaphysics of Love. Studies in Renaissance love poetry from Dante to Milton* (Cambridge: Cambridge University Press, 1985), pp. 221–53.

[7] See Smith, *Metaphysical Wit*, p. 26. For a general study of Aquilano, see Antonio Rossi, *Serafino Aquilano e la poesia cortigiana* (Brescia: Morcelliana, 1980).

[8] See *Poesie varie*, ed. by Benedetto Croce (Bari: Gius. Laterza, 1913), p. 86; and *Marino e i Marinisti*, ed. by Giuseppe Guido Ferrero (Milan and Naples: Riccardo Ricciardi, 1954), pp. 398, 370, 331. See also Tommaso Stigliani's poem on a lap-dog and Paolo Zazzaroni's on a woman's mole, *Marino e i Marinisti*, pp. 643, 976. Marino was heavily influenced by, and indeed consciously imitated, the poetry – and in particular the sonnets – of Lope de Vega. In turn, Marino was himself an important and lasting influence on seventeenth-century Spanish poetic practice. For a consideration of the fluidity of cultural exchange between Spain and Italy, see Juan Manuel Rozas, *Sobre Marino y España* (Madrid: Editora Nacional, 1978); Joseph G. Fucilla, *Relaciones hispanoitalianas* (Madrid: CSIC, 1953), and *Estudios sobre el petrarquismo en España* (Madrid: CSIC, 1969).

cursory acquaintance with Spanish lyric poetry of this period is sufficient to make clear how "conservative" the list of objects mentioned by Forster is. Items of jewellery are written about, but instead of simple rings and necklaces, the pieces become peculiarly specific (as in the example just cited by Marino), such as a diamond necklace shaped like a phoenix, or a pair of earrings in the form of sundials.[9] Objects associated with the woman come to include such macabre items as glass hearts or ornamental skulls.[10] The reification of the body of the idealized woman continues, but absolute perfection is replaced by a more realistic portrayal of women, whose very "blemishes" – birth marks,[11] scars,[12] freckles,[13] and pox marks[14] – are revelled in. The woman's domestic pets loom large, but, like Lesbia's renowned sparrow, they are usually dead.[15] Even children have a tendency to die in her vicinity.[16]

The seventeenth-century lyric was thus marked by a pronounced drive towards novelty of subject matter on the one hand, and absolute particularity and specificity on the other. The idealization of the beloved which Petrarch offers is a world away from this more mundane and materialistically contex-

---

[9] See, respectively, Quevedo, *Poesía original completa*, ed. by José Manuel Blecua, 2nd edn (Barcelona: Planeta, 1983), p. 344, no. 305, and Antonio de Solís, *Varias poesías*, p. 320. For more domestic items, compare the *décima* on a lost hairpin by Agustín de Salazar y Torres, *Cítara de Apolo, varias poesías divinas y humanas. Primera parte*, (Madrid: Antonio González de Reyes, 1694), p. 165.

[10] See Hurtado de Mendoza, *Obras poéticas*, ed. by Rafael Benítez Claros, 3 vols (Madrid: RAE, 1947–48) I, pp. 277–79, 279–82.

[11] See Soto de Rojas, *Obras*, p. 60.

[12] See Manuel de Faria y Sousa, *Fuente de Aganipe o rimas varias* (Madrid: Carlos Sánchez Bravo, 1646), divided into six parts separately paginated, Part 2, fol. 42r. See also Soto de Rojas, *Obras*, pp. 60–61.

[13] See Juan Bautista Felices de Cáceres in *La poesía aragonesa del barroco*, ed. by José Manuel Blecua (Zaragoza: Nueva Biblioteca de Autores Aragoneses, 1980), pp. 123–24.

[14] See Ana Abarca de Bolea, in *Antología poética de escritoras de los siglos XVI y XVII*, ed. by Ana Navarro (Madrid: Castalia, 1989), pp. 254–55.

[15] Antonio de Solís, *Varias poesías*, p. 118; and Quevedo, *Poesía original completa*, p. 518, no. 482 and p. 526, no. 494. On Quevedo's treatment of this topos, see Smith, *Quevedo on Parnassus*, pp. 74–77. Smith argues that Quevedo's preference for genus over species, "animal" rather than "dog", is evidence of his greater idealization and abstraction of Petrarchan motifs and his presupposition that his readers would be familiar with this long-popular topos. In an academy context, the topos is frequently given further novel twists precisely to revivify the long-familiar: see, for example, the *endechas* on a lover who kills the lady's favourite bird by accident whilst attempting to catch it and return it to its cage (*Sol de academias*, pp. 38–39). Compare the three poems on a woman teaching her parrot to speak, in *Badajoz*, fols 16r–19v; and the poem on a woman who, having lost a cat, has a dog returned to her, in *Academia que se celebró en el convento de los Padres Clérigos Reglares [. . .] día primero de la Pascua de Pentecostés, este año de 1681 [. . .]* (Madrid: Atanasio Abad, 1681), pp. 76–78, a reference I take from Simón Díaz, *Bibliografía de la literatura hispánica*, IV (1955), p. 386.

[16] See Hurtado de Mendoza, *Obras poéticas*, III, pp. 240–41

tualized milieu of the seventeenth-century lady and her lover. In such compositions a specific and particular object is made to carry general and universal significance, as the poet uses it to describe his emotions and his experiences of love. What unites all these poems is their argumentative procedure, which may be termed metonymic. By means of metonymy the poet is able to saturate the trivial object and the particular moment with interpretative and illustrative importance. Metonymy transforms that which appears contingent and marginal into something central and essential. The rhetorical procedure is similar to that in the majority of occasional and political sonnets: the incidental and the peripheral are transformed; the particular is made the embodiment of the universal. The argumentative format of such compositions falls within what Gracián terms "argumentos conceptuosos"; more specifically, they enact an argument "a minori ad maius".[17] Gracián states that the purpose of poetic wit based upon argument is to "exprimir y exagerar los sentidos" (II, p. 80). Further, in this type of wit the poet must establish an "hermosa correlación" between the terms of the comparison in order to "argüir del uno al otro" (II, p. 83). Both these procedures are especially evident in the various poems which treat more mundane or domestic objects. Typical of the latter is the "búcaro", or Portuguese clay, eaten by women to sweeten their breath (and possibly also for the supposed narcotic and contraceptive properties of the clay).[18] Rather than simply writing a poem on this habit, which strikes us as highly unusual but which was mundane and therefore presumably banal to the seventeenth-century reader, Luis de Ulloa y Pereira chooses to make the clay a dynamic component in his emotional drama:

> Ya con las alas del favor osado
> la púrpura flamante competía,
> búcaro, que entre aljófar se movía,
> no sin las presunciones de animado.
>   Mirábale yo triste y asustado,
> y en Celia despreciada su osadía;
> para remedio de la envidia mía
> obró la contingencia, no el cuidado.
>   Así arrojó a mis ojos el destino,
> sin desdén ni favor, la tierra unida,
> memoria de pesar y de contento;
>   porque, alentado del calor divino,

---

[17] See Gracián, *Agudeza y arte de ingenio*, ed. by Evaristo Correa Calderón, 2 vols (Madrid: Castalia, 1969), II, p. 83.

[18] In an article by José Angel Montañés, "Las meninas comían barro", *Babelia* (Literary Supplement), *El País*, 2 May 1992, p. 10, a ceramics expert, Natacha Seseña, suggests that the effects of eating clay were various: it made the skin paler, but also prevented menstruation and may have been used, therefore, as a kind of contraceptive. She also notes its possible narcotic effect.

> fue imagen a la muerte y a la vida,
> el barro, con el nombre y el aliento.[19]

Initially envious of the intimacy and proximity which the "búcaro" has with the beloved, his emotions are assuaged by the fact that, whilst the clay has enjoyed unparalleled intimacy with Celia, it has now been violently ejected from her presence. The poet-lover thus establishes an implicit comparison between the "búcaro" and his own fate at the hands of Celia and thereby makes a particular event emblematic: the "búcaro", to which the Petrarchan antithesis of life and death are applied (lines 13–14), comes to stand as an emblem of the fate of all lovers. The explanation of why, and in what ways, the "búcaro" is exemplary is offered in the final tercet: the poem thus exhibits the binary format of problem-solution which is the favoured argumentative format of such sonnets. The mundane object, seemingly unpromising material for a love sonnet, comes to signify something beyond its own immediate inconsequentiality.

I have concentrated in some detail on non-academy poetry in order to emphasize how love poetry in general is, by the seventeenth century, developing a taste for the particular and the circumstantial. This both enables the poet to exercise his wit whilst also allowing a greater degree of domestic contact and intimacy. Literary academies also reflect this broader move to contextualization. What seems to motivate the secretaries in prescribing topics on ever more specific objects, however, is less a desire for realism and intimacy and more a constant desire for unfamiliarity and surprise, for clearly once the initial motif is familiar this can only be achieved by the accrual of details to the original or by the invention of entirely new subjects, something which, perhaps surprisingly, rarely happens in the academies which prefer instead to compose endless variations on more-or-less standard amatory topics. The academies also manage to renew a sense of novelty in another way, for fetishistic reverence often simply gives way to humour and parody.

A list of the objects treated by academy topics includes, not surprisingly, a large number of commonplace amatory "accessories" such as the mirror and the ubiquitous butterfly. Such topics are often framed in a straightforward and conventional manner, although there is sometimes an attempt to revivify otherwise clichéd subject matter by giving it an extra twist which invariably takes the form of expanding on the context in which the object itself is found. Thus whilst Petrarch simply mentions Laura's mirror and Tasso, more

---

[19] See Ulloa y Pereira, *Obras*, ed. by Juan Antonio de Ulloa Pereira (Madrid: Francisco Sanz, 1674), p. 27. The specific (and indecorous) dynamism of the object in this poem strongly suggests to me that it is an academy piece. Compare Quevedo, *Poesía original completa*, p. 354, no. 320; Soto de Rojas, *Obras*, p. 111; and Góngora, *Obras completas*, ed. by Juan and Isabel Millé y Giménez, 3rd edn (Madrid: Aguilar, 1951), p. 385.

specifically or interactively, holds it up for his lady,[20] the academy love poet looks at the woman in a mirror when it unexpectedly breaks;[21] or alternatively describes how the wind closes the window whilst the lady is lost in rapt self-contemplation.[22] Similarly, whilst the butterfly, like most Petrarchan butterflies, may simply choose to die near the dazzling light of the woman's eyes,[23] it may be involved in more unusual activities such as being killed by the woman annoyed at its fluttering around her face,[24] or landing on a flower dangling from her mouth.[25]

In each of these poems, as a description of their contents makes clear, the object itself is largely subsumed into the broader situation into which it is placed. Of no intrinsic interest either to the lover or the poet, items are rather catalysts for a single dramatic interchange. Thus in the poem just mentioned on the poet looking at his lady in a mirror, the way in which the topic itself is framed ("A un galán que, mirando en un espejo a su dama, se cayó el espejo") encourages the poet assigned the piece, Manuel Freire de Andrade, constantly to deflect our attention away from the object itself, the mirror, towards the lovers for whom it serves briefly as a means of specular union:

> Embelesado en el puro
> cristal de un brillante espejo
> Fileno estaba, exhalando
> por los ojos su amor dos mongibelos.
>   Miraba en él de su Clori
> los bellísimos reflejos,
> porque el sol de su hermosura

---

[20] See Petrarch, *Rime*, p. 155, no. 45; and Torquato Tasso, *Poesie*, ed. by Francesco Flora (Milan and Naples: Riccardo Ricciardi, 1952), p. 705.

[21] See *Pascua de Reyes*, fols 29v–30v (corrected foliation). The Petrarchan norm is for the lady either simply to contemplate herself in the mirror or to break it herself. See, for example, the sonnets by Bocángel, *Lira*, p. 356; Pedro de Quirós, *Poesías divinas y humanas*, ed. by M. Menéndez Pidal (Seville: Sociedad del Archivo Hispalense, 1887), p. 2; Lope de Vega, *Obras poéticas*, p. 1414; and López de Zárate, *Obras varias*, II, p. 95, and *Sesenta y seis poemas inéditos*, ed. by José Simón Díaz (Logroño: Editorial Gonzalo de Berceo, 1976), p. 37.

[22] See *Sol de academias*, p. 36.

[23] See *Fonseca Feb 1663*, fols 29v–30v. Compare *Fonseca April 1662*, fols 23r–24v.

[24] See *Fonseca April 1662*, fol. 29r. Compare the two identical *liras* by Salazar y Torres, *Cítara de Apolo*, pp. 130–31, 137–38. These poems literalize the opening simile of one of Petrarch's most imitated sonnets, "Come talora al caldo tempo sòle", attributing the insect's death to the woman's active rather than passive involvement. See *Rime*, p. 304, no. 141. For a study of the topos, see Alan S. Trueblood, "La mariposa y la llama: motivo poético del siglo de oro", in *Letter and Spirit in Hispanic Writers: Renaissance to Civil War. Selected Essays* (London: Tamesis, 1986), pp. 26–34.

[25] See *Real Aduana*, pp. 39–40.

se ocultaba entre nubes del respeto.
   Absortamente elevado
en su amante devaneo,
le dijo tierno y rendido,
rompiendo las clausuras del silencio:
   "¡O tú!, misterioso Apeles,
que en el cristalino lienzo
de tu misma esencia imprimes
el bello encanto de mi rendimiento.
   ¡O tú!, retórico mudo,
que con elegante afecto
animado estás la sombra
de aquella imagen de mi dulce objeto.
   Pues en tu cristal se estampa
ese admirable bosquejo
del más hermoso milagro
que por culto el Amor cuelga en su templo.
   Dile a ese bello imposible
de mi soberano dueño
que acrisole sus desvíos
en la amorosa fragua de mi pecho.
   Mas, ¡ay de mí!, que al impulso
del aire de mis acentos
se cayó desvanecido
el atractivo imán de mi embeleso.
   ¡O terrible, o duro trance
del más fino sentimiento!;
Amor, si éstas son tus glorias
muy cerca del abismo está tu cielo.
   Tú la reflexión hermosa
del esplendor, que venero,
me robaste, porque gustas
de aumentar con el llanto los incendios.
   Falsa deidad te imagino,
y en tu ceguedad contemplo
que premias con el castigo,
si en tu breve placer fundas el premio.
   Que unidas viven tus glorias
con tu alado movimiento,
pues para quien las anhela,
tan fugitivas son como tu vuelo.
   De injusto dios te acreditas;
pues son con engaño expreso
tus placeres ilusiones,
tirana astucia de tu falso imperio.
   Huyendo de tus cautelas,
y al rigor de Clori huyendo,

> del desengaño impelido,
> la senda seguiré del escarmiento".[26]

As with Ulloa y Pereira's sonnet on sweet-smelling clay what happens to the object is as important as the object itself. Here the mirror is important precisely because it directs the attention of poet, lover and reader beyond itself, deflecting our gaze to the amatory crisis which its own shattering emblematically mirrors. Greater contextualization serves therefore to defamiliarize a traditional long-standing topic, and so gives the poet greater room for developing the subject. Moreover the mirror's "double" action means that the poet must exercise greater wit in drawing significance from both its reflective qualities and its breakage.

The broadening of the frame in which the lovers are set leads to an excess of detail becoming the substitute for a portrayal of psychological realism. The emotions remain on the level of mere platitude, whilst the situations which express them become more complex. The interest of such academy poems lies in their manipulation of amatory props, rather than in the depth or subtlety of the participants' emotional involvement, for as the emotions ossify into inert cliché so the external world intrudes, with poets not using the objects they describe to revivify their emotional discourse but more to conceal its very absence. The intrusion of the "real world" into the academy poem is a means of developing wit rather than conveying emotion as it had initially been when objects were introduced into the lyric around the beginning of the century. By the second half of the century the academy has not only particularized objects to the exclusion of emotion, but also begins to treat the dramatized object in an overtly theatrical way. A 1698 *romance* on a "búcaro", for example, written to answer the question set by the topic "¿De qué debe de estar más desvanecida la tierra, de ser de lo hermoso comida en barro, o pisada en polvo?" takes the form of a dramatic dialogue. Part of the poem is taken up with a lament by the "triste barro" itself, bemoaning its own fate in comparison with the earth on the ground:

> Estas dichas envidiaba
> otro barro al verse entero,
> y de un triste escaparate
> estos dijo tristísimos lamentos:
> "¿Qué delito cometí
> para vivir siempre preso,
> estrechado entre cristales
> a sólo ser alhaja de deseos?
> ¿No surqué yo de los mares
> estos piélagos inmensos

---

[26] See *Pascua de Reyes*, fols 29v–30v (corrected foliation).

> que hay desde el Austro triste al Bóreas
> y desde Chile al gaditano fiero?
> ¿Si a sus embates furiosos
> fui de bronce, fui creciendo,
> qué resistencias de firme
> no habían de labrarme monumento?
> Mas ya reconozco: soy
> de barro perecedero;
> duren mármoles y bronces
> que de tanto durar estoy que muero.
> ¿Que le falte a mi desgracia
> un acaso, un contratiempo,
> un descuido, un no sé que
> le falte que conmigo dé en el suelo?
> Por deshacerme en pedazos
> diera el alma que no tengo,
> porque el morirme de sano
> ha de ser para mí el mayor tormento["].[27]

What is of interest in the poem is the absence of the lover himself; the personified object has assumed his position in the amatory dynamic and is expressing the longings normally voiced by the lover directly. Although by no means a burlesque poem, the effect is bathetic and slightly ludicrous.

In a similar way to this increased specificity, the standard practice of praising and reifying individual features of the woman's face or body which thereby gain iconic status as amatory "objects" occurs within academies which constantly introduce a note of derogatory particularity. There are various poems, for example, on the woman's excessively large feet;[28] and she may suffer from such unlady-like aliments as scabies,[29] or merely from a

---

[27] See *Señoras*, pp. 153–54. Despite the dramatic exchange between the "barro" and the "polvo", the editor's comments (p. 153, n. 149) that this speech explicitly recalls Segismundo's soliloquy in the first act of *La vida es sueño* seems far-fetched. Compare *Valencia, Real Palacio*, pp. 27–28.

[28] See *Repetida carrera*, pp. 45–46. Compare Salazar y Torres, *Poetas líricos de los siglos XVI y XVII*, ed. by Adolfo de Castro, 2 vols, vols 32 and 42 of the Biblioteca de Autores Españoles (Madrid: Ediciones Atlas, 1951), II, p. 219; and Antonio de Solís, *Varias poesías*, pp. 154–55. In his satire on a young poet's attempt to compose an academy piece, Zabaleta ridicules poets who exaggerate the smallness of their ladies' feet, commenting: "Si los pies de un cuerpo humano no tuvieran correspondencia en la cantidad con los demás miembros, fueran feos y erraran hacia la pequeñez; fueran pies de oso, que ni son hermosura ni firmeza". See *El día de fiesta por la tarde*, p. 392. The academy pieces on large feet do the same, implicitly ridiculing the gulf between Petrarchan hyperbole and the "real world". Alfay's anthology of 1654 contains pieces both on a woman's large hands and her large mouth: see *Poesías varias de grandes ingenios españoles recogidas por Josef Alfay*, ed. by José Manuel Blecua (Zaragoza: CSIC, 1946), pp. 185, 194.

[29] See *Fonseca April 1662*, fols 33r–34v.

common cold.³⁰ More striking are those topics which subvert the most sacred of Petrarchan clichés, the perfection of the lover's eyes: sometimes it is simply a question of one eye being larger than the other;³¹ or of a woman with a small body possessing, in contrast, large eyes;³² but the most bizarre topic in this category, given at one of Fonseca de Almeida's academies, is on a woman losing her glass eye, a far cry from the "sol de' begli occhi sereno" of Laura.³³

Whilst there are clear European precedents for such notes of "realism" being treated in a serious manner, as a basis for a meditation on the lover's own mortality, for example, or on youth's vanity, it is relatively rare to find this in Golden Age poetry. In Spain, within the academies, "bodily realism" or imperfection somewhat inevitably leads to decorous humour or causes the poet to adopt a lighter and less reflective stance. The very nature of this subject matter makes it ripe for parody, and not simply within the academies. Lope's *Rimas de Tomé de Burguillos* (Madrid, 1634), for example, offers a sustained parody of this style of poetry, its subject matter and its rhetorical procedures. The volume includes sonnets on Juana's dog which bites whoever touches her hand, her large shoes, a toothpick, a pet bird which pecks her tongue, and one on her comb, made either of boxwood or ivory (the poet is uncertain, but note the parodic emphasis on specificity).³⁴ As well as being a parody of a Petrarchan *canzoniere*,³⁵ the collection can also be viewed as an obvious product of academy culture and its mentality. Moreover, it may well have influenced the choice of certain academy topics later in the century: as well as those on large feet which I have already mentioned, for example, topics such as a woman pecked on the lips by a goldfinch after she has been

---

³⁰ See Polo de Medina, *Obras escogidas*, ed. by José María de Cossío (Madrid: Clásicos Olvidados, 1931), p. 126.

³¹ See *Repetida carrera*, pp. 47–48. Compare Salazar y Torres' eulogistic sonnet to a lady's spectacles which, at least implicitly, implies less than perfect vision. See *Poetas líricos de los siglos XVI y XVII*, II, p. 218.

³² See Navarro, *Poesías varias*, pp. 195–97 (the rubric states that this was an academy piece).

³³ See *Academia que se celebró en siete de Enero, en casa de Don Melchor de Fonseca de Almeida, siendo Presidente Don José Porter y Casanate, Secretario D. Luis de Oviedo y Fiscal D. Juan de Montenegro y Neira* (Madrid: Francisco Nieto, 1663), fol. 25r, a reference I take from Simón Díaz, *Bibliografía de la literatura hispánica*, IV (1955), p. 373; Petrarch, *Rime*, p. 338, no. 173. Such topics recall various sonnets by Quevedo, which may well have been academy pieces, treating respectively ladies who are cross eyed, one-eyed, or blind: see *Poesía original completa*, pp. 350–52, nos 315–16.

³⁴ See Lope de Vega, *Obras poéticas*, pp. 1366, 1360–61, 1351, 1394, 1345. The situations described range from a woman who eats salt and ash to the beloved cutting her nails on a balcony, or having her measurements taken by a tailor – much to the poet's envy (pp. 1397–98, 1373–74, 1348).

³⁵ On this point, see Felipe Pedraza Jiménez, "La parodia del petrarquismo en las *Rimas de Tomé de Burguillos* de Lope de Vega", in *Homenaje a Gonzalo Torrente Ballester* (Salamanca, 1981), pp. 615–38.

trying to feed it with her mouth,[36] or on a toothpick which hits the lover in his eye after the woman has spat it out,[37] are clearly thematically very close to Lope's parodic compositions.

This rapid survey of objects establishes the ubiquity of the trend towards the particular in the seventeenth-century lyric. Of the three types of topics which I have distinguished, only this type was more actively pursued outside literary academies. The only significant ways in which the academies developed the long-established Petrarchan tradition of hymning individual objects was either to emphasize its humorous potential or to establish the object in question in a highly specific and unusual anecdotal context. In contextualizing and dramatizing the object by placing it as a "participant" in a clearly delineated amatory situation, the set topic itself often constitutes the most novel and original element of the poetic process. Within the academy it is not only the poet's skill and ingenuity which is on show, but also that of the academy secretary who has invented the topic. Furthermore, the treatment given to this Petrarchan style of verse in the academies brings it far closer to the type of subject matter which was the most popular, as well as the most influential, in literary academies throughout the century, the amatory scenario, which, whilst similarly stemming from the Petrarchan tradition, enjoyed a far greater degree of sustained and independent development within the academies.

ANECDOTE AND MELODRAMA: THE AMATORY SCENARIO AND ACADEMY TOPICS

As with those poems based around a particular object or feature of the beloved, poems which establish and explore specific amatory situations or scenarios are common to both academy and non-academy verse. However, this type of topic receives a more exaggerated treatment within academies. It is therefore legitimate to see academies playing a significant and substantial role in the development of this particular strand of amatory poetry in the seventeenth century. To highlight the significant differences between academy and non-academy treatment, I shall again begin by briefly exemplifying the latter, seeing how such subject matter arises from various poetic traditions only to be developed fully in the academy.

The origins of this type of verse are again to be found in the Italian Petrarchan tradition. To take only one example, in the poetry of Giambattista

---

[36] See *Fonseca Feb 1663*, fols 19r–20r.

[37] See *Sol de academias*, p. 34. Compare Lope's sonnet, p. 1351. Salazar y Torres also composed some *endechas* on a willow toothpick in a woman's mouth. See *Cítara de Apolo*, pp. 134–37. Polo de Medina includes a *décima* on a toothpick given by a lady to her lover in his academy novel: see *Obras escogidas*, p. 127.

Marino there are poems on such subjects as the lady bathing, sewing, out on a carriage ride, and milking a sheep.[38] Although Italian Petrarchan practice was undoubtedly the most important influence, it is worth emphasizing that there is a precedent for this type of poetry in the *cancionero* tradition. Writing of fifteenth-century poetry, Pierre le Gentil states that such "poésie de circonstance" was peculiar to Spain and Italy: "Tandis qu'en Espagne on semble prendre plaisir à trouver, dans les plus menus faits de la vie quotidienne, un prétext à versifier, en France au contraire on s'efforce plutôt de s'élever au-dessus des contingences."[39] It seems possible, then, that the native tradition of the *cancionero*, which, as I shall discuss in detail in the next section, played an immensely influential role in shaping academy poetry, may also have played a part in disseminating a taste for this kind of particularizing verse. Indeed, one of Quevedo's most anthologized sonnets, "Aminta, para mí cualquiera día", an excellent example of this type of occasional verse, in which the poet draws out the significance for him of the ash smeared on Aminta's forehead on Ash Wednesday,[40] for all that it owes its language and attitude to Petrarchism also has a thematic precedent in a *cancionero* poem written by Antón de Montoro.[41]

By the seventeenth century the mundane or trivial incident connected with, or involving, the woman and/or the poet had become a standard part of the poets' repertoire. Again, a summary of a handful of the situations dealt with will give some impression of the nature of such trivial compositions. The lady covers and uncovers her face;[42] she is jealous of her own reflection;[43] she may tune a musical instrument with her mouth (being deaf);[44] she prefers looking at a corpse to her lover;[45] she cuts her hair,[46] and burns it by accident whilst

---

[38] See *Poesie varie*, pp. 77, 69–70, 87, 70. See the comments by James V. Mirollo in *The Poet of the Marvellous. Giambattista Marino* (New York and London: Columbia University Press, 1963), p. 126.

[39] See *La Poésie lyrique espagnole et portugaise à la fin du moyen âge*, 2 vols (Rennes: Plihon, 1949), vol. 1: *Les Thèmes et les genres*, p. 210. See also his list of *cancionero* examples, pp. 206–07.

[40] See *Poesía original completa*, p. 346, no. 308.

[41] See *Segunda parte del Cancionero General, aora nuevamente copilado de lo más gracioso y discreto de muchos afamados trovadores*, ed. by Antonio Rodríguez-Moñino (Oxford: The Dolphin Book Co., 1956; facsimile of Zaragoza 1552 edn), pp. 185–86.

[42] See Carrillo y Sotomayor, *Obras*, ed. by Rosa Navarro Durán (Madrid: Castalia, 1990), pp. 178–79; and Quevedo, *Poesía original completa*, pp. 344–45, no. 306. Compare Petrarch, *Rime*, p. 148, no. 38.

[43] See Miguel de Colodrero Villalobos, *El Alpheo, y otros asuntos en verso, ejemplares algunos* (Barcelona: Sebastián y Jaime Matevad, 1639), fol. 27r; and Moncayo, *Rimas*, pp. 93–94.

[44] See the sonnet by "Tineo" included in Blecua (ed.), *Poesía de la edad de oro, Barroco*, pp. 412–13.

[45] See Hurtado de Mendoza, *Obras poéticas*, I, pp. 287–91.

[46] See Ulloa y Pereira, *Obras*, p. 39; and López de Zárate, *Obras varias*, I, p. 301.

curling it;⁴⁷ she drowns;⁴⁸ she spits water into a fountain;⁴⁹ she turns a weapon on the poet;⁵⁰ she is stung by bees;⁵¹ she throws a variety of objects at her lover, including a lemon, a snowball, a capsule of perfumed water, and an orange;⁵² she extinguishes a candle only to rekindle the flame with her breath;⁵³ she cuts her finger on a piece of jewellery;⁵⁴ and she suffers various illnesses.⁵⁵

Again the primary appeal of such subjects for contemporary poets and their audience was presumably that it offered a means of dressing up tired amatory clichés. Indeed, if the primary condition for such love poetry was to bring together the beloved and some – any – detail of her life, then the possibilities for such a "renewal" were potentially infinite. Here was a means of making the long-familiar appear pleasantly and unexpectedly different. Incidents

---

⁴⁷ See Quevedo, *Poesía original completa*, p. 349, no. 313; Faria y Sousa, *Fuente de Aganipe*, Part 2, fol. 46. Compare Bocángel, *Lira*, p. 143.

⁴⁸ See Bocángel, *Lira*, p. 149; López de Zárate, *Sesenta y seis poemas inéditos*, pp. 39–40; Moncayo, *Rimas*, pp. 220–22; Ulloa y Pereira, *Obras*, pp. 208–09; and Salcedo Coronel, *Cristales de Helicona*, fol. 7v.

⁴⁹ See López de Zárate, *Obras varias*, I, p. 187.

⁵⁰ See Antonio Alvares Soares, *Rimas varias* (Lisbon: Mattheus Pinheiro, 1628), fol. 10r. For an academy topic by Salazar y Torres similar to this last poem, see *Carnestolendas*, pp. 47–48; and in the same volume, pp. 82–84, on a woman shooting at a statue of Cupid.

⁵¹ See Torre y Sevil, *Entretenimiento de las musas*, p. 179; and Gaspar Sotelo, in Alfay, *Poesías varias*, p. 99. Compare Tasso, *Poesie*, p. 720.

⁵² See, in order, Carrillo y Sotomayor, *Obras*, p. 191; Moncayo, *Rimas*, pp. 89–90, and Hurtado de Mendoza, *Obras poéticas*, I, pp. 26–27 (for snowballs); Moncayo, p. 91, for the "huevo de azahar". For an academy piece written at the close of the sixteenth century at precisely the time when this style of verse was becoming popular in Spain, whose topic is a lover knocked out by an orange thrown by his mistress, see *Academia de los Nocturnos*, II, p. 107. See also Juan de Salinas, *Poesías humanas*, ed. by Henry Bonneville (Madrid: Castalia, 1987), p. 410. On the poetic topos in general, see Stephen Reckert, *Beyond Chrysanthemums: Perspectives on Poetry East and West* (Oxford: Clarendon Press, 1993), pp. 66–89. For an example from the *cancioneros*, see Nicolás Núñez, in *Poesía de Cancionero*, ed. by Alvaro Alonso, 2nd edn (Madrid: Cátedra, 1991), pp. 376–77. Compare Garcilaso, *Obras completas*, ed. by Elias L. Rivers (Madrid: Castalia, 1974), pp. 61–62. Keith Whinnom makes the point that *cancionero* compositions like this which treat concrete objects are, despite their popularity with modern critics, very much the exception, the norm being poems of a more severely abstract character. In this type of academy topic, therefore, the influence of the *cancionero* is minimal, unlike the other two types. See Whinnom, *La poesía amatoria de la época de los Reyes Católicos* (Durham: University of Durham, 1981), pp. 41–43.

⁵³ See Quevedo, *Poesía original completa*, p. 346, no. 309; Moncayo, *Rimas*, p. 92. An identical academy topic is recorded in one of Fonseca's academies. See *Jardín*, I, fol. 19.

⁵⁴ See Góngora, *Sonetos completos*, ed. by Birutė Ciplijauskaité, 6th edn (Madrid: Castalia, 1990), p. 160; Navarro, *Poesías varias*, pp. 3–4 (compare pp. 18–22).

⁵⁵ See Solís, *Varias poesías*, p. 269; Alfay, *Poesías varias*, p. 201; and Salazar y Torres, *Cítara de Apolo*, pp. 115–16 (this is an academy piece).

drawn from the domestic, private world of the beloved, just like the objects associated with her already discussed, also give a poet ample opportunities to exercise his wit. In a poetic centred upon ingenuity, surprise and wonder, what could test the poet's wit more than having to establish a "significant" link, that is a link beyond the merely circumstantial and transitory, between the beloved and an object as unpromising as clay chewed to sweeten the breath, or an incident as mundane as covering the face with a veil? It is the challenge of making the insignificant significant, of endowing the particular with universal meaning, that lies behind the initial diffusion of this kind of love poetry in the seventeenth century.

A further attraction of exploring the trivial minutiae of the beloved's world is that such an approach allows the poet greater scope for introducing an erotic element into his otherwise chaste relationship with the beloved. Given the domestic and intimate nature of so many of these recurrent incidents, the poet-lover becomes, in describing them, a not-so-gentlemanly voyeur who offers a titillating intrusion into the intimacy of a lady's private world. Even Petrarch's founding text stresses the voyeuristic potential of the domestic or intimate scenario: in a madrigal describing the washing of a veil, for example, the poet's comparison of himself with Actaeon explicitly emphasizes this aspect.[56] However, despite such nascent voyeurism in Petrarch, it was the seventeenth century which fully exploited this potential in domestically intimate situations. Feet in particular became a favourite focus of attention, as when a woman faints on realizing her lover has been watching her put on her shoes,[57] or the lover marvels whilst his lady's feet are bled.[58] Indeed bloodletting becomes a standard means of dwelling on the prone and vulnerable body of the woman and on her exposed flesh, often in a strikingly perverse and macabre fashion.[59]

In line with these possible reasons for the widespread popularity of poetry which emphasizes the incidental the topics set by academies tend to become both more bizarre and unusual (less domestic and realistic) and more

---

[56] See *Rime*, p. 165, no. 52. For an excellent discussion of this madrigal, see Mazzotta, *Worlds of Petrarch*, pp. 67–69.

[57] See Antonio Enríquez Gómez, *El siglo pitagórico y Vida de don Gregorio Guadaña*, ed. by Teresa de Santos (Madrid: Cátedra, 1991), pp. 243–49. These poems, on the same subject but in a variety of styles, come from an account of an academy contained within the novel; they are reproduced with various errors by Sánchez, *Academias*, pp. 188–91.

[58] See Faria y Sousa, *Fuente de Aganipe*, Part 2, fol. 41v; and Góngora, *Sonetos completos*, p. 146.

[59] The number of poems on blood-letting is enormous. For a representative selection, see Lope, *Obras poéticas*, pp. 97–98; Hortensio Félix Paravicino, *Obras póstumas, divinas y humanas* (Madrid: María Fernández, 1650), fol. 88r; Moncayo, *Rimas*, p. 90; Soto de Rojas, *Obras*, pp. 61–62; Alvares Soares, *Rimas varias*, fol. 5r; and Faria y Sousa, *Fuente de Aganipe*, Part 2, fols 41r, 49v, 51v (four compositions).

salacious and risqué. In fact, this last aspect provoked the censure of Juan de Zabaleta. As I discussed in the first chapter Zabaleta, despite important and specific reservations, was basically in favour of the literary academy as a formative social and literary experience. However, one point on which he is most insistent is that amatory topics should be banned. The reason he gives for this is simply that he views them as morally pernicious. His criticism is worth citing, for the academy's influence was, as he implies, instrumental in the development of this style of composition along ever more frivolous, sensual and suggestive lines, precisely because the atmosphere of the occasion encouraged rather than censored poetic freedom by removing the restraints of thematic decorum:

> Lo que culpo en las academias es la mala elección de los asuntos. Debiéranse desterrar totalmente los amatorios. No los pretendo tan severos como si los repartiera Catón. Quiérolos festivos, pero quiérolos honestos. Ellos son la espada negra del entendimiento que le habilita para cosas de grande importancia. Mas nadie me negará que fuera locura grande tomar espada negra, que cortase, por la empuñadura. Asuntos poéticos que hieren la razón del alma que se encarga de ellos, son muy malos asuntos. El acónito es veneno tan cruel que aun con el contacto mata. Los asuntos sin honestidad, aunque el que los discurre piense que no los bebe, es peligro mortal del alma el tocarlos. Huyamos, por Dios, huyamos de ellos.[60]

It is certainly possible to find plenty of examples of academy pieces which treat salacious and titillating subject matter, the type of topics which Zabaleta would presumable condemn as not being "honestos". However, poems on such topics as "[A] una mujer, que entrando a bañarse en Manzanares, volvió la cabeza y vio un viejo en carnes que la seguía",[61] and "A un galán, que enamorado de su dama, viéndola encinta, logró su desengaño, viendo que parió un hijo negro", are far from being in the majority.[62] Zabaleta's objection

---

[60] See *Fiesta por la tarde*, pp. 392–93.

[61] For this topic, set by Bocángel, see Brown, "Gabriel de Corral: sus contertulios y un MS. poético de academia inédito", *Castilla*, 4 (1982), 9–56 (pp. 42–46).

[62] See *Ciudad Real*, fols 12v–13r. In its salacious sensationalism this topic broadly recalls a purportedly true verse account published in Cuenca in 1603 telling of a "lady of Seville who gave birth to a black boy after making love to her husband while her black maid's baby was in bed with them". See Henry Ettinghausen, "The Illustrated Spanish News. Text and Image in the Seventeenth-Century Press", in *Art and Literature in Spain: 1600–1800. Studies in Honour of Nigel Glendinning*, ed. by Charles Davis and Paul Julian Smith (London: Tamesis, 1993), pp. 117–33 (p. 124); and, in the same volume, Juan Carrete Parrondo, "Estampas fantásticas: Imágenes y descripciones de monstruos", pp. 55–67. Clearly a sensationalist mentality was common to academies and news accounts, being the more popular manifestation of the emphasis on novelty and wonder which were central to contemporary poetics. On Spanish news, see Ettinghausen, "The News in Spain: *Relaciones de sucesos* in the Reigns of Philip III and IV", *EHQ*, 14 (1984), 1–20; "Sexo y violencia: noticias sensacionalistas en la prensa española del siglo XVII", *Edad de Oro*, 12

to "immoral" love poetry is presumably focused primarily on the domestic and physical intimacy which is not only unavoidable but positively cultivated in topics such as the blood-letting of the woman. Of course, Zabaleta's blanket condemnation probably owes as much to the rhetorical exaggeration of the moralist as to poetic reality.

This having been said, poems could be extremely explicit. An excellent example is a poem by Castillo Solórzano whose scenario has Filis fast asleep whilst a monkey, chained near her, splits open and eats pine nuts. After describing Filis asleep in mock "culto" language, the poem introduces the lascivious monkey:

> En tanto pues que soñaba
> empleos de sus melindres
> en el zaguán de su idea
> si no palpables, visibles,
> un remedo de los hombres,
> un epítome risible,
> sagaz, si animal, que dio
> oficio a los boratines:
> un mono, por no deciros
> palabras por alambiques,
> escolta hace a su dueño,
> doméstico como humilde,
> si bien su entretenimiento,
> goloso cuanto apacible,
> era comer de la fruta
> de quien Atis fue su origen.
> Con lascivo natural,
> con objeto apetecible,
> y con piñones por pasto,
> ¿quién habrá que se averigüe?
> Disculparle quiero al mono,
> que con la fruta y el brindis
> no era mucho acumular
> incentivos varoniles.
> Mal puede hacer la razón,
> que sus impulsos corrigen
> ligaduras de metal
> que a los cautivos oprime.
> ¡Cuánto diera por traer
> en ocasión tan felice
> la fuerte insignia que dio

(1993), 95–107; and "Prensa comparada: relaciones hispano-francesas en el siglo XVII", in *Estado actual de los estudios sobre el Siglo de Oro. Actas del II Congreso Internacional de Hispanistas del Siglo de Oro*, ed. by Manuel García Martín, et al. (Salamanca: Ediciones Universidad de Salamanca, 1993), pp. 339–45.

> a los Mazas noble timbre!
> Culpa se tuvo la dama
> en el casero combite,
> que en cada piñón sus ganas
> cobran filos más sutiles.
> ¡Guárdate, Filis! ¡Despierta!
> Que si atropella imposibles
> te espera una tarquinada,
> si no es gozo de Pasife;
> que si en la tal calabriada
> inadvertida concibes,
> nos darás un filimono,
> por esos bajos países.[63]

Unlike the standard Petrarchan poem which seeks to set the woman in an intimate environment, the scenario here, whilst in part by no means unrealistic or unbelievable, has clearly been established for its erotic possibilities rather than its domestic accuracy. Each detail is selected purely for its potential to contribute to the sexual interpretation of the whole. This is partly because this is a burlesque piece. Nevertheless, this emphasis on the incongruity of the initial scenario in which the woman is placed is shared by the majority of topics of this type set in academies, whether they are treated humorously or not. What the burlesque genre of Castillo's *romance* enables is a frank exposure of the desire motivating both poet and lover in more serious poems of this type: the desire for physical intimacy and erotic contact with the woman's body. It is this desire, whether occluded or explicit as here, which Zabaleta would have seen as being far from "honesto".

The amatory situations proposed in literary academies are many and are often very similar in their subject matter and its treatment to mainstream love poetry of the period: thus the same academy which set the topic of a lover discovering that his lady has given birth to a black child, also set a completely decorous topic on a standard subject, the lady pricking her finger on a rose, printing no less than six compositions on the subject.[64] Similarly, Lope de Vega submitted two sonnets to Saldaña's Madrid academy in 1611 on a woman who, having eye trouble, is advised to cut her hair;[65] and the subject of blood-letting, frequent in non-academy verse, was even more popular within

---

[63] See Soons, *Castillo Solórzano*, pp. 103–04, whose text I reproduce. What makes this burlesque poem of probable academy origin is the specificity and artificiality of the situation which it describes.

[64] See *Ciudad Real*, fols 29v–34r. On the same topic, see *Sol de academias*, p. 29; and the nine compositions in *Seville*, fols 6r–8r. The subject of the lady being pricked or cut by accident whilst picking flowers was a popular one: see, for example, Quevedo, *Poesía original completa*, p. 342, no. 303; and Sor María de Santa Isabel, in *Antología poética de escritoras*, p. 202.

[65] See J. P. Wickersham Crawford, "Some Unpublished Verses of Lope de Vega",

the academies throughout the century.⁶⁶ Normally, however, the topics set are far more detailed and unusual than their non-academy equivalents:

> A Filis, que teniendo su galán en compaña, deseaba el cierzo, para que le apagara su amor, y el bochorno, para que lo encendiera.⁶⁷
>
> A una dama que, con agua de la boca, se lavaba las manos.⁶⁸
>
> A un galán que huyendo en camisa de otro, que pensó ser el marido de su dama, al salir por la puerta encontró con el marido verdadero.⁶⁹
>
> Se queja un amante de que estando su dama escribiéndole un papel a la luz de una bujía, en que le favorecería, el aire mató la luz, impidiéndole el que persiguiese; cuyo acidente le mudó la voluntad.⁷⁰
>
> A un galán que, yendo a ver a su dama, fue a tiempo que a ella se le quemaba la casa; y al oír que le llamaba para que la socorriese, él se desmayó; y al volver en sí, la vio en brazos de otro.⁷¹
>
> A un celoso que haciendo un agujero para acechar a su mujer, derribó un pedazo de la pared, cuyo polvo le dio en los ojos, y le cegó.
>
> De un galán aborrecido que no pudiendo ver sino a la criada, y pensando hablar con ella una noche, a la luz de un relámpago vio que era su dama aquella con quien hablaba.
>
> A una dama que escribió a un galán un papel quejándose de él porque decía que era vieja, y él respondió con solo enviarle la fe del bautismo, en que constaba tener 68 años de chanza.⁷²
>
> A un galán que haciendo aire a su dama no pudo quitarle las moscas que se le pegaban al afeite.⁷³

The last two examples cited here show how, as with topics treating objects, there is also a tendency to parody Petrarchan idealism by injecting into it a large dose of often humorous "realism": indeed, the last mentioned topic

---

RH, 19 (1908), 455–65 (p. 461). Lope mentions these poems being submitted to the academy in a letter to the Duke of Sessa. See *Cartas*, p. 106.

⁶⁶ See Pantaleón, *Obras*, II, p. 58; Bocángel, *Lira*, p. 357; Corral, *La Cintia*, p. 108; *Badajoz*, fols 21v–22v; Valencia, *Real Palacio*, p. 32; Solís, *Varias poesías*, pp. 268, 273; Hurtado de Mendoza, *Obras poéticas*, I, pp. 229–32; Cáncer, *Obras varias*, pp. 179–82; and *Pascua de Reyes*, fols 14r–15v. This last parodic poem is an excellent example of the use of increased specificity to offset familiarity: the lady is bled, and she faints, and she bemoans the fact that her lover is not to be bled.

⁶⁷ See Navarro, *Poesías varias*, pp. 204–06 (an academy piece).
⁶⁸ See Polo de Medina, *Obras escogidas*, pp. 153–54.
⁶⁹ See *Badajoz*, fols 14r–15r.
⁷⁰ See *Carnestolendas*, pp. 48–50.
⁷¹ See *Real Aduana*, pp. 41–44.
⁷² See *Sol de academias*, pp. 43–44, 42, 45–46. For a further case of "mistaken identity" to the poem cited here, see Salcedo Coronel, *Cristales de Helicona*, fol. 11v.
⁷³ See *Repetida carrera*, pp. 44–45.

recalls Quevedo's diatribes against cosmetics and the fact that "beauty" is often the product of artifice and deception, except that the academy poet destroys Petrarchan idealism for comic rather than moral effect.[74] An excellent example of this type of risqué humour which grounds the Petrarchan lady, and her lover, firmly in physical, bodily reality are the following *quintillas* on a woman who, having been praised for her sweet smelling breath with which she has just rekindled a flame, breaks wind in front of her lover:

> Si [de] tu aire he de pintar
> las propiedades en suma,
> no sé cómo comenzar,
> que no he podido cortar
> hoy de buen aire la pluma.
>
> Pero, Inés, pues ya tu aliento
> me huele, y no me lo excusa,
> habréme de ir con gran tiento,
> que si he de hablar lo que siento,
> no me sopla bien la musa.
>
> Fuego añades a mi fuego,
> si das aliento a la pira.
> Y si haces tiro a mi ruego,
> arde con mi amor, mas luego
> ¡fuego de Dios lo que tira!
>
> Ya yo sé de tu cuidado
> lo que tengo que temer;
> pues estando enamorado
> pienso que te has olvidado
> de un descuido sin querer.
>
> Extraño, en tu buena fe,
> que estés así tan penada,
> porque, aunque el aire se fue,
> ¿quién ha de probar el que
> tú quedaste desairada?
>
> Es tu boca, por juguete,
> del ámbar la maravilla;
> y el aire de su retrete,
> por encenderse el pebete,
> se le corrió una pastilla.
>
> Bien del aire y fuego mides
> los dos contrarios intentos,
> pues en sus forzosas lides
> se vienen (si a uno despides)
> abajo los elementos.

---

[74] For a typically grotesque passage which deconstructs a woman's beauty and shows it to be no more than the product of cosmetic illusion, see Quevedo, *El mundo por de dentro*, in *Sueños*, ed. by Ignacio Arellano (Madrid: Cátedra, 1991), pp. 299–306.

ACADEMY TOPICS AND SEVENTEENTH-CENTURY LOVE POETRY 81

>   Mi amor se queda en su punto,
> aunque tu aire me provoca,
> divídelo, porque junto,
> no hablaré más del asunto,
> por no tomarlo en la boca.
>   Inés, pues con tu donaire
> tengo ya tanto interés,
> no me hagas otro desaire,
> que entenderé que es tu aire,
> siendo el aire de tus pies.[75]

Such a topic subverts the popular amatory topic mentioned above in which the lady extinguishes a flame only to rekindle it with her "life-giving" breath in so far as the poem turns on the unexpected and scatological contrast between the breath's marvellous "ámbar" and the "aire de su retrete" which, whilst providing inspiration, does little for the poet's respiration.

In contrast to such scatological humour, many academy poems, particularly in the early decades of the century, often fail to engage with the thematic potential of the unusual topic, skirting the dynamics of the scenario set to concentrate instead on describing them in purely Petrarchan terms. In a *romance* included in Polo de Medina's *Academias del jardín* (1630), a topic was set on the subject of a woman spitting on her lover from a balcony; in composing a piece on this promising situation the poet concentrates almost exclusively on describing the action of spitting via the elegant and euphemistic terms of ice and fire:

>   En la ventana de un cielo,
> gloria de un ingrato amor,
> Amarilis, sol de nieve,
> una tarde amaneció.
> Por el rubí de una boca,
> de un cielo hermoso arrebol,
> por un rasgo de clavel,
> breve herida de otra flor,
> sobre un amante de fuego
> copos de nieve llovió;
> que es posible que en su beldad
> que pueda nevar un sol.
> Eran centellas de nieve,
> injurias de su rigor,
> las que fueron en su boca
> perlas que el alba rió.
> A tan nevado desdén

---

[75] See *Ciudad Real*, fols 13v–14r. See also fol. 14v. for a sonnet on the same subject. Compare *Badajoz*, fol. 25v, on bad breath.

> el desprecio agradeció;
> que aun una crueldad alivia
> excesos de su dolor.
> En su constancia la nieve
> ya sus efectos trocó
> que se abrasa en lo menudo,
> y se enciende en su candor.
> Como se niega a deseos,
> que es alma todo su amor,
> crecen el hielo, que lleva
> todo el fuego al corazón.
> Pastores, que en las riberas
> de Sigura, cisnes sois,
> ¿quién vio que la nieve abrase?
> ¿quién vio que el fuego nevó?[76]

Despite the subject matter the treatment here is elegant but largely traditional; its conceits, far from being far-fetched, are rather tired Petrarchan clichés. It is as if the poet was unable definitively to break away from Petrarchan norms to explore the unusual and indecorous behaviour of the lady set out in the topic itself. In the early decades of the century poems often disassociate themselves from direct involvement with the triviality of their subject matter by retreating into the familiar territory of Petrarchism; far from revelling in the scenario envisioned, the poet recoils from it and cloaks it in Petrarchan decorum. In contrast, once such subjects have become standard it is precisely the scenario proposed by the topic that becomes the focus of attention with poets using it as the basis to create endless extravagant conceits which interpret and reinterpret it from every conceivable angle. In a poem such as Polo de Medina's the interpretative and ludic edge of wit has not yet broken free from the restraints of sixteenth-century idealism and propriety. The academy would play a crucial role in encouraging poets to abandon the latter and fully utilize their wit in exploring the increasingly unlikely and unrealistic scenarios set by academy secretaries.

Although there is great diversity in treatment, thematic groups of the most popular topics can be readily discerned. Perhaps not surprisingly the procedure behind composing a list of topics for the next meeting owed as much to setting variations on established and popular themes as on genuine originality and novelty. More popular themes include love letters, portraits, either the man or the woman being asleep, and wedding-night "dramas". The first two types are obviously very similar to those poems centred upon a particular object, differing only in their ever greater specificity and precision. The love letters are returned to the woman secured by a golden chain; they are dropped by accident into a fire before being read; are so treasured and hoarded that

---

[76] See *Obras escogidas*, pp. 124–25.

mice eat them; and are burnt causing the lover's moustache to catch fire.[77] Portraits are similarly treated: the woman, furious, stabs her lover's picture; lightening strikes and destroys another; whilst a third saves the lover from a bullet.[78]

More typical of this type of composition in the academy, however, are the other two topics centred upon the man or the woman being asleep (or unconscious), and the wedding-night and its attendant problems. The dream motif plays an important part in the first group of poems and all are clearly distantly related to a topos which was exceedingly popular in sixteenth-century Spanish poetry, the erotic dream.[79] Variations on this topic include the lover who re-enacts the woman's disdain by dreaming of her fleeing his embrace; the woman who paradoxically dreams nightly of the man she loathes; and the lover who dreams his beloved is dead, only to awake and discover his premonition is partially fulfilled when he learns she is ill.[80] More melodramatic are the *endechas* on the subject of the *galán* who falls asleep next to his lady on the shore – itself a suggestive degree of intimacy which is obviously totally anti-Petrarchan – only to awake and find she has been abducted.[81] Furthermore, as with other types of topics, our poetic expectations can be neatly reversed, as when the lover is brought round from a swoon by his lady's sighs – fainting normally being the prerogative of the Petrarchan mistress.[82]

The group of poems which take as their setting the wedding night are more humorous and entertaining. Some of these pose a dilemma for the bridegroom which the poet must resolve and are thus similar to the debate topics which I shall consider in the next section, whilst others establish patently ridiculous situations:

> Duda y resuelve si un novio a quien desafían la noche de la boda debe salir o no.[83]

---

[77] See, respectively, *Pascua de Reyes*, fols 15v–16r; *Sol de academias*, pp. 49, 39–40; *Fonseca Feb 1661*, fols 27v–28v. See also *Repetida carrera*, pp. 40–41; and Fonseca, *Jardín*, I, fols 48v–49r, "A la oblea que una dama puso en los labios para cerrar un papel, que llegó a manos de un galán sin enjugarse". Also Góngora's sonnet comparing a box containing a lady's returned letters and a funeral urn: *Sonetos completos*, p. 150.

[78] See *Real Aduana*, pp. 70–72; Cáncer, *Obras varias*, pp. 85–86; and *Sol de academias*, p. 27. See also *Valencia, Real Palacio*, pp. 19–20.

[79] On this topos, see Christopher Maurer, " 'Soñé que te ... ¿Dirélo?': El soneto del sueño erótico en los siglos XVI y XVII", *Edad de Oro*, 9 (1990), 149–67.

[80] See *Real Aduana*, pp. 86–88; *Sol de academias*, p. 37; and Salazar y Torres, *Poetas líricos de los siglos XVI y XVII*, II, p. 219. The *romance* cited earlier on the sleeping woman and the lascivious monkey obviously belongs in this category too.

[81] See *Repetida carrera*, pp. 43–44. Compare a related topic on a man who, unable to save his beloved from the Turks who are abducting her, kills her so as not to see her in another man's arms: *Fonseca Feb 1661*, fols 16r–18r.

[82] See *Sol de academias*, pp. 46–47. For an example of the normal Petrarchan procedure, see Navarro, *Poesías varias*, pp. 189–91.

[83] See *Pascua de Reyes*, fols 30v–31v (corrected foliation).

A un novio que la noche de su boda se levantó a oscuras a beber y al volver a la cama con su novia se perdió en el aposento.[84]

A un novio, tan flaco de memoria, que la noche de la boda se le olvidó que había de dormir con la novia, y se fue.[85]

Al suceso de un novio que trocó la noche de su boda una bebida con la purga de un enfermo.

Al suceso del enfermo, con la confección que estaba para el novio.[86]

Obviously the humour of all of these poems hinges simply on the sheer incongruity of the scenario and all of them share a similar "adolescent" bawdy humour revolving around the one topic expressly forbidden in Petrarchan poetry, sex: as the disappointed *novia* whose husband has forgotten his marital "duties" puts it:

>   Causa es para descasarme
>   ese achaque que padeces,
>   que es gran falta en un marido,
>   ser hombre que no se miembre.[87]

This attitude, together with an ill-concealed misogyny, can be seen in the first of the poems cited above by Francisco de Lezcano:

>   Como el casarse y reñir
>   no son lances diferentes,
>   a un novio le desafían
>   porque a casado se enseñe.
>   Salir debe al desafío,
>   y aun morir, que es excelente
>   medio para no reñir

---

[84] See *Real Aduana*, pp. 34–38.

[85] See Cáncer, *Obras varias*, pp. 116–19.

[86] These companion pieces are printed in full in Soons, *Castillo Solórzano*, pp. 99–102. Quevedo has a *romance* which deals with an identical scenario and which carries the following note by González de Salas: "El doctor Andrés de Laguna, doctísimo español, afirma en la ilustración que hizo a Dioscórides haber sucedido ansí a un novio y a un fraile, estando él en Mets, ciudad de la Francia bélgica; y lo refiere con no menor travesura de donaire, que aquí viene a ser forzosa". See Quevedo, *Poesía original completa*, pp. 1004–09 (p. 1004). See also Juan de Salinas, *Poesías humanas*, pp. 239–42. Whether these pieces, clearly inspired by the sixteenth-century Segovian doctor's anecdote, were actually written at the instigation of an academy is uncertain, but it seems fair to assume that they were, particularly as the two showing the closest similarity were written by Castillo and Quevedo who were members of the *Academia de Madrid* in the early 1620s.

[87] See Cáncer, *Obras varias*, p. 118. Compare the opening lines of Francisco de Avellaneda's poem in *Real Aduana*, p. 34.

> con su mujer muchas veces.
>   Mas no salga, que los novios
> decir necedades suelen,
> y matar con necedades
> es trato doble, y no puede.
>   Salga la novia, y es logro,
> pues quedará de esa suerte,
> sin contrario, si ella mata,
> o sin mujer, si ella muere.
>   Si es cuñado el enemigo,
> ya se ve que reñir deben;
> pero si no es cuñado
> riñan, porque lo parece.
>   Mas las paces los casados
> hacen en la cama siempre,
> y será mejor que el novio
> con su contrario se acueste.
>   Pero, pues es pecador,
> salga y tendrá buena muerte;
> pues al punto que se casan
> los maridos se arrepienten.
>   Pero, aunque esté arrepentido
> cualquier casado merece
> irse vestido y calzado
> al limbo por inocente.
>   A estas horas mi buen novio
> muy bellaco pleito tiene,
> si triunfa, queda casado,
> y rendido, si le vencen.
>   Si los necios son dichosos,
> muy bien la novia merece,
> pues que fue necia en casarse,
> la ventura de perderle.
>   Salga y muera en la campaña,
> que mis coplas le conceden,
> por librarle de marido,
> el bien de que muerto quede.[88]

The difference between this poem and one like Polo de Medina's cited above has far less to do with genre and the relative relaxation of propriety allowed in humorous poetry and far more to do with the whole manner in which the topic has been approached. By 1674, the date of this poem, the *conceptista* manner has so overtaken Spanish poetry that an emotional synthesis and a Petrarchan linguistic sensibility have yielded to a witty analysis of all the possible angles of a given subject. The topic is here approached in each stanza from a

---

[88] See *Pascua de Reyes*, fols 30v–31v (corrected foliation).

different perspective; the result is a seemingly exhaustive consideration of the initial scenario, in stark contrast to Polo's all but total avoidance of it. Such a poem, devoid of all lyricism and replete with facetious reasoning, is absolutely typical of academy poetry by the second half of the century.

The type of topic which sets a scenario and leaves the poet to describe, resolve or further it introduced a note of raucous humour into a long-standing part of the Petrarchan thematic repertoire. Although such topics are often decorous and serious, the format also enabled the composition of more explicitly erotic verse. In contrast to non-academy poetry in which such eroticism is present but left discreetly implicit in the very subject matter, academy poetry often actually draws the hearer's attention to the ribald and erotic aspects of the topic in hand. The result is poetry often every bit as sexually explicit as the type of *poesía erótica* collected by Pierre Alzieu, Robert Jammes and Yvan Lissorgues.[89] Perhaps more significantly, this type of topic also fully exploits the performative nature of the academy format and occasion: topics set, in their clear delineation of events and action, frequently read, as do the poems themselves, like scripts or summaries of the convoluted plots of Golden Age comedies and *capa y espada* plays.[90] The oral reception of such poems must have been an essential factor in contributing to their popularity, with voice, gesture and facial expression being deployed to emphasize the often bawdy nature of the lines being recited. Of all the types of topics, this is the most truly performative, being potentially dramatic both in its subject matter and in its delivery.

THE CASUISTRY OF LOVE: PARADOXES, DILEMMAS AND CONUNDRUMS

I have mentioned at various points the influence of the Castilian *cancioneros* on the choice and treatment of topics set in literary academies. Nowhere is the influence of the *cancionero* stronger than in those poems which set out to resolve or simply analyze the paradox or dilemma posed by the academy secretary in the set topic. The closest precedent for this type of composition is the *cancionero* debate poem. This was presented in the form of a single poem with two parts, the *pregunta* being written by one poet and the *respuesta* by another. The poet composing the *respuesta* was normally obliged to use the

---

[89] See *Poesía erótica del siglo de oro*, 2nd edn (Barcelona: Editorial Crítica, 1984).

[90] This is equally true, of course, of many pieces which have come down to us with no clear indication that they originated in an academy, but whose detailed specificity suggests that they did. Compare, for example, the following title of a *romance* by Hurtado de Mendoza: "Estando un caballero con una señora y una hija suya, avisaron que estaba allí un astrólogo, de que ella gustaba mucho, y fue necesario que se escondiese, y también la hija, y en la pieza a que se fue halló la moza, que se ofendió de que hubiese entrado donde ella estaba" (*Obras poéticas*, I, pp. 212–15).

same verse-forms and rhymes as had been employed in the *pregunta*.⁹¹ The form originated in the Provençal *tenso* and the French *jeu-parti*: in the former a wide range of themes were used and the discussion was freer, whilst the latter normally dealt with courtly love and the initiator of the debate would give his fellow poet various hypotheses to pursue, he himself being then obliged to defend whichever was not chosen.⁹² The *pregunta/respuesta* debate was often performed orally and then judged, both procedures providing further native precedent for academy practice.

The hypothetical dilemmas posed by debate poetry typically involve endless variations on the paradoxes of love: is a man in love without hope of happiness better off than a man not in love at all?; is it better to serve an unresponsive woman or to turn to a responsive one whom you love less?; which is preferable, to be present or absent if love is not reciprocated?; is an ugly but intelligent woman to be preferred to a stupid but beautiful one?⁹³ As we shall see, examples of subjects like this can be found in every seventeenth-century academy.

The strict *pregunta/respuesta* format is not often used in academies; most frequently poets are simply asked to discuss and analyze the type of paradox or dilemma which the *cancionero* poet had been required to resolve. Nevertheless some examples of poems following the proper debate format do exist. Several occur in a manuscript account of academy verse probably written by Pedro Méndez de Loyola, a member of the *Academia de Madrid* in the 1620s. A lewd example is the following:

    PREGUNTA
    Clori por Fabio muriendo
    no puede con él gozarse,
    sin reducirse a casarse
    con quien está aborreciendo.
    Por gozar a quien adoras,
    Fili, entre año raras veces,

---

⁹¹ This procedure of being tied to certain rhyme words is also employed in some academies and *justas* in the seventeenth century. For an example of the former, see the various sonnets cited in Kenneth Brown, "Gabriel de Corral", pp. 26–29; and for the latter, see *Relación de las exequias que en la muerte del rey nuestro señor don Felipe Cuarto el Grande, rey de Españas, y emperador de las Indias hizo la Universidad de Oviedo en el Principado de Asturias. Ofrécela en la real mano de la reina nuestra señora doña María Ana de Austria* (Madrid: Pablo de Val, 1666), p. 99.

⁹² This account is indebted to the articles of John G. Cummins, "Methods and Conventions in the 15th-Century Poetic Debate", *HR*, 31 (1963), 307–23, and "The Survival in the Spanish *cancioneros* of the Form and Themes of Provençal and Old French Poetic Debates", *BHS*, 42 (1965), 9–17. See also Pierre le Gentil, *La Poésie lyrique espagnole et portugaise*, I, pp. 461–69; and Alonso (ed.), *Poesía de Cancionero*, pp. 38–40.

⁹³ I take these examples from those debate topics mentioned by Cummins, "The Survival in the Spanish *cancioneros*", pp. 14–16.

>   ¿fueras de quien aborreces
>   todas las noches seis horas?
>
>   RESPUESTA
>   Casándome el que aborrezco,
>   suya con razón me llama;
>   y sin casarme la llama
>   me consume, en que padezco.
>   Cásome en fin, que el dolor
>   poco es, se templa, se cura,
>   en la esperanza segura
>   de gozarme con mi amor.
>   Y mayor gloria consigo
>   en la que gozar pretendo,
>   pues la aumento destruyendo
>   el honor de mi enemigo.[94]

More normally, the *pregunta*'s place is simply taken by the set topic in prose, which obviously serves exactly the same function in delineating the precise terms and content of the subsequent composition. A good example of a straightforward academy dilemma is the following poem by Agustín de Salazar written to resolve whether a man can love something perfectly if the object of his love is incapable of responding to him:

>   ¿Puede amar, sin ser amado,
>   un corazón? ¿Quién lo ignora?
>   ¿Cuándo el amor no mejora
>   lo fino en lo desgraciado?
>   Un imposible adorado
>   es el afecto mayor;
>   que quien aspira al favor
>   en su pasión importuna,
>   idolatra a la fortuna,
>   no sacrifica al amor.
>   Si de mi conocimiento
>   depende mi voluntad,
>   ¿me ha de pagar la beldad
>   que yo tenga entendimiento?
>   ¿Qué más agradecimiento

---

[94] See Brown, "Gabriel de Corral", p. 28. Brown argues for Méndez's authorship in "El cancionero erótico de Pedro Méndez de Loyola: parte segunda del «Gabriel de Corral: sus contertulios y un MS. poético de academia inédito»", *Castilla*, 11 (1986), 57–80. Compare Solís, "A una recien casada que dejó de ver a su amante", *Varias poesías*, pp. 189–90. Bawdy debate poems are found in the *cancioneros* too. See, for example, the exchange between Baena and Alvaro de Cañisares on the subject of whether it is preferable for the lady to be dressed or naked: *Cancionero de Juan Alfonso de Baena*, ed. by José María Azaceta, 3 vols (Madrid: CSIC, 1966), III, pp. 880–82.

busca una amante pasión,
que amar, y amar con razón?
Si es obligación querer
lo hermoso, ¿por qué he de hacer
mérito la obligación?
  El amor correspondido
no es perfectamente amar;
que no se ha de equivocar
lo amante y lo agradecido.
Siempre contingencia ha sido
el rigor o la clemencia;
y si la correspondencia
hiciera la voluntad,
no fuera Amor deidad,
pues no lo es la contingencia.
  El amante que procura
ser en su afecto dichoso
tiene ambición a lo hermoso,
mas no amor a la hermosura.
El que adoró la luz pura
de una beldad rigurosa,
con pasión más generosa
ama, Clori, despreciado;
porque el ser yo desgraciado
no te quita el ser hermosa.
  El mayor bien que se alcanza
en un soberano empleo
es que no sepa el deseo
donde habita la esperanza.
Amar con desconfianza
es la pasión más segura,
pues el que necio procura
en amor correspondencia,
adora la conveniencia,
desairando la hermosura.
  En el no ser admitido
acredito mi cuidado;
luego ¿de ser despreciado
debo estar agradecido?
Clori, rigores le pido,
no clemencia, a tu beldad,
que es fácil la voluntad,
que no olvida en su fineza,
por cultos a la belleza,
los templos a la piedad.[95]

---

[95] See *Pascua de Reyes*, fols 16v–17v.

What is typical in this poem is its unadorned exploration of the Golden Age conception of love which, being largely conceptualized via paradox and antithesis, allows a poet endless argumentative possibilities. It is therefore in these types of composition that love, if not sincerity, is most squarely the focus of poetic wit within the academy.

The most recurrent types of dilemmas, problems and paradoxes set by academies tend to be framed around one of three sets of antithetical terms, beauty/ugliness, love/hate, absence/presence, the last two of which are of obvious Petrarchan origin. The opposition absence/presence was particularly popular throughout the whole of the century and gave rise to a variety of topics in which the poet was asked to consider or simply describe various paradoxes occasioned by this antithesis:

> Pondérase un amante, poseído de dos contrarias pasiones, que viendo a su dama la aborrecía y dejando de verla, la amaba.
>
> A una dama, que al mismo a quien había favorecido ausente, presente despreciaba.
>
> A una dama que favorecía a un galán, teniéndole ausente, y en viéndole, se entibiaba.[96]
>
> A un galán, que no viendo a su dama la adoraba, y en viéndola, la aborrecía.[97]
>
> Pregúntase que debe elegir este galán: ¿vivir a vista de su dama aborrecido, o favorecido en su ausencia?[98]

Occasionally this long-worn topic is given a certain formal twist. Thus in the 1678 Ciudad Real academy the topic stipulated that the poet must discuss a lover's feelings about his lady's absence "con precepto de no decir razón afirmativa". This gave rise to two compositions, a set of three *décimas* (which will be discussed in the next chapter) and the following sonnet whose novelty, and indeed interest, lies not in the subject matter but in its formal treatment:

> ¡Qué pena! ¡Qué rigor! ¡Qué sentimiento!
> ¿Te vas Clori? ¿me dejas? ¡qué inclemencia!
> ¿No he de verte, ni hablarte? ¡qué impaciencia!
> ¿Me olvidarás? ¡qué ahogo! ¡qué tormento!
>   Pero ¿cómo respiro, cómo aliento?
> ¿cómo me animo y tengo resistencia?
> ¿hay tormento más duro que la ausencia?
> En mal tan rigoroso, ¿hay sufrimiento?

---

[96] See *Real Aduana*, pp. 29–33, 59, 83.
[97] See *Fonseca Jan 1661*, fols 16v–17v.
[98] see *Valencia, Real Palacio*, pp. 30–31.

>   Pues ¿cómo vivo? ¿cómo con mi vida
>   el tósigo no acaba en un instante?
>   ¿Soy insensible o fiera enfurecida?
>   ¿soy tigre, soy león, o soy amante?
>   ¿se olvida ya el amor? ¿la fe se olvida?
>   ¿soy mármol, peña, bronce, soy diamante? [99]

With poems such as these whose innovation is formal rather than thematic the performative aspect would have been central to its success and we see here how the academy by the second half of the century frequently adopts and adapts theatrical language or rhetoric in treating its topics.

The beauty/ugliness antithesis usually takes the straightforward form of choosing between the two, or explaining how a man can fall in love with an ugly woman, though variation is introduced as in the *certamen* topic "¿por qué razón llaman entendidas a las feas, si no hay mayor necedad que ser feas".[100] Similarly the love/hate antithesis, already obviously present in the absence/presence paradox, is usually treated in an uncomplicated manner, though sometimes this topic shows the same tendency towards the anecdotal that we saw in the topics which treat mundane objects, whilst still being specifically framed within the debate format. An example of the uncomplicated treatment of this subject, by which I mean that the poem simply addresses the central paradox without recourse to any detailed narrative context, is Bocángel's *romance* described as follows by the seventeenth-century heading: "Si un amante se ve entre dos damas, una que amada le aborreció, y otra que le amó aborrecida, ¿a cuál debe más?"[101] The same amatory dilemma is treated in a variety of forms by other academy poets,[102] but Bocángel's piece is particularly suggestive because of the nautical simile it introduces in lines 17–20:

>   Luchaba yo bien así
>   como el náufrago que, viendo
>   la nave arder, ni se otorga
>   a las aguas ni al incendio.

These lines are of interest because the sinking ship itself becomes the setting for a poem by Ulloa y Pereira which thereby further dramatizes this particular debate topic. In Ulloa's sonnet the lover, for no very clear reason, has to

---

[99] See *Ciudad Real*, fol. 12r.
[100] See, respectively, *Pascua de Reyes*, fols 27r–28r (corrected foliation); and Antonio de Solís, *Varias poesías*, pp. 293–94, 246–47.
[101] Bocángel, *Lira*, pp. 409–10.
[102] See, for example, the rather incomprehensible *romance* included in Camerino, *La dama beata*, pp. 108–09; or the sonnet by Juan de Olivenza in *Fonseca April 1662*, fol. 26r. Camerino's poem was in all probability composed for the same academy as Bocángel's.

decide which of the two women to throw overboard, the one he loves but who hates him, or the one he loathes but who adores him in turn:

> Voz de oráculo fue que se entregara
> de dos ninfas al mar la que eligiera
> amante, que forzado en la ribera,
> el destino cruel executara.
>   El caso fue que en una idolatrara,
> y otra en el hielo de su amor ardiera.
> Fue de razón librarse la postrera;
> y fue de amor que la razón faltara.
>   Premio fue, no castigo, que ofreciese
> sepulcro un elemento a la fineza
> de la que ya murió cuando vivía.
>   Y al desdén fue lisonja que se viese
> suceso que animase la dureza,
> ejemplo que templase la porfía.[103]

The seventeenth-century editor's epigraph to this sonnet in Ulloa y Pereira's *Obras* informs us both that it was a topic set by an academy and, more interestingly, that the subject was later turned into a play, possibly one of the academy's *comedias de repente*, a fact which underlines the inherently dramatic conception and style of topics of which this is such an excellent example.[104] It comes as a surprise, though, to realize that this archetypal academy topic was actually far from novel. Exactly the same dilemma and nautical scenario are treated in a *pregunta/respuesta* format by the late fifteenth-century *cancionero* poet Antón de Montoro, "el ropero de Córdoba". It seems clear that Ulloa y Pereira was aware of Montoro's poem, for the opening quatrain lifts a specific detail direct from the latter's poem, attributing the idea of throwing one of the women into the sea to a "voz de oráculo" (in Montoro the notion is suggested by a "voz muy pavorosa").[105] Ulloa's poem, being a sonnet, is far more tightly constructed than Montoro's which spends a considerable amount of time describing the narrative situation in a prosaic fashion. The fact that the unusual scenario need not be explained by Ulloa in the poem itself, because the audience would have been aware of it from the rubric set out in the topic, is one clear advantage of the academy format which enables the poet, at least in restricted verse-forms, to develop a heightened sense of

---

[103] See *Obras*, p. 32. Compare the *romance* on pp. 208–09.
[104] The epigraph reads: "Hallándose un galán obligado a echar en la mar una de dos damas con quien estaba, que de la una se hallaba muy enamorado, y le aborrecía, y la otra le quería, y la desdeñaba. Fue asunto de una Academia que el que escribiera echase la que le pareciese, y diese la razón en un soneto. Después se hizo comedia de esto" (p. 32).
[105] See Antón de Montoro, *Cancionero*, ed. by Emilio Cotarelo y Mori (Madrid: José Perales y Martínez, 1900), pp. 111–14 (p. 112). The "answer" suggested is to save the beautiful woman loved by the "escudero" and "a la otra condenar / a cualquier tribulación" (p. 114).

narrative drama and specific context without necessarily any loss of poetic impact.

Apart from the three most popular antithetical variations, the amatory problems posed in academies usually involve the poet in a similar process of having to decide between two mutually exclusive options or choosing which is the lesser of two evils:

> ¿Cúal es mayor dolor, el que se explica o el que se calla?
>
> Discurre un galán cúal fue mayor pena, llorar a su dama ingrata o borrar con sus lágrimas su retrato.
>
> Pondérase cúal es más dicha, la de una mujer casada con un ciego o la de una necia con un sordo.[106]

Equally the poet is often called upon to pronounce on what is the most suitable behaviour for a lover, as when he must state which is the greatest indication of a lover's feelings, going pale or blushing at the sight of the lady he loves; or on the finer points of Petrarchan psychology, such as determining whether feigning indifference when actually in love or pretending to be in love when actually you are indifferent causes the most pain.[107] (Despite the marked prevalence of a binary presentation of subject matter, poems can occasionally offer a simple exploration of a paradox or dilemma, such as Castillo Solórzano's academy piece "a una dama, que no pidiendo, recebía cuanto le daban", or the *décimas* composed by Bocángel on a woman who, when promised anything by her lover, however impossible the demand, requires him to stop loving her altogether.[108]) Sometimes the topic is framed in strikingly similar ways to existing *cancionero* debate poems. In the *Cancionero de Baena*, for example, there is a *pregunta/respuesta* series in which Baena poses the following problem to Ferrant Manuel de Lando:

> Desidme, señor gentil, enperante,
> ver mi amiga e nunca fablalla,

---

[106] See *Fonseca Jan 1661*, fols 11v–12v; and *Repetida carrera*, pp. 15–16, 34–35. The choice between two undesirable things is a popular subject for non-amatory topics: in the *Repetida carrera*, for example, poets are asked to decide which is worse, being bald and wearing a wig, or not wearing one at all (pp. 41–42); whilst in the Ciudad Real academy of 1678 the topics included one asking which was the worst error, the fact that Rome had exiled all doctors or that it had allowed prostitutes (fols 21r–22v). Similarly many of the topics set in the famous Buen Retiro academy of 1637 involve the poet in deciding between two equally preposterous options, such as which is more stupid, to be occasionally stupid or to be permanently intelligent; or whether Diego de Covarrubias y Leyva could better defend the Retiro with his vigilance or his pronounced paunch. See *Academia burlesca*, pp. 646–47, 641–42.

[107] See *Valencia, Real Palacio*, pp. 35–36; and *Fonseca April 1662*, fols 18v–19v.

[108] See Soons, *Castillo Solórzano*, pp. 93–94, and Bocángel, *Lira*, pp. 428–29. For an identical poem to Bocángel's, see Castillo Solórzano, *Las harpías en Madrid*, pp. 140–41.

o syenpre fablalla e nunca miralla;
de quel faga, d'esto me dat conssonante.[109]

This is directly echoed by a sonnet written for one of Fonseca de Almeida's academies on the topic "¿Quién enamora más, una mujer hermosa que se ve y no se habla, o una mujer discreta, que se habla y no se ve?":

> Quedó a una discreción Fabio rendido,
> sin ver al dueño, pero fue excusado,
> que le habló tan perfecto imaginado,
> que aun dudó si era menos lo entendido.
>   Vio Fabio una hermosura, y suspendido
> quedó a sus luces, ciego y elevado,
> como dando a entender que había encontrado
> desempeño en los ojos el oído.
>   Mas no fue así, que en Fabio conseguida
> de amor la palma la hermosura alcanza,
> toda una alma por triunfo a su luz pura
>   tuvo imperiosamente reducida,
> que si la discreción dejó esperanza,
> no tuvo que esperar con la hermosura.[110]

Topics such as this, like the *pregunta/respuesta* format itself, are clearly variations of the *cuestión de amor* in which the lover has to resolve an amatory dilemma – usually, as here, in the form of deciding between two difficult options – using all the casuistry of love. This debate format was popularized by Boccaccio in his novel *Filocolo*, which presents thirteen *questioni d'amore*, some of which have echoes in academy topics. The topics structured around the notions of presence and absence, for example, find a distant parallel in Boccaccio's eleventh *questione*, namely whether seeing a lady in person or thinking lovingly of her gives more pleasure.[111] Similarly the two *décimas* by Méndez de Loyola cited earlier which raise the question of whether a woman should marry a man she hates in order to be able to sleep with the one she loves is comparable to the twelfth *questione* in which a man who has been found with both a bawd and a lady is given the stark option by the latter's brothers of either first sleeping with the bawd for a year and then with the lady for a further year or reversing this and sleeping with the lady first and then the bawd, both under the condition that he must sleep with whomever he chooses in the second year as frequently as he has with his choice in the first (pp. 531–36). The popularity of such *cuestiones* in Spain, and their particular connection with literary academies, is underlined in

---

[109] See *Cancionero de Baena*, III, p. 822.
[110] See *Fonseca April 1662*, fol. 20r.
[111] See Giovanni Boccaccio, *Filocolo*, ed. by Mario Marti (Milan: Rizzoli Editore, 1969), pp. 528–30.

Calderón's *Los tres mayores prodigios* (1636). In the play Medea organizes an "academia de amor" during which she presents her two suitors, Friso and Jason, with a knotty amatory puzzle taken directly from the first *questione* in *Filocolo*: Medea presents Friso with her ribbon whilst accepting a ribbon from a rival suitor, Jason; she then asks them which of them has been shown the greatest favour.[112] This scene in a production written expressly to be performed in the newly rebuilt Buen Retiro palace thus stages the type of occasion and its poetic topics which enjoyed immense popularity at the court of Philip IV.[113]

As we have seen, academy poetry has both general and specific thematic parallels with *cancionero* poetry. Julio Rodríguez's recent characterization of the typical *cancionero* poet as "amoroso, burlesco, satírico, obsceno, ocasionalmente religioso",[114] gives some idea of the close similarity between the fifteenth-century poets and their seventeenth-century academy counterparts who exhibit exactly the same range of thematic attitudes with the exception of the last. The *cancioneros* remained popular throughout the Golden Age, being diffused both via such works as Hernando del Castillo's *Cancionero general* (first printed in Valencia in 1511, and going through nine editions in total in the sixteenth century) and, especially, via the plethora of *pliegos sueltos* and smaller *cancionero* anthologies both of which exercised even greater influence because of their ready availability and their relative cheapness.[115] Such poetry was not simply the preserve of the *vulgo*: Gracián includes many fifteenth-century poems in his *Agudeza y arte de ingenio*, and is full of admiration for their poets. The seventeenth-century academies were drawing on and developing a tradition in Peninsular verse stretching back in an unbroken line to the fifteenth century. The *cancioneros*, therefore, with their debate poems and their occasional verse, provide a clear native precedent for academy poetry.

---

[112] See Pedro Calderón de la Barca, *Obras completas*, ed. by A. Valbuena Briones, 3 vols, vol. 1, *Dramas*, 5th edn (Madrid: Aguilar, 1966), pp. 1557–58. In Boccaccio, the object in question is a garland of flowers. See *Filocolo*, pp. 459–65. On the popularity of this particular *cuestión* in Spain, see José F. Montesinos, "Una cuestión de amor en comedias antiguas españoles", *RFE*, 13 (1926), 280–83; and Joaquín Casalduero, "Parodia de una cuestión de amor y queja de las fregonas", *RFE*, 19 (1932), 181–87: neither critic mentions Calderón's court drama.

[113] Compare Hurtado de Mendoza's *décimas* answering a *pregunta* posed by the Count de la Roca as to whether it is better to be near the beloved, but behind her back, or far away but facing her. See *Obras poéticas*, I, pp. 221–27. As Davies points out, this poetic form was a standard part of the palace poet's repertoire: *Poet at Court*, p. 101.

[114] See *Poesía crítica y satírica del siglo XV*, ed. by Julio Rodríguez Puértolas (Madrid: Castalia, 1981), p. 298. This comment is made with particular reference to Antón de Montoro.

[115] For the predominance of *cancionero* poetry in *pliegos sueltos*, even at the close of the seventeenth century, see E. M. Wilson, "Quevedo para las masas" in *Entre las jarchas y Cernuda*, pp. 276–97. On the *pliegos* themselves, see Julio Caro Baroja, *Ensayo sobre la literatura de cordel* (Madrid: Ediciones Istmo, 1990).

Conclusion

Having considered the types of topics set and the subject matters written about in the academies, I would like to return to the two questions I posed at the start of the chapter: the role of the academy in originating and promoting such poetry and, parallel with this question of the exact relationship between academy and non-academy verse, the extent to which the distinctive thematics of academy poetry are determined by the formal characteristics and the ambience of the social occasion itself.

As we have seen, academy topics have their origins firmly in contemporary amatory practice, itself largely based upon late sixteenth-century Italian developments in the Petrarchan tradition which greatly expanded upon Petrarch's own occasional muted gesture towards empirical reality in the *Canzoniere*. The exception to this is the debate style poem, popular in the academy precisely because of its inherently discursive presentation of an argument and its readily exploitable potential for oral, declamatory presentation. Such topics show a closer affinity to the native *cancionero* tradition, a tradition which was itself influential in fostering a conceited style of verse and, arguably more importantly, in thereby providing a native precedent for seventeenth-century Spanish *conceptismo*, allowing Spanish theoreticians to claim that wit is inherent to Spain and not a cultural implant from Italy. The academy seems to have latched onto early an innovative strand of late sixteenth-/early seventeenth-century love poetry – the cult of particularization – and transformed it by substantially developing it along more specific, anecdotal lines. As the century proceeds, so this anecdotal framing of the amatory topic becomes increasingly melodramatic and far-fetched. That the academy should have picked up and developed this latest development of the Petrarchan tradition is hardly surprising. Not only was this subject matter novel at the start of the century, but its very ubiquity guaranteed its incorporation into the academy's range of topics. Furthermore, the academy was an environment ideally suited to its development. The informality and communality of its sessions clearly worked against the cultivation of both amatory sincerity and idealization, as we shall see in the next chapter, and so favoured a wholesale exploitation of the incidental and contingent elements of the lovers' milieu. The light-hearted and amusing atmosphere also allowed a greater degree of poetic licence and poets, unfettered from considerations of decorum, could develop these topics either along salacious and ribald lines or into the realms of the ever more farcical and bizarre. In this way academies helped to acclimatize this particular lyric innovation. In so doing they also gave it its own particular momentum and cultural legitimacy, such that by the 1620s, at the latest, it is the academy which is propagating this style and, at least in this thematic area, consequently influencing wider amatory practice, if only because in quantitative terms this type of subject matter (whether treated humorously or seriously) dominated academy production. This was in sharp contrast to non-academy poetry where a more traditional, idealizing and formalized love lyric continued to predominate, a lyric exemplified by the court poetry popularized by a poet such as Hurtado de Mendoza based on what Gareth Davies aptly labels the "Manzanarian idyll".[116] By taking this thematic development to extremes, the academy ensured its continuation in a less dramatic or exaggerated form beyond its confines. Within the academy, however, such topics, despite tracing their roots back to contemporary Petrarchan practice, nevertheless radically deviated from it: Petrarchan origins did not mean Petrarchan poetry, in style or intent.

The precedents for academy topics which I have cited – namely *cancionero* verse, early sixteenth-century Italian Petrarchan poetry as exemplified by Aquilano Serafino, and the poetry of Giambattista Marino – were all products of social and cultural climates similar to that prevailing in seventeenth-century Spain. Trevor Dadson, in a discussion of the close similarity between *cancionero* poetry and the verse of the Count of Salinas, has drawn attention to the fact that the socio-literary conditions of Habsburg Spain in the late sixteenth and early seventeenth centuries were very similar to those in fifteenth-century Castile which gave rise to the *conceptista* style characteristic of *cancionero* poets. Indeed, he goes as far as to argue that literary academies were thus the direct descendants and inheritors of this native *conceptismo*.[117] Similarly, writing of the formative context in and for which Serafino, Cariteo, Tebaldeo and their fellow poets composed their verse, A. J. Smith comments that their poetry is "court art through and through" which attempts to "transform into lively art the casual traffic of court life".[118] This equally applies to poets such as Tasso and Marino, the latter aptly described as a "poet-entertainer" by Mirollo, who also attributes his distinctive style to the fact

---

[116] See Davies, *Poet at Court*, p. 109. For a broad discussion of this type of poetry, see Luis Rosales, *El sentimiento de desengaño en la poesía barroca* (Madrid: Ediciones Cultura Hispánica, 1966), pp. 134–205; and Arthur Terry, *Seventeenth-Century Spanish Poetry: The Power of Artifice* (Cambridge: Cambridge University Press, 1993), pp. 208–18.

[117] See Trevor Dadson, "El Conde de Salinas y la poesía cancioneril", in *Actas del Congreso Internacional sobre literatura hispánica en la época de los Reyes Católicos y el descubrimiento* (Barcelona: PPU, 1989), pp. 270–78 (pp. 275, 278 n.17). On the court as a source of patronage and hence of great literary influence during this period, see Angus MacKay, *Spain in the Middle Ages. From Frontier to Empire, 1000–1500* (London: Macmillan, 1977), pp. 207–08.

[118] See *Metaphysical Wit*, pp. 25, 26. Regarding these poets, Forster comments that "theirs was an uncommitted art suited to court life and court entertainment", and argues that only with the work of Pietro Bembo (1470–1527) did Petrarchism return to its more "serious" origins (*The Icy Fire*, p. 26). Certainly the first generations of Petrarchists in Spain – Boscán, Garcilaso, Cetina, Acuña – continued this "serious" approach, fusing the Petrarchan discourse with the courtly model, and more openly Neoplatonic ideas, of Castiglione's *Cortegiano*.

that much of the Neapolitan's verse is directed at an audience at various courts or academies.[119] Not surprisingly, this more courtly or communal forum led to an increase in themes and subjects dealing with specific social activities, thereby effectively grounding the lyric space firmly in the intimacy and particularity of its audience or readership. Poets were writing for closed circles of acquaintances, a coterie world in which great premium was set on mental acuity and ingenuity and in which friends, writing expressly for the amusement of friends, could make satirical allusions and knowing references to each other's private lives, their amatory and social successes and failures, whilst poets, seeking status, patronage and preferment could make elaborate courtly compliments and gestures towards real or potential patrons. (Hence, in seventeenth-century Spain, the inclusion of laudatory poems to royalty among academy topics, and the use of the academy itself as a means to mark a specific royal event which became so widespread in the second half of the century.) Poetry became both a means of conducting social interaction and of staving off the boredom of life in societies bound by rigid etiquette and formal conventions.

In each of these environments the composition of verse within the narrow world of court or academy produced a similar type of witty, urbane, circumstantial and "light" poetry. The court cultures that emerged in Europe in the fifteenth and sixteenth centuries, which were given definitive literary expression in Castiglione's *Il Cortegiano* (1528), gave particular prominence to poetry as both a courtly pursuit and, consequently, a suitable gentlemanly pastime. Indeed, it has recently been argued that the Renaissance courtly code drew many of its procedures from contemporary poetics, both sharing a common basis in ornament, play and dissemblance.[120] Whilst in Spain the notion of a gentleman-courtier predates Boscán's 1534 translation of *Il Cortegiano*, being apparent, for example, in the fifteenth-century Castilian

---

[119] See Mirollo, *Poet of the Marvellous*, p. 195. For a consideration of the kinship between Serafino and Marino, see Lorch, "Petrarch", pp. 90–91. For a succinct overview of Tasso's lyric poetry and its social milieu, see C. P. Brand, *Torquato Tasso: A Study of the Poet and his Contribution to English Literature* (Cambridge: Cambridge University Press, 1965), pp. 133–55.

[120] Daniel Javitch, for example, argues that the "basic reason why [poetry's] artifices were so esteemed was their resemblance to the artifices courtiers themselves sought to display in their conduct", and notes that "poetry had always possessed and been seen to possess the ornamental, deceptive, and playful properties that proper court conduct eventually shared with it. In fact, the Renaissance courtly code, as Castiglione defines it, drew many of its rules for beautifying the self from traditional procedures in verbal and pictorial art". See *Poetry and Courtliness in Renaissance England* (Princeton: Princeton University Press, 1978), pp. 6, 105. On the centrality of the ludic in Castiglione, see Thomas M. Greene, "*Il Cortegiano* and the Choice of a Game", in *Castiglione. The Ideal and the Real in Renaissance Culture*, ed. by Robert W. Hannard and David Rosand (New Haven and London: Yale University Press, 1983), pp. 1–15.

emphasis on the need for a lettered and classically educated aristocracy,[121] what Boscán and Garcilaso did in appropriating *Il Cortegiano* and both Italian metres and the Petrarchan discourse for a Castilian audience was, in the words of Ignacio Navarrete, "to assert that poetry is not only an aristocratic activity, but an exclusively aristocratic activity from which those not graced with courtly *sprezzatura*, those who must labor to learn rules, are excluded".[122] In the seventeenth century, at a time when the "democratization" of literature and the ensuing encroachment and influence of the *vulgo* on matters of literary taste were greatly resented and despised, the academy enabled the lower nobility, the *caballeros*, a group which continued to rise in administrative importance and dominance throughout the century, to gain access to the cultural exclusivity of poetry and hence to the appearance, if not the actual status, of the "leisured" aristocracy. The academy is thus in a very real sense the result of a broadening of the courtly ethos of exclusivity and its concomitant view of poetry as a suitable social activity for an educated elite at leisure to include the aspiring courtiers, the minor officials, functionaries and bureaucrats, but in such a way as to retain still a sense of the elitism and exclusivity which typified court culture throughout Europe.

Whilst the closed and intimate nature of both court and academy in Renaissance and Baroque Italy and Spain tended to foster wit and conceited language, in seventeenth-century Spanish academies they surprisingly did not tend to encourage novelty and variety. The relative lack of diversity in topics set is one of the more striking features of this type of verse. As the examples cited in this chapter reveal, academies adhered to a relatively reduced number of tried-and-tested topics, with meetings held towards the close of the century still often setting topics centred on similar scenarios, objects and emotions to those set at the start. Academy poetry thus becomes an extended exercise in composing variations on a limited number of themes, in a way that recalls contemporary theatre with its endless variations on basically similar plots and dramatic scenarios, its *refundiciones*, and – in a dramatist such as Calderón – its use from play to play of identical images, concepts and vocabulary to express common emotions such as jealousy and love. What strikes us as a relative lack of imagination and poetic invention can be viewed as part of the very challenge and interest of academy topics: minor variations, added rhetorical or metrical difficulties, and the setting of ever more specific (and humorous) scenarios in which the poet had to set the clichéd emotions and

---

[121] See J. N. H. Lawrance, "On Fifteenth-Century Spanish Vernacular Humanism", in *Medieval and Renaissance Studies in Honour of Robert Brian Tate*, ed. by Ian Michael and Richard A. Cardwell (Oxford: Dolphin, 1986), pp. 63–79 (pp. 73–75). Also see Peter E. Russell, "Las armas contra las letras", in *Temas de "La Celestina" y otros estudios. Del "Cid" al "Quijote"* (Barcelona: Editorial Ariel, 1978), pp. 209–36.

[122] See Ignacio Navarrete, *Orphans of Petrarch. Poetry and Theory in the Spanish Renaissance* (Berkeley, Los Angeles: University of California Press, 1994), p. 48.

amatory situation – all confronted the poet with the difficult task of making the familiar seem interesting, new and entertaining. In this way we need to revise our conception of the relationship between wit and novelty, for the academics suggest that novelty lay more in a poet's resourceful and ingenious approach to a subject than in the subject matter itself. Such paucity of invention in the setting of topics can also be taken, of course, as a clear indication that amatory poetry in Golden Age Spain was, finally, exhausted. Either way, the performative and occasional nature of the event, together with the fact that its immediate purpose was entertainment, did undoubtedly introduce a new current into contemporary poetry, theatricality. Both the subject matter and its style tend towards the dramatic and the declamatory, the incidental and the impersonal. Consequently, theatricality is the dominant characteristic of both academies themselves and of much of the poetry they produced. The result is a poetry which is truly occasional and ephemeral, written to be delivered and performed for a specific audience: out of this context and on the page, the performative edge is lost with the result that academy verse too frequently appears insipid, forced, and utterly trivial.

4

FROM LYRICISM TO PERFORMANCE: THE POETIC PERSONA IN ACADEMY LOVE POETRY

In his *Carta a un amigo suyo, nuevo en la corte* published in 1654 Alvaro Cubillo de Aragón offers the following advice to the aspiring courtier on attending and writing for a literary academy:

> Si en Academia alguna te hallares
> donde ya por costumbre recibida
> algún señor presida,
> obedece el asunto y no repares
> en que sátira sea;
> que como se usa allí de impersonales,
> ya pintando una vieja, ya una fea,
> un miserable, un calvo, un antojado,
> y en esta acción lucida
> no se tira a ventana conocida,
> puedes, sin que tu pluma desmerezca,
> decir cuanto al ingenio se le ofrezca.[1]

These twelve lines neatly encapsulate the literary academy; in particular they foreground one aspect of academy compositions which I wish to consider in detail in this chapter, namely the cultivation of impersonality. Cubillo de Aragón himself makes no mention of love poetry. Indeed, from the examples of poetic characters which the poet-courtier will be required to write about within the academy it seems clear that he probably has in mind the more satirical and parodic type of composition – the "vieja", "fea" and "calvo" are all standard subjects of humorous academy verse. Nevertheless the poet-dramatist has here touched upon one of the most significant aspects of academy poetry, the fact that the nature of the event leads to a more dispassionate approach to love poetry. Poets may assume the guise of the lover whose situation and emotional reactions have been laid down by the set topic but, in the majority of cases, they abandon altogether the intimacy of the "confessional mode" of the first-person singular and write instead totally impersonal

---

[1] Alvaro Cubillo de Aragón, *El enano de las musas* (Madrid: María de Quiñones, 1654), p. 46.

verse using the third person. The impersonality adopted by academy poets alters the founding fiction of the whole Petrarchan enterprise whose linguistic universe has as its "(pro)nominal center" the first-person singular, the "I" who is both poet and, most importantly, lover.[2] The result is a style of poetry which constitutes a definitive modification of, and substantial break with, the mode of love poetry which had dominated Spanish poetry since Boscán and Garcilaso introduced the Italianate style in the first quarter of the sixteenth century.

A further important distinguishing feature of academy poetry and one intimately connected to the projection of a textual persona is metatextuality. Metatextual commentary on the literary task in hand, made using the first person, becomes an institutionalized characteristic, even within poems which actually convey their amatory content via the third person. In this way poets create lyrics which combine both amatory distance and poetic or literary intimacy, using a persona to relate not to the amatory content but to the academy context. Hence the addressee of such poems is always primarily the academy audience rather than the fictitious woman internal to the poem's drama. This is not to argue that academy verse is more sophisticated because more obviously the self-reflexive product of artifice and performance. Indeed, in many ways such poetry is less sophisticated precisely because it is one dimensional and little concerned with combining and exploring the different and competing elements of amatory fiction, rhetorical self-projection and poetic dexterity. Most academy poetry stands in contrast then to poets such as Góngora, Quevedo and Lope, as well as Garcilaso and Herrera, who composed love poetry which is aware of, and therefore attentive to, its dual status as the product of love and art.[3]

To set academy developments in the projection of lyric personae in context it is important to appreciate just how central the creation of a plausible amatory presence was to Golden Age love poetry. Enormous emphasis was

---

[2] See Marguerite R. Waller, *Petrarch's Poetics and Literary History* (Amherst: University of Massachusetts Press, 1980), p. 51. As Thomas M. Greene writes: "One could argue that the fundamental subject of the *Canzoniere* is not so much or not only the psychology of the speaker as the *ontology* of his selfhood, the struggle to discern a self or compose a self which could stand as a fixed and knowable substance". See *The Light in Troy. Imitation and Discovery in Renaissance Poetry* (New Haven and London: Yale University Press, 1982), p. 124.

[3] For the recent critical re-evaluation of Garcilaso, for long regarded as the archetypal Spanish voice of Petrarchan authenticity, see Mary E. Barnard, "Garcilaso's Poetics of Subversion and the Orphean Tapestry", *PMLA*, 102 (1987), 316–23; Anne J. Cruz, *Imitación y transformación. El petrarquismo en la poesía de Boscán y Garcilaso de la Vega* (Amsterdam, Philadelphia: John Benjamins Publishing Company, 1988); Caroll B. Johnson, "Personal Involvement and Poetic Tradition in the Spanish Renaissance: Some Thoughts on Reading Garcilaso", *RR*, 90 (1989), 288–304; and E. C. Graf, "Forcing the Poetic Voice: Garcilaso de la Vega's Sonnet XXIX as a Deconstruction of the Idea of Harmony", *MLN*, 109 (1994), 163–85.

placed on what Paul Julian Smith has astutely labelled the "rhetoric of presence".[4] Petrarchan poetry sought to create the illusion of authentic utterance via the amatory persona and the confessional mode: the psychological credibility of emotion and voice was paramount. Rhetorical manuals taught ways in which the poet could artificially produce the impression of the emotions which he claimed to feel, thereby enabling him to move his audience with their veracity.[5] This should remind us that contemporary readers did not assume that a poet's amatory fiction was literally true, although some critics did seek a factual basis for a poet's emotions, but without ever taking a sustained biographical approach.[6] The purpose and nature of this "rhetoric of presence" is most clearly and explicitly stated in the introductory sonnets of lyric sequences. Such sonnets leave us in no doubt that the emotional and linguistic dominance of the poet-lover is a central feature of the Petrarchan discourse. Indeed it is the primary function of the introductory sonnet to present the amatory persona as pivotal to the success of the entire Petrarchan enterprise. A brief consideration of the prologue-sonnet will thus enable us to establish Petrarchan priorities in the creation of a lyric persona, and so to appreciate the degree to which academy poets deviate from the amatory norm, both in their serious love poetry and in their humorous verse, the parodic and comic impact of which rests upon our awareness of their subversion of standard amatory practice.

Functioning partly as a form of *captatio benevolentiae*, the introductory sonnet attempts to involve readers emotionally in the fiction of the love sequence by engaging their empathy.[7] It thus acquires a position of strategic importance in the presentation of the poet's romance for it foregrounds the centrality of an affective first-person singular and assures the emotional

---

[4] This notion is developed in the second chapter of Smith's *Writing in the Margin. Spanish Literature of the Golden Age* (Oxford: Clarendon Press, 1988).

[5] See, for example, Miguel de Salinas, *Retórica en lengua castellana* (Alcalá, 1541), in *La retórica en España*, ed. by Elena Casas (Madrid: Editora Nacional, 1980), pp. 163–66. On this point see also Rosemund Tuve, *Elizabethan and Metaphysical Imagery* (Chicago and London: University of Chicago Press, 1947), pp. 180–91.

[6] In their comments on Garcilaso's poetry, for example, both El Brocense and Herrera mention biographical details in their discussions of the eclogues; whilst Quevedo's editor, González de Salas, comments in his 1648 edition of the poet's verse on the autobiographical nature of the amatory sequences of both Petrarch and Quevedo. See the *Anotaciones* in Garcilaso, *Garcilaso y sus comentaristas*, ed. by Antonio Gallego Morell, 2nd edn (Madrid: Gredos, 1972), pp. 281, 301, 475–76; and Quevedo, *Obra poética*, ed. by José Manuel Blecua, 4 vols (Madrid: Castalia, 1969–81), I, p. 117. For a recent discussion of Garcilaso and the question of sincerity, see Daniel L. Heiple, *Garcilaso de la Vega and the Italian Renaissance* (University Park, Pennsylvania: Pennsylvania State University Press, 1994), pp. 3–72.

[7] For a general survey of the introductory sonnet, see Juan Manuel Rozas, "Petrarca y Ausias March en los sonetos-prólogo amorosos del siglo de oro", *Homenajes. Estudios de filología española*, 1 (1964), 57–75.

sincerity and credibility of the amatory experiences described. The opening sonnet of Petrarch's *Canzoniere* is the canonical text in this rhetorical strategy:

> Voi ch'ascoltate in rime sparse il suono
> di quei sospiri ond'io nudriva 'l core
> in sul mio primo giovenile errore
> quand'era in parte altr'uom da quel ch'i'sono,
>   del vario stile in ch'io piango e ragiono
> fra le vane speranze e 'l van dolore,
> ove sia chi per prova intenda amore
> spero trovar pietà, non che perdono.
>   Ma ben veggio or sì come al popol tutto
> favola fui gran tempo, onde sovente
> di me medesmo meco mi vergogno;
>   e del mio vaneggiar vergogna è 'l frutto,
> e 'l pentersi, e 'l conoscer chiaramente
> che quanto piace al mondo è breve sogno.[8]

Various elements of the sonnet, such as the dichotomy it establishes between youthful error and mature experience, and its emphasis on suffering, elements that are central to the Petrarchan experience and portrayal of love in Golden Age Spain, need not concern us here. What I wish to draw attention to is the emphasis which it places on an affective bond which will link the poet-lover and the reader within, and by means of, the text itself. The poet informs the reader that the collection will not simply convey information about the course of a love affair, but that the poet-lover will himself speak through the medium of his verse to a receptive audience. According to Petrarch, such an act of communication should create a bond of empathy between the poet-lover and all those who have experienced love themselves: thus the poet hopes to arouse compassion and pity in his audience (lines 7–8).[9] Consequently our perception of the intensity of Petrarch's emotions is tied to his rhetorical dexterity as a poet: to convince us of his virtuosity as a lover he needs to move us through his success as a poet. Thus whilst Laura is presented as the catalyst of the lyric sequence, the poet-lover persona, the "I", is the centre of the poetic and amatory enterprise and the element upon which the success of the whole undertaking depends.[10]

---

[8] See Petrarch, *Rime*, p. 89.

[9] Compare *Rime*, p. 228, no. 95.

[10] Compare Mazzotta, *The Worlds of Petrarch*, p. 3; and Waller, *Petrarch's Poetics and Literary History*, p. 51. I am not trying to suggest that the first-person singular presented in and by Petrarch's *Canzoniere*, or indeed that presented by any Spanish Petrarchist, is a unified and non-problematic element, or that it necessarily has, or was perceived as having, any degree of authenticity, only that it normally presents itself as

In Spain poets had largely broken with an important aspect of the Petrarchan model from the very introduction of the Italian mode in the early sixteenth century in so far as they tended to prefer to write self-contained Petrarchan poems rather than larger lyric sequences. However the emphasis on emotion and voice (the "rhetoric of presence") was still central, the difference between Petrarch and the majority of his Spanish imitators being one of scale and emphasis, necessarily occasioned by their respective uses of the sequence and the single poem. Nevertheless various poets over the course of the Golden Age did write Petrarchan sequences, including Boscán and Herrera[11] in the sixteenth century, and Lope de Vega,[12] Soto de Rojas,[13] Bocángel[14] and Quevedo[15] in the seventeenth. Inevitably these are prefaced with a prologue-sonnet in which both the amatory and the literary endeavours are presented as intertwined; like Petrarch they therefore employ metatextuality to further both the text's and the lover's integrity and plausibility.[16] The two recurring features of such poems are an emphasis on the exemplary

such. Both Mazzotta and Waller offer a detailed consideration of the complexities and contradictions of Petrarch's employment of the first person.

[11] On Herrera's *Algunas obras* (Seville, 1582), see Antonio Prieto, *La poesía española del siglo XVI*, vol. II: *Aquel valor que respetó el olvido* (Madrid: Cátedra, 1987), pp. 570–85.

[12] For a consideration of Lope's *Rimas* as a Petrarchan sequence, see Antonio Carreño, "Amor 'regalado'/amor 'ofendido': las ficciones del yo lírico en las *Rimas* (1609) de Lope de Vega", in *Hispanic Studies in Honour of Geoffrey Ribbans*, ed. by Ann L. Mackenzie and Dorothy S. Severin (Liverpool: Liverpool University Press, 1992), pp. 73–82. Of course Lope also wrote a parodic anti-sequence, the *Rimas de Tomé de Burguillos*.

[13] On the Petrarchan affinities of Soto de Rojas' *Desengaño de amor en rimas*, see Antonio Prieto, "El *Desengaño de amor en rimas* de Soto de Rojas como cancionero petrarquista", in *Serta Philologica F. Lázaro Carreter*, 2 vols (Madrid: Cátedra, 1983), II, pp. 403–12; and Aurora Egido, "La enfermedad de amor en el *Desengaño* de Soto de Rojas", in *Al Ave el Vuelo*, pp. 32–52.

[14] In Bocángel's *La lira de las musas*, for example, despite the fact that a significant proportion of the poems in the collection were composed for the *Academia de Madrid* in the 1620s, it is possible to discern a small but unified mini-sequence dedicated to Filis. This is a good example of how the academic and Petrarchan styles coexisted in the seventeenth century. See *Lira*, pp. 27, 73–80; and Trevor J. Dadson, "La psicología del amor en los sonetos a Filis de Bocángel", in *Actas del X Congreso de la Asociación Internacional de Hispanistas*, ed. by Antonio Vilanova, 4 vols (Barcelona: PPU, 1992), I, pp. 863–71.

[15] For a reasoned attempt to view Quevedo's *Canta sola a Lisi* as a Petrarchan cycle, see D. Gareth Walters' introduction to his edition of Quevedo, *Poems to Lisi* (Exeter: University of Exeter, 1988), pp. vii–xxxii.

[16] Ignacio Navarrete's comments on Juan Boscán, the first Spanish Petrarchist, are pertinent here: "There is a double didacticism at work in these early poems. On the amatory, thematic level, they are meant to admonish people not to make Boscán's mistake, not to fall in love as he has done [. . .] But on a metapoetic level, Boscán provides instruction both in Petrarchan love and in writing Petrarchan sonnets, so that in spite of the stated aim of warning people away, he actually seeks to be imitated." See Navarrete, *Orphans of Petrarch*, p. 78.

nature and purpose of the collection and on the affective relationship between poet-lover and reader. Both can be found in the introductory sonnets of two of the earliest Spanish Petrarchists, Boscán and Hernando de Acuña.[17] Such was their importance to the Petrarchan mode in Spain that they are present in the love poetry of seventeenth-century poets as diverse as Villamediana, Esquilache, Trillo y Figueroa and Bocángel.[18] Typical of these introductory compositions is the opening sonnet which introduces the first section of Soto de Rojas' *Desengaño de amor en rimas* (Madrid, 1623):

> Tristes quejas de amor dilato al viento;
> serán, por tristes, de mi error castigo;
> por quejas, nuevo honor de mi enemigo;
> y por de amor, de amantes escarmiento.
> Será también la voz de mi instrumento
> en el proceso de mi edad testigo;
> y yo el áspero actor, que a mí me sigo,
> y el culpado que canta en el tormento.
> Vosotros, o jueces, o fiscales,
> bien así que mis malos infinitos
> no me juzguéis, si no sentís mis males.
> Que si buscáis castigo a mis delitos,
> castigos tienen a su culpa iguales:
> fuegos de amor abrasan mis escritos.[19]

Here the poet-lover's experience is presented as exemplary (line 4).[20] More importantly his presence is evoked, following Petrarch's example, by the privileging of speech with its connotations of presence and hence plenitude. This is done both explicitly (lines 1, 5–6) and implicitly (the address to his readers in the sestet links poet and reader into a fictional dialogue). In calling himself an actor the poet-lover underscores the importance of his role and his performance to the collection which will unfold the vicissitudes of his emotional drama. As with Petrarch our focus is squarely directed to this "yo", the

---

[17] See Boscán, *Obras*, ed. by Carlos Clavería (Barcelona: PPU, 1991), pp. 235–38; and Acuña, *Varias poesías*, ed. by Luis F. Díaz Larios (Madrid: Cátedra, 1982), p. 89.

[18] See Villamediana, *Poesía impresa completa*, ed. by José Francisco Ruiz Casanova (Madrid: Cátedra, 1990), p. 77; Francisco de Borja, Prince of Esquilache, *Obras en verso* (Brussels: Baltasar Moreto, 1663), p. 1; Trillo, *Obras*, p. 5; Bocángel, *Lira*, p. 131. Bocángel composed another introductory sonnet for his first volume of poetry, *Rimas y prosas* (Madrid, 1627): see *Lira*, p. 347. On this sonnet, see Mauricio Molho, "El soplo y la letra: Gabriel Bocángel ante sus escritos", *Edad de Oro*, 6 (1987), 189–99. Compare, too, the famous opening sonnet of Lope's *Rimas: Obras poéticas*, p. 23.

[19] See Soto de Rojas, *Obras*, p. 34.

[20] Compare Soto de Rojas' comments in the volume's prologue, *Obras*, p. 24. On this point see Andrés Soria Olmedo, " 'Fuegos de amor abrasan mis escritos': La conciencia literaria en el 'Desengaño de amor en rimas' ", in *Al Ave el Vuelo*, pp. 139–57.

linguistic, dramatic and emotional centre of the cycle of poems; the beloved, the "enemigo", is peripheral to the drama. What matters most in the enterprise upon which the poet-lover is embarked is our relationship as readers to him as protagonist, a relationship which is initially characterized as being either judgemental or empathetic and forgiving (lines 9–11), but which is ultimately made redundant by the poet himself: the lover's presence is sufficient unto itself; the performance, he implies, is basically a self-centred soliloquy since in his role as poet he is already the judge of his own drama (lines 12–14). Whilst the poem is mainstream in its Petrarchan concerns, Soto de Rojas' active role in Madrid academies leaves its trace here, and in so doing evokes contemporary academy practice: not only does he choose to present his persona in overtly theatrical terms (line 7), but he significantly refers to his readers as "fiscales" (line 9).

From this brief excursion into mainstream love poetry we can establish the parameters of normal Petrarchan practice. One of the central aims of the "rhetoric of presence" is to fuse the two facets of the persona, poet and lover, into a seamless whole. This is desirable since for Petrarchan poets a consistent portrayal of a strong poetic voice and an authoritative presence via the immediacy of the first-person is seen as the guarantor of the credibility of the emotions expressed and hence of the successful reception of the poetry. It is this endeavour to create an empathetic bond between poet-lover and reader which imbues Petrarchan love poetry with its characteristic pursuit of credibility and sincerity and which establishes it as a discourse inextricably linked to, and dependent upon, the successful presentation of the poetic persona.

By the seventeenth century various factors were contributing to the decline and disintegration of classic Petrarchism, not least the very longevity of the dominance of the discourse itself in the peninsula. The increased emphasis on ever more elaborate rhetorical figures, the shift from *res* to *verba* which upset the Renaissance "virtues" of clarity and decorum, jeopardized the Petrarchan mode by shifting attention from the emotional intensity of the lover's vicissitudes to the language used to convey them. As early as 1619 the poet Francisco de Rioja feels the need to defend Herrera's poetry, somewhat half-heartedly, against the accusation of an excess of figures and tropes. Rioja writes:

> Los versos que [Herrera] hizo en la lengua castellana son cultos, llenos de luces y colores poéticos, tienen nervios y fuerza, y esto no sin venustidad y hermosura; ni carecen de afectos, como dicen algunos, antes tienen muchos y generosos; sino que se esconden y pierden a la vista entre los ornatos poéticos, cosa que sucede a los que levantan el estilo de la humildad ordinaria. Los sentimientos del ánimo afectuosos, cuanto más delgados y sutiles, se deben tratar con palabras más sencillas y propias, sólo porque se

descubran a los ojos y hieran el ánimo con su viveza; en fin, ellos se han de ofrecer, no se han de buscar entre las palabras.[21]

The theory apparent here, a theory already by 1619 largely outstripped by contemporary practice, is that an excess of figurative language serves only to obliterate the necessary creation of an affective poet-lover persona. The language of Petrarchan poetry was thus coming to threaten the entire enterprise. A further important factor in the decline in or dissolution of the Petrarchan model was the greater metrical heterogeneity of seventeenth-century verse. The expansion of the Petrarchan idiom beyond the Italian verse-forms such as the sonnet and *canción* to include native Spanish forms such as the *romance* and *letrilla*, and the consequent use of the terser octosyllabic line, opened up amatory poetry by grafting the native tradition – the *cancionero* style and the *romance* narrative prolixity – onto the intensity of the Petrarchan idiom to a far greater degree than had occurred with the earlier generations of Petrarchan poets in Spain. Moreover the increasingly sophisticated deployment of intertextual references also served to undermine the supremacy of the original model. As Ignacio Navarrete has shown, a poet such as Góngora, by drawing on love poets as diverse as Petrarch, Garcilaso, Ovid, Tasso and Claudian, effectively ends the privileged hegemony of the Petrarchan discourse's originator; whilst Quevedo, by refusing to assimilate his intertextual borrowings and models and choosing instead to make them stand out, radically underlines the conventionality, the rhetoricity, of the emotions he expresses, even whilst simultaneously conveying a strong poetic voice.[22]

Despite all the transformations experienced by Petrarchism as it evolved over the seventeenth century, however, the hegemony of the empathetic immediacy of the first-person singular remained largely in place as one of its enduring legacies to Spanish amatory poetry. The academy's development of a style of love poetry not necessarily centred upon such a Petrarchan persona is consequently one of its most striking features. As I mentioned in the introduction, academy poetry ranges from the satirical and burlesque, genres which had long parodied the Petrarchan role, through bizarre scenarios and far-fetched situations, to traditional unadorned Petrarchan subject matter: within each of these this lynch-pin of the dominant amatory discourse was either abandoned, distorted or severely compromised. The academy thereby further contributed to the debasement and loss of cultural and poetic authority of the prevailing amatory style, for in its poetry the persona projected is characterized either by its absolute impersonality or by its ironic and

---

[21] See Herrera, *Poesía castellana original completa*, ed. by Cristóbal Cuevas (Madrid: Cátedra, 1985), p. 481.

[22] See *Orphans of Petrarch*, pp. 204, 219. For a general survey charting the decline of Petrarchism in the latter half of the century, see Arthur Terry, *Seventeenth-Century Spanish Poetry*, pp. 208–37.

performative distance, both styles being, as the preceding discussion should have made clear, the antithesis of the intense, personal nature of the Petrarchan model. In this way the academy deviated from the amatory paradigm in three closely connected areas: in the projection of sincerity and credibility; in the type of textual relation fostered between the poet and his audience; and in the separation of the twin facets of poet and lover so carefully united in Petrarchan verse. It is with these three areas that the remainder of this chapter is concerned.

The illusion of sincerity and credibility which poets writing in the Petrarchan mode actively seek to establish is not generally a priority of academy poets. The cultivation of the first-person singular is frequently abandoned in marked preference for the third. Thus, whilst the emotional range and amatory concepts of a poem may still broadly derive from Petrarchan poetry, what is fundamentally unPetrarchan is often simply its dispassionate detachment, as in the following poem "a un imposible conseguido" by Juan Pellicer de Tovar:

> Belisa, deidad suprema,
> yace rendida a un acaso,
> logrando Fabio en delicias
> cuanto le ocultó el recato.
>   ¡O, cómo de lo imposible
> triunfa solamente el hado!;
> pues para hacer un dichoso
> intervinieron los astros.
>   Aquel a quien la fortuna
> le va regiendo los pasos
> tropieza con los desprecios
> para dar en los halagos.
>   Los rigores de Belisa,
> que eran asombro de Fabio,
> le estaban haciendo hora
> para llegar a los brazos.
>   Ya dueño el alma le invoca,
> y él el nombre está dudando;
> porque lo extrañó el decoro,
> aunque lo pronuncia el labio.
>   Más y más favores goza,
> que en Belisa el duplicarlos
> es justificar la queja
> por si llega a ser ingrato.
>   Aun exteriores desvíos
> que son del honor reparos,
> los comienza hacia desdenes
> y acaban en agasajos.
>   Fabio quiere, Fabio adora,

> mas como se ve envidiando
> de los méritos ajenos
> labra propios sobresaltos.
>   Con la caricia presente
> teme que lo soberano
> suele adolecer las almas
> con achaques de lo vario.
>   Pero no recele, no,
> que superiores cuidados
> antes de hacer la fineza
> la consultan con el mármol.
>   Y más Belisa, que siendo
> dulce homicida de tantos,
> deja al que nace deseo
> en respectos sepultado.
>   No obstante Fabio repite
> en medio de sus aplausos,
> "o si viviésemos siempre
> queridos, y no olvidados".[23]

Indeed it often seems fair to say that the unquestioning critical disfavour shown towards academy poetry actually stems from its impersonal and occasional nature; critics implicitly follow the Petrarchan paradigm which privileges "presence" as a guarantee of sincerity in dismissing such poetry as "academic exercises" simply because its production is visibly occasioned by external circumstances rather than personal sincerity.[24]

The shift from the personal to the impersonal, from the proximity of the first person to the remoteness of the third, is a direct consequence of the nature and format of the academy itself which makes poets develop a style and adopt a role suited to the exigencies of the occasion for which they are writing. As Willard King has commented: "no era de esperar que una organización que exigía al poeta producir una nueva composición cada semana y leerla ante una reunión de colegas satíricos fuese un ambiente fecundo para la creación de poesía seria u hondamente personal".[25] As I have mentioned, even more detrimental to any attempt to cultivate a credible amatory persona is the need to produce love poetry to order according to the conditions of the

---

[23] See *Fonseca Feb 1663*, fols 27r–28r.

[24] The condemnatory comments of Parker and Jammes are representative of this preference for the personal over the impersonal. See A. A. Parker, *The Philosophy of Love in Spanish Literature, 1480–1680*, ed. by Terence O'Reilly (Edinburgh: Edinburgh University Press, 1985), p. 232 n. 23; and Robert Jammes, *Etudes sur l'oeuvre poétique de Don Luis de Góngora y Argote* (Bordeaux: Institut d'Etudes Ibériques et Ibéro-américaines de l'Université de Bordeaux, 1967), p. 316. Compare E. M. Wilson, "La estética de don García de Salcedo Coronel y la poesía española del s.XVII", *RFE*, 44 (1961), 1–27.

[25] See *Prosa*, p. 54.

set topic. Topics set not only dictate the subject and the metre, but, as Cubillo de Aragón acknowledges in his advice to an aspiring courtier cited at the start of this chapter, they often actually require an objective or neutral approach by stipulating that the poem be addressed "a un galán/una dama que . . .". Furthermore, the nature of the types of topic most often set is such to encourage actively the abandonment of emotions in favour of a full and witty exploration of the ramifications of the bizarre and elaborate scenarios, objects, and dilemmas. These popular types of topics dispel all notions of plausibility. Most are so clearly far-fetched that even when they are credible, in the sense of realistically possible, they are frankly improbable. This is so because the academy developed this type of subject matter far beyond its range in non-academy poetry where it tends to be deployed to introduce a note of relative realism and a type of domestic intimacy otherwise denied the unrequited lover. Given the exaggerated and dramatic twists invariably added to this type of subject, it is hardly surprising that poets abandoned the attempt to present the scenarios set as capable of provoking genuine and credible emotional responses in the lovers who must describe or narrate them. Consequently, one of the paradoxes of the academies propagating and further developing the emphasis on particularity and specificity, a stylistic and thematic trait of seventeenth-century Spanish poetry in general, is that such an emphasis far from fostering a greater sense of realism actually serves to detract from this: the more the lovers are grounded in mundane reality, as they invariably are in academy topics, the less credible and realistic they and their emotions appear. With such topics, therefore, emotion is consistently subordinate to the incident described; emotion itself becomes incidental.

Even when a poet does opt to employ the first person, the limitations imposed on the projection of a poetic persona by having to treat a particular incident are apparent. The more a poet concentrates on an external object the more our sense of the poet as a speaking voice diminishes. As Smith comments, "The domestic banality of much seventeenth-century lyric is the practical demonstration of the traditional theoretical proposition that particularizing detail both lowers the stylistic register and impoverishes poetic effect."[26] On an even more basic level, an audience of friends, unlike a solitary reader, cannot as easily go along with the fiction of the poet's personal involvement. Similarly the possibility of reflection which enables an emotive, empathetic response is considerably reduced when a poem is heard rather than read. Such limitations often give rise to a sense of indeterminacy and confusion as poets seem to struggle between the competing – and conflicting – demands of two distinct discourses, the Petrarchan and the academic. In Gaspar de Medina's poem on a lady bitten by a snake, the poet is effectively forced by both his subject matter and the prevailing academy style

---

[26] See Smith, *Quevedo on Parnassus*, p. 164. Compare *Writing in the Margin*, p. 63.

to relegate the lyric "yo" to a position of secondary importance, thereby lessening its potential rhetorical impact:

> Herida al mortal veneno
> de la ponzoña de un áspid,
> padece Lisi divina
> del rigor que sus amantes.
>   Despojos son de sus iras,
> finezas siempre constantes,
> y a fementidas lisonjas
> benigno ofrece hospedaje.
>   Sin duda de tus rigores
> éste, o Lisi, es el más grande,
> que no logre el rendimiento
> lo que la ofensa halla fácil.
>   Del veneno las congojas
> humana te persuaden,
> y del voto despreciabas
> divinas inmunidades.
>   Nunca pedí tal venganza
> de Amor, Lisi, a los altares,
> porque el demérito ignora
> del ofendido las frases.
>   Tú solo el cruel has sido,
> ¡o veneno inexorable!,
> pues de Lisi hermosa has hecho
> imposibles las crueldades.
>   De humanos méritos sólo
> hizo su rigor examen,
> pero tú osado atropellas
> el indulto a las deidades.
>   Y tanto más, cuanto ofreces
> en efectos desiguales,
> que Lisi cruel dé vida,
> y que tú halagüeño mates.
>   ¡O Lisi!, no de la ofensa
> se enmienden tus impiedades,
> ni del peligro te informen
> los escarmientos vulgares.
>   No deba a ajeno accidente
> lo que mi ruego no alcance,
> ni sea dichoso a costa
> de tus infelicidades.
>   Padezca yo, si adoleces,
> igualmente de tus males,
> y en tanto dolor no ofrezcas
> alivio que le disfraze.

>   Firme siempre en tus rigores
>   te admire el dolor constante,
>   y de la vida no excedan
>   las amenazas de frágil.[27]

The first two stanzas, following normal academy practice, reiterate the scenario given in the topic, and do so here in the third person: Medina appears to be adopting the impersonal mask of the academy poet. A switch to a more personal and involved tone, signalled by the possessive adjective ("tus") and the direct address ("o Lisi") of lines 9–10, unsettles our initial expectations by alerting us to the presence of a poetic presence, the speaking subject. However, given the impersonal opening there remains an essential ambiguity as to the exact relationship between this speaker and Lisi: is he merely the detached academy poet addressing his subject, or the poet-lover more intimately involved with Lisi's sufferings and, in turn, one of the objects of her "rigor"? This ambiguity is in turn resolved in the fifth stanza when the verb "pedí" brings us the expected intimate relationship between "yo" and "tú", poet-lover speaker and woman addressee. Stanza six introduces yet another switch with the vocative now invoking the snake's poison, not Lisi, who returns as the addressee again in stanza nine. Such oscillations in voice and addressee detract from sustained emotional intensity, offering instead the spectacle of a poet at once totally distanced from, and hence unaffected by, his subject (lines 1–8), and intimately involved with and moved by it (lines 41–48). The effect is thereby to foreground the poem's artificiality (its origin in a set topic) and its academy context, and so to undermine the relationship it also seeks to convey via the unfortunate incident of the snake bite. This use of the personal and impersonal encapsulates the essential dilemma facing an academy poet over whether to use a Petrarchan persona or a more distanced and disinterested one.

Having discussed some of the causes and consequences of the academy's marked preference for impersonal love poetry, and having established the sharp contrast thereby between standard academy practice and the Petrarchan norm, I propose now to turn to those poems in which the poet does adopt the lyric persona and treat the most hallowed of Petrarchan *topoi* with the accustomed unalloyed lyrical sincerity. Even on such conventional pieces the academy exerts a kind of pressure which is detrimental to what I have called the Petrarchan enterprise. Put simply, no poem can be divorced from, and hence remain unaffected by, the occasion; the influence of the academy as a whole on its constituent elements is unavoidable. Poets most often resort to the use of the first person in those topics which offer clichéd Petrarchan subject matter. If the topic suggests a routine Petrarchan subject then poets adopt the appropriate lyrical persona and compose perfectly poised verse enlivened

---

[27] See *Pascua de Reyes*, fols 32v–33v (corrected foliation).

where possible and appropriate with flashes of wit and ingenuity. Such familiar verse can be exemplified in a poem by Felipe Muñiz Delgado. Required to gloss the following lines,

> ¿Qué será, zagala, qué,
> aqueste dolor que tengo?
> Si es amor, válgame el tuyo;
> si es querer, ¡o qué bien quiero!,

he chooses to do so by adapting them to another of the topics (on which he had already composed two poems) which stipulated, "A una dama que, cogiendo una rosa, se hirió en una espina y viendo la sangre quedó desmayada" (itself something of a thematic cliché by the 1670s):

> Las selvas hacen alarde,
> Laura, a lograr tus favores.
> Mira que el andar con flores
> puede dolerte, aunque tarde.
> Si por cogerlas se arde
> tu deseo, temeré
> el que diviertas tu fe
> con ellas. Si has de quedar,
> sin que puedes pronunciar,
> ¿qué será, zagala, qué?
>   No a cogerlas te destines
> con mano tan prodigiosa,
> que por cortar una rosa
> puedes manchar los jazmines.
> Por no verte en tales fines,
> con cariño te prevengo,
> y si te cortas yo vengo
> a padecer mucho más,
> pues no cesará jamás
> aqueste dolor que tengo.
>   Mi prevención es en vano,
> pues la flor quieres tomar,
> y llegándola a cortar
> parece rosa tu mano.
> El buril se queda ufano,
> viendo el carmín, triunfo suyo.
> Tú desmayas y yo arguyo
> si es de la herida dolor,
> si es otra causa mayor,
> si es amor. Válgame el tuyo.
>   Ya su deidad misteriosa,
> cuanto esplendor adquirió,
> sólo a un filo se rindió

> como culpa al nacer rosa.
> No por frágil, por hermosa
> padeces; y de aquí infiero
> las prendas que en ti venero,
> y me arrastran con rigor,
> si es impulso, es superior;
> si es querer, ¡o qué bien quiero![28]

I cite the poem in full as an example of the endurance of the Petrarchan mode within the academies: academy poets are well able to compose such verse, and indeed frequently do so outside the academies themselves. The "yo" and "tú", lover and beloved, exclude the listener/reader so that the act of enunciation is entirely amatory in its formulation; the poem, in other words, makes no mention of its status as a poem. The poet thereby make us encounter the piece as a love message first and as a rhetorical and aesthetic construct second. As we shall see, this communicative priority, which is standard in Golden Age verse, is not the normal textual relation posited by academy poetry. Despite their exploitation and cultivation of standard Petrarchan procedures – the first person, concentration on emotional reaction rather than incident, primacy of love over rhetoric – the fact that such poems were performed alongside other academy poems written to meet different priorities undermines their very credibility and hence weakens the rhetorical efficacy of their protagonists. Felipe Muñiz Delgado's poem, for example, takes its place next to poems on a woman breaking wind and on the disillusion of a lover discovering that his lady has given birth to a black child, as well as more rhetorically exhibitionistic poems written entirely in questions and exclamations.[29] These more customary academy topics serve only to reduce more straightforward Petrarchan pieces to their own level or status by underlining that they too are occasional compositions. The sincerity and amatory credibility sought and conveyed in such poems is thus undermined by the fact that the majority of other poems on the same occasion flaunt their lack of sincerity and plausibility. (This is somewhat similar to what happens to those poems which celebrate or commemorate a royal event in an elevated and lofty tone when they are placed in an academy alongside poems which adopt a lower register or a more humorous or parodic vein, namely the sentiments and attitudes of the former become rhetorically transparent.) We are of course faced here once again with the question of the ability of academy members to discriminate between genres and registers and to disassociate the style and subject of one composition from that of another. Such discrimination is arguably easier when the poems are read rather than recited one after another, for encountering a poem orally

---

[28] See *Ciudad Real*, fols 33r–34r. For the other two compositions mentioned, see fols 31v–33r. As I commented in Chapter 3, this was a popular Petrarchan subject.

[29] See *Ciudad Real*, fols 13v–14v, 12v–13r, 11v–12v.

within an academy differs markedly from the printed reception of verse in which it is standard practice (both in our own century and the seventeenth) to group poems by genre as well as by verse-form. This is not to suggest that the more subdued and traditional type of composition would have been received in the same manner as other academy poems, or even that it would have been evaluated by the same criteria. Rather the coexistence of poems of divergent style – and, moreover, with those poems seeking to embody a "rhetoric of presence" via the first person being very much in the minority – implicitly reveals the Petrarchan sensibility to be simply one poetic mode amongst many, and hence equally the product of artifice. The much sought after illusion of authentic utterance is thus shattered as Petrarchism looses its poetic hegemony. Against this must be set the fact that the poems are normally recited and that, consequently, to the degree that a poet is prepared to "perform" his composition as if it were a piece of dramatic verse for the stage such a performance may project the desired illusion of authenticity. The importance of performance as a defining factor in the reception of academy verse is something to which I shall return.

As well as the detrimental effect of the academy itself on the reception of individual poems, the integrity and impact of the first-person singular, when this is used in serious academy compositions (as opposed to burlesque or satirical poems where it is more frequently employed), is also equally affected by the tendency of poets to accentuate their poetic rather than their amatory virtuosity. A desire to perform rhetorically and to produce a masterful poem which will make an immediate impression is more important than the fact that the composition in question is a love poem; technical and thematic mastery always seem to matter more than the expression of feeling. Consequently academy poems tend to draw attention to their own textuality, their own nature as products of wit and ingenuity, more insistently and consistently than any other category of Golden Age poetry. This exhibitionistic tendency is encouraged by the way many topics are framed. For example, a topic given in one of Fonseca de Almeida's academies requires the poet, Sebastián Ventura de Vergara Salcedo, to produce a verbal portrait of his lady, but this task is substantially complicated by the additional requirement to do so only employing "esdrújulos" as rhyme words. The subject matter itself has a long and respectable Petrarchan pedigree, and indeed Vergara's actual manner of treating it is entirely conventional for he simply slavishly follows the long-established manner for the composition of verbal icons by starting with the hair, moving over the facial features, down past the breasts to the legs and feet.[30] The additional difficulty of the rhymes, however, requires the poet to

---

[30] On the vogue for verbal portraiture in Golden Age Spain, see Gareth Alban Davies, " 'Pintura': Background and Sketch of a Spanish Seventeenth-Century Court Genre", *JWCI*, 38 (1975), 288–313. As Davies' discussion of the topos makes clear (p. 304), Vergara's treatment is totally conventional. See also *Fonseca April 1662*, fols 20v–21v.

accentuate his poetic skill, with the result that the topic becomes primarily a lexical challenge. Consequently the poem submitted is an excellent example of poetic virtuosity displacing amatory sincerity, although the poet manages as skilful a fusion of the two as could have been hoped for given the stipulations of the topic itself:

>   Una copia tuya Fílida
> quiero sacar hoy mi cálamo,
> y ha de ser en todo única,
> con licencia de los clásicos.
>   Tu cabello en ondas nítidas,
> el cuello ilustra magnánimo,
> sin que obscurezca el negro ébano
> la cándidez de su páramo.
>   La frente es de nieve sólida,
> siendo su espacioso ámbito
> blanco donde el amor teórico
> dirige sus flechas práctico.
>   Los ojos dos astros fúlgidos
> son, mas de rayos tan máximos,
> que no hieren los del Délfico
> jámas con ardor tan cálido.
>   La nariz en perlas líquidas
> vierte olores aromáticos,
> sirviendo al certamen bélico
> de tus dos luceros, árbitro.
>   El breve rasgo de búcaro,
> y tan breve que es un átomo,
> tu boca labios de púrpura
> ostenta con dientes cándidos.
>   Las mejillas con dos fértiles
> primaveras, olor plácido
> respiran, porque en benévolo
> favonio, se vuelve el ábrego.
>   El talle es gentil y tímido,
> se manifiesta mirándolo;
> pues que en un puño el más mínimo
> le meterá con poco ánimo.
>   De jazmín diez hojas cándidas,
> sino son puros carámbanos,
> tus manos con rayos frígidos
> conservan en pozos cálidos.
>   Tus pies inquiero solícito,
> pero los miro tan párvulos,
> que temo al sondar el piélago
> por falta de pie ser náufrago.
>   Mas dos columnas de pórfido,

> mucho más que el cristal diáfano,
> todo el *non plus ultra* de Hércules
> sostienen, con brío Atlántico.
> Este en todo celebérrimo
> retrato, del orbe escándalo
> ha de ser, sin que los críticos
> pongan el menor obstáculo.[31]

A proclivity for exhibitionism readily deflects poetry towards a more overtly dramatic and performative style. On occasions the peculiar demands made on the poet by the topic produce love poetry which resembles nothing more than a dramatic soliloquy. When required to compose a poem using only questions and exclamations to express the feelings of a lover on seeing his lady depart, José Díaz Jurado's piece, whilst recalling sixteenth-century Petrarchan dialogue sonnets such as those by Gutierre de Cetina, bears a striking resemblance particularly in its final stanza to Calderón's stylized form of dialogue in which a speech is carefully constructed and interspersed with rhetorical asides and declamatory phrases. Whilst such rhetoric conveys emotion and the poet's turbulent mental state, its excess surpasses credibility. However, this matters less than the fact that the poet shows that he has successfully risen to the challenge set. In doing so the poem once again reveals the affinity between the academy and theatre, and it is not difficult to imagine the poem being melodramatically declaimed by the poet:

> ¡Di! ¿Te ausentas? ¿Qué te mueve?
> ¿Es tu alivio mi pesar?
> ¿Por qué me quieres dejar?
> ¿Quieres ver mi muerte breve?
> ¿Te he sido falso o aleve?
> ¿Mis cariños no te obligan?
> ¿Gustas de que su mal digan?
> ¿En qué los premias constante?
> ¿No se lo ofreciste amante?
> ¿Es bien que engañados vivan?
>   ¿Dónde el mal ha de llegar?
> ¿Quién me obliga a padecer?
> ¿Son efectos del querer?
> ¿Es acaso no gozar?
> ¡O, dura ley del penar!
> ¿Es soledad o es temor?
> ¿Es desdicha o es rigor?
> ¡O qué tormenta sin mar!
> ¿Ha de ser todo llorar,

---

[31] See *Fonseca Feb 1663*, fols 22v–23v. Compare the *romance en esdrújulos* in *Badajoz*, fol. 9.

> o dar la vida al dolor?
> Corazón, ¡dolor terrible!,
> ¿qué te aflige? ¡Rigor fuerte!
> ¿De qué nace? ¡Dura muerte!
> ¿Padecer? ¡Golpe sensible!
> ¿Olvidar? ¡Caso imposible!
> ¿Aborrecer? ¡Quién pudiera!
> ¿Divertirse? ¡Ojalá fuera!
> ¿Buscar ocasión? ¡Bajeza!
> ¿No hay consolarse? ¡Fineza!
> ¿Y dejar de ser? ¡Quimera![32]

What both these examples have in common is the complication of conventional amatory subject matter by lexical or rhetorical difficulties. The fact that clichéd subjects are chosen in such topics indicates that their purpose was essentially to test the poet as a craftsman. The attention of both poet and audience is directed at the final piece's rhetorical construction rather than its amatory content.

The distinct poetic priorities as well as the thematic heterogeneity of literary academies necessitate a revision of our expectations of the first-person persona. Attuned by over a century of traditional love poetry to regard the persona as the indispensable element of Petrarchism, the audience/reader of academy poetry finds that the persona, when employed, is decentred. A further distinctive and, to a large extent, innovatory way in which the academy defamiliarizes and destabilizes the amatory persona is to incorporate an element of metatextual commentary within a poem on its amatory content. The academy poet's presence can be introduced directly or indirectly. If directly, the poem will treat the amatory content dispassionately in the third-person singular whilst incorporating the first-person into the poem as a projection of the "real" poet; whilst if indirectly, the poem will be written entirely in the first person but with a process of disassociation taking place within the persona between the poet and the lover (and hence between the academy context and the amatory text). Either way, the result is the creation of a polyphonic discourse in which a variety of voices, perspectives and attitudes exist, a situation which is inimical to the creation of a seamless Petrarchan presence. The academy poet's presence thus becomes a substitute for that of the lover and the result of this is that our attention is constantly drawn from text to context, from the inner fictional world of the poem and its lovers to the "real" site of its actual performance, to the degree that the poem enacts its own process of composition, interpretation and enunciation. It is as if the

---

[32] See *Ciudad Real*, fols 11v–12r. A sonnet, which I quoted in Chapter 2, was also composed for the same topic (fols 12r–v). For Cetina's dialogue sonnets, see *Sonetos y madrigales completos*, ed. by Begoña López Bueno (Madrid: Cátedra, 1981), pp. 158–59, 213, 307–08.

cultivation of subjectivity, the "yo" created and sustained by the Petrarchan lyric momentum, is replaced by that of performance. Consequently what comes to characterize academy poetry is a rhetoric of performance rather than one of presence.

The frequency with which poems refer to their own academic context and construction is a further manifestation of the theatrical or performative nature of the seventeenth-century literary academy to which I have constantly drawn attention. Both the occasion itself, with its attentive audience of fellow poets (many of them actual playwrights) and "silent" women, and the topics set, with their tendency towards overstatement and melodramatic amatory scenarios, encourage such theatricality. Indeed the innate sense of theatre probably lies at the heart of the academy's popularity and success in Spain. This supposition gains credibility by the fact that over the course of the century academies become increasingly stylized and theatrical in their format and presentation. There are numerous examples of occasions when this ever-present theatricality takes on a more prominent and substantial form, often coming to dominate the occasion. One such occasion was the *certamen poético* held in the Buen Retiro in 1638 for which the Italian stage-designer Cosme Lotti constructed a stage, as well as various stage-machines, on which laurel-crowned individuals representing the poets of antiquity read out the poems submitted.[33] Less elaborate than this, but no less theatrical, was the setting for an academy held in the viceregal palace in Valencia in 1669 to celebrate Charles II's birthday at which Charles and Mariana, the Queen Mother, were present in the form of their portraits, a common device on such occasions and one later used by Calderón to represent on stage Charles and his wife Marie-Louise of Orleans during the *loa* to his play *Hado y divisa de Leonido y Marfisa* in 1680.[34] More significant than this theatrical touch, however, was the format taken by another literary academy session organized in 1691 by the *Academia de Valencia*, a body which, despite its name, was more akin to the eighteenth-century usage of the term, consisting as it did of five distinct bodies devoted to politics, mathematics, poetry, music and dance.[35] The "poética festiva" which this group organized was an extraordinary

---

[33] See Bergman, "El «Juicio final»", pp. 554–57. The setting of this *certamen* was described in greater detail in Chapter 1. Teresa Ferrer Valls mentions briefly the theatricality of sixteenth-century academies and *justas*. See her *La práctica escénica cortesana: de la época del Emperador a la de Felipe III* (London: Tamesis, 1991), pp. 109–11.

[34] See the full title of the *Real academia* cited in the Works Consulted. On Calderón, see Sebastian Neumeister, "Los retratos de los Reyes en la última comedia de Calderón (*Hado y divisa de Leonida y Marfisa*, Loa)", in *Hacia Calderón. Cuarto coloquio anglo-germano*, ed. by Hans Flasche, Karl-Hermann Körner and Hans Mattauch (Berlin: Walter de Gruyter, 1979), pp. 83–91. Also see Shergold, *History*, p. 344; and, more generally, María Alicia Amadei-Pulice, *Calderón y el barroco. Exaltación y engaño de los sentidos* (Amsterdam, Philadelphia: John Benjamins Publishing Company, 1990), pp. 153–67.

[35] See *Poética festiva*, Introduction, pp. 11–14 (p. 12).

session of the *Academia a Nuestra Señora de los Desamparados y San Javier*, a group which met regularly from 1690–92.[36] The introduction to the published account of these festivities, held in the presence of the Viceroy, Carlos Homo Dei Moura, Marquis of Castel-Rodrigo, to celebrate the king's birthday, informs us that there were not enough poets to take part in a full-blown academy. Consequently the "fiesta" was held in the form of a dramatic dialogue in which five academy poets – Antonio Pallás, José Ortí, Francisco Figuerola, Pedro Valterra and Vicente Blanquer – played the roles of interlocutors but "sin perder la formalidad de cedulillas, asuntos poéticos y vejamen".[37] This dramatic academy dialogue, acting as a running metacommentary on the event, served to bind together the disparate elements (drama, music, dancing) which, given the lack of poets, constituted the occasion. A taste of the rather pedestrian interchange which resulted can be gleaned from its opening lines:

Pallás:	Introducción. Silencio.
Figuerola:	Cedulillas.
Blanquer:	Asumpto que me han dado, seguidillas a nuestro heroico rey, seriojocosas.
Pallás:	Cierto que ustedes tienen lindas cosas: ¿No le dije, señor, que no empezase, hasta que yo primero le avisase?
Figuerola:	Dice bien, cedulillas lo primero es en toda academia.
Pallás:	Ni eso quiero. Yo empiezo: Introducción.
Figuerola:	Eso es porfía, ¿no son primero en toda academia las cedulillas siempre?
Pallás:	Pues pregunto si ésta mi idea es.
Blanquer:	Este es mi asumpto.
Pallás:	Aún no lee usted.
Blanquer:	Yo leer quiero que el asumpto se lee lo primero.
Pallás:	Digo, pues, que no lea,

---

[36] See *Señoras*, pp. 23–24. Mas i Usó comments that holding an extraordinary session of an academy was common practice in Valencia during the final decades of the century (p. 24). This was however common practice across Spain throughout the academy's history in the seventeenth century: as we have already seen, the *Academia burlesca* was probably a special session of the *Academia de Madrid*, whilst Fonseca de Almeida's academy devoted a session to celebrating Charles II's birth.

[37] See *Poética festiva*, p. 14. José Ortí had been the secretary at a further Valencian academy to celebrate Charles' birthday held in 1683. See *Segundo día de ejercicios . . . Academia de Valencia . . . día de los años de S.M. Carlos II . . .*, MS, bound in a volume containing other printed academy accounts (NLS: G.24c.1).

	porque en mi introducción tengo la idea de leer primero.
Figuerola:	En casos semejantes, nunca la introducción la he visto antes de leer cedulillas.
Pallás:	No es abuso porque el ir al revés todo es del uso.[38]

These examples are significant not so much because they differ from the run-of-the-mill academy, which they most certainly do, but because they formalize the theatricality inherent in the format itself. Such theatricality normally manifests itself in the performative nature of the poetry: in its conception, its composition and its delivery academy poetry is, above all else, a performance. In this way, academy poetry is in the Golden Age sense "poesía dramática" rather than "poesía lírica", and has closer affinities with dramatic verse as employed in the *comedia* than with normal lyric poetry. As such it is perhaps somewhat inevitable that the persona which comes to predominate in academy love poetry belongs to the actual poet himself, whose ironic and sardonic "presence" projects itself as skilfully performing and adroitly manipulating his seemingly unpromising material. Such a persona comes to inject a ludic element into academy verse, making it more consistently playful than love poetry written outside the academy. The 1691 Valencian academy, therefore, in turning the entire event into an academic colloquy was merely formalizing and expanding a preexisting tendency of academy poets to comment on their compositions, their fellow poets, and the academy itself, and to thereby endow the individual poems and indeed the entire occasion with an ironic self-referentiality.

The amatory persona adopted by generations of Golden Age love poets is obviously itself a rhetorical performance. As we have already seen, in the introductory sonnet it is normal practice, following Petrarch's example, to allude explicitly to the circumstances and purposes behind the composition and completion of the entire collection. The sequence thus shows an awareness of itself as a poetic product but importantly this metatextual level is incorporated to enforce, rather than to work against, the amatory or thematic level: such comments are made in the voice of the poet-lover who is thus

---

[38] See *Poética festiva*, p. 15. Ortí and Figuerola also composed full-blown theatrical pieces: they wrote, for example, the *baile* (Ortí), and the *loa*, *entremés* and *mojiganga* (Figuerola) for a 1690 production of Calderón's *La fiera, el rayo, y la piedra* in the royal palace in Valencia. On the theatricality of academies, compare Egido, *Fronteras de la poesía*, pp. 158–59. Plays were sometimes performed as part of an academy: Pantaleón de Ribera, for example, composed a *loa* for a play performed in the *Academia de Madrid* during carnival (*Obras*, II, pp. 147–48); whilst in his *Comentarios* Duque de Estrada mentions the performance of a "comedia de repente" as an integral part of an academy held in Naples under the auspices of the Count of Lemos. See *Comentarios*, pp. 195–97.

speaking "in character", and are an integral part of the dramatic project, namely the credible self-projection of the poet-lover who forms the centre of the collection. Where the academy persona differs in this process of self-projection is in its overt signalling of its own self-awareness of performing – in the sense of composing and reciting – a poem to order. Thus the notion of delivery and performance, or voice and gesture (*pronuntiatio* and *actio* in Classical rhetoric), is frequently made an explicit and integral part of the finished poem itself, contributing to the effective reception of the piece in the academy session for which it was written.[39] Self-referentiality becomes a means of foregrounding the patent implausibility of the amatory enterprise and of disassociating the academy poet proper from the poetic persona, be that in the first- or the third-person singular. In other words it becomes a means of deliberately shattering rather than enforcing the normally carefully-wrought amatory illusion, and the poet deploys it as part of a nonchalant and dismissive gesture to make his audience aware of the gulf between the Petrarchan and the academy poetic. It hardly needs saying that such self-referentiality differs markedly from the metatextuality of much seventeenth-century drama in that it is never used as a means of seriously questioning the ontological or epistemological status of the work of art vis-à-vis reality.

Though self-referentiality is regularly present in serious compositions, it is more pronounced, because more developed and sustained, in humorous pieces. The opening two stanzas of Pedro de Torres Granero's poem on a lady breaking wind by accident (cited in full in Chapter 3) are typical of the way in which poets alert the listener of the poem to the context of, and thereby the reason for, its production, signalling thus its status as a work of artifice and occasion, rather than as an expression of amatory sincerity and truth:

>   Si [de] tu aire he de pintar
>   las propiedades en suma,
>   no sé cómo comenzar,
>   que no he podido cortar
>   hoy de buen aire la pluma.
>   Pero, Inés, pues ya tu aliento
>   me huele, y no me lo excusa,
>   habréme de ir con gran tiento,
>   que si he de hablar lo que siento,
>   no me sopla bien la musa.[40]

The poet, assuming a first-person role, combines his dual identities as amorous lover and academy poet by fusing metatextual commentary with the

---

[39] For a succinct overview of these terms in Classical rhetoric, see Brian Vickers, *In Defence of Rhetoric* (Oxford: Clarendon Press, 1989), pp. 65–67.

[40] See *Ciudad Real*, fol. 13v.

topic in question via the dual significance of "aire" in the opening stanza.[41] Moreover, like many such poems, he parodies the normative opening invocation to the muses, here undercutting this with his two oblique references to the fact that he is writing not from private inspiration but simply from academic compulsion ("he de pintar"/"he de hablar"). Likewise in the opening to some *redondillas* on a lover's cold included in Polo de Medina's *Academias del jardín* the poet refers to the composition arising from an academic exercise rather than spontaneously, again wittily fusing the topic to his treatment by his lady:

> Por Dios, Fili, que me río
> cuando a vuestro resfriado
> hacer versos me han mandado,
> tratándome así de frío.
>   Mas no serán novedades;
> porque si es mi vena fría
> ¿quién como la musa mía
> dirá de vuestras frialdades?[42]

In poems such as these which use the first-person singular, particularly when dealing with subject matter which is clearly comical rather than simply farfetched, the opening stanzas are thus used as a means of disassociating the dual strands (lover and poet) normally presented as indivisible in the seamless Petrarchan "yo", and of doing this whilst actually seemingly projecting just such a persona. The Petrarchan persona is thus humorously undermined from within, and the amatory role is subsumed within the more prominently projected academy persona.

Rather than internally split the poet-lover persona itself into its constituent elements as a means of refering to the academy context of the love poem, many poets choose instead to create two distinct personae, with the amatory content normally being treated in the third person and the first person being reserved for the sarcastic comments of the academy poet. In the opening of José Miravet del Castillo's poem written on the topic "A una dama que escribió a un galán quejándose de él porque decía que era vieja, y él la respondió con sólo enviarla la fe del bautismo en que constaba tener 68 años de chanza", for example, the woman is addressed directly, but by the poet, not her lover:

> Dos papeles son el blanco
> del mío, mi musa quiera
> que con chanzas y con burlas

---

[41] Compare the opening lines of a poem by Alonso de Zárate y la Hoz which do likewise, *Fonseca Feb 1663*, fol. 30v.

[42] See *Obras escogidas*, p. 126.

> acierte al blanco de veras.
>   Como a escribano esta vez
> me ha tratado el academia,
> pues que quiere entre papeles
> darme este rato tarea.
>   En efecto a tu papel
> voy Filis, que mi obedencia
> aun en asuntos livianos
> que tiene higados muestra.[43]

The sheer triviality of the assigned task is referred to, as is, more importantly, the fact that it is this very triviality which constitutes the poetic challenge of the topic. By mentioning the poem's thematic triviality the poet is adapting the opening rhetorical strategy of *captatio benevolentiae* (employed so often in the opening sonnets of amatory sequences), but whereas this had initially been used as a means of gaining the readers' goodwill and sympathy, here it is used as the primary means of drawing the attention of an audience to the difficulty of his task and hence, implicitly, to his own skills as a poet in rising to the challenge and overcoming it.[44] When both the opening and closing stanzas are used in this way, the effect of the polyvocal presentation of the topic is to set the dispassionate amatory content within a more "personalized" performative framework. Fermín de Sarasa y Arce's *coplas* on the misfortune of a man who loves a foolish, one-eyed woman fully utilize such academic inclusivity by having the poet use the first person in the framing stanzas to refer to his own act of composition and in the body of the poem as part of the reported speech of the lover; the lover's "yo" thereby exists only as part of the poet's own act of enunciation:

> Un galán, enamorado
> de una mujer tuerta y boba,
> (si no me engaño) es la trova
> que me han dado.
>   Y que el amante cuitado
> se querelle de su fe,
> en doce coplas de pie
> quebrado.
>   "No acierto, aunque más me pida",
> dice, "a servirla cortés,
> porque una boba no es

---

[43] See *Sol de academias*, p. 45. Compare the opening to another poem read at the same academy by Pedro Juan Espí, pp. 43–44.

[44] Compare the opening stanza of a poem on a lover who falls over and breaks his nose whilst dancing which also uses the subject matter as a means of referring to the difficulties of the topic: "Si el caer has de cantar, / Musa, de aquel que danzó / anteayer, / cuando quiero tropezar / ayúdame, porque no / me dejes caer." See *Repetida carrera*, p. 19.

>   entendida.
>   Y el errar yo se concierta
>   entre dudas y sospechas,
>   que nunca manda a derechas
>   una tuerta".
>   . . .
>   Diez coplas de hierro o bronce
>   están hechas, juro a tal
>   y ésta (si no cuento mal)
>   es la once.
>   Razón es que me remoce,
>   viendo que están acabadas,
>   pues tras once badajadas
>   dan las doce.[45]

The poems so far cited to illustrate the self-referential aspect of academy verse have been humorous. However, even love poetry accorded serious treatment exhibits a penchant for self-commentary, although in contrast to humorous poems these tend only to allow the intrusion of the context and the academy poet's comments at the end of the composition. Luis Nieto, for example, devotes twenty-seven stanzas to a consideration of a favourite academy subject, a man who loves his mistress when they are apart but abhors her when they meet, only to finish not with a conclusive summary, a witty resolution, or a final epigrammatic twist to end the poem on a definitive and decisive note, but with a brief and oblique reference to the difficulty – and implicitly the futility – of the poetic task which he has just accomplished:

>   Rara tarea del alma,
>   la que entre afectos distintos
>   se abrasa en lo imaginado,
>   cuando se hiela en lo activo.
>   ¿De qué materia se ceba
>   incendio tan exquisito,
>   que si es actual, vives muerto,
>   y si es mental, mueres vivo?
>   En dos accidentes, Fabio,
>   de una causa procedidos,
>   para el amor, ¿qué no ves?
>   y para el odio, ¿qué has visto?
>   Viendo aborreces, formando

---

[45] See *Real Aduana*, pp. 56–58. See also pp. 23–24 of this same volume for another humorous poem which opens with references to its composition. Compare Lope de Vega's famous sonnet from *La niña de plata* which likewise never manages to rise above the pedestrian. See *Poesía selecta*, ed. by Antonio Carreño (Madrid: Cátedra, 1984), pp. 587–88. See also *Badajoz*, fols 14r–15r.

> nuevo dolor del alivio;
> pues ¿cómo, teniendo lumbre,
> están tus ojos tan fríos?
>   ¿No viendo adoras? ¿Qué es esto?
> ¿para el afecto remiso
> tiene acaso la memoria
> términos más persuasivos?
>   Pero no ves, y eso basta,
> que en el interior estilo,
> bien sé que de lo privado
> se ceba lo apetecido.
>   Pero has visto, y eso sobra,
> pues con más seguro arbitrio
> por lograr lo deseado
> desdeñas lo poseído.
>   En tu amante frenesí
> parece que han concurrido
> para un influjo dos astros,
> uno adverso, otro propicio.
> . . .
>   No más discurso, porque
> en este opuesto ejercicio,
> si se busca la razón,
> se tropieza en el delirio.[46]

The final stanza marks a break in both the stylistic and compositional format of the preceding stanzas, bringing the composition back to its academy context and signalling the impossibility of ever actually reaching a definitive conclusion. Indeed the conclusion recognizes that any ending to paradoxes such as the one Nieto has been required to consider is inevitably arbitrary given that the way poems are created from such topics both within academies and beyond is, as here, to produce a series of ingenious but provisional statements. Given the flexibility of this compositional procedure and the resulting provisional character of its constituent arguments, the poem is potentially interminable.

In a manner similar to Nieto, Juan de Vera y Villarroel concludes a piece in which he has adopted the role of a lover bemoaning the fact that his lady only allows herself to be seen on days when there is an eclipse by wittily combining the quibbling style he has used throughout the piece with a reference to the conclusion of the poem itself, suggesting thus that he has exhausted the topic on which he has discoursed:

> Debate mi amor la causa,
> ya que el efecto consigue;

---

[46] See *Real Aduana*, pp. 29–33.

>   que quien duda los principios,
>   a despechos tropieza con los fines.[47]

As we shall see in Chapter 5, this method becomes simply a convenient way of rounding off the poem by signalling closure, creating thereby a formal break between the amatory and the academic discourses and, as with the above examples, bringing the listener back to the academy context and hence to the poet himself.[48]

In both serious and humorous poems, then, it is standard practice to refer to the act of composition and performance and thereby to draw attention away from the intimate and closed world of the Petrarchan lover to the public forum of the academy itself. Whether the poet decides to disassociate himself entirely from the amatory topic by relegating the lovers to the third person and keeping the first purely for his own comments, or to have the first-person persona speak both as a lover to his lady and as a poet to his academy audience, the opening and closing stanzas have several features in common: they serve as an apology for the banality of the subject matter, they invoke the muses' help with the difficult task in hand, and they indicate that the subject of the poem has been forced upon the poet. In short, they denigrate their very subject matter and depict the poet as critically self-aware of the limitations of academy thematics. In so doing their effect is both to reverse Petrarchan priorities and to recast the nature of the relationship between poet and audience, so that empathy is evoked for the poet's plight in having to compose something on singularly unpromising material rather than for the lover's sufferings. The intrusion of the occasion for which the poem has been composed, albeit in only one or two stanzas of what may be a long poem, consequently emphasizes the fictionality of the amatory scenario treated and the reality of the academy setting.

These features of academy verse are present in the last poem I would like to consider which includes references to the poem's composition and context in both its opening and concluding lines. In combining ludic self-referentiality with a basically serious treatment of its trivial subject matter it is a good example of the different priorities and practices employed by academy poets to overcome the shortcomings of the typical topics set, as well as typifying how poets adapted the normal strategies of contemporary love poetry to meet

---

[47] See *Real Aduana*, pp. 69–70.

[48] Often this is done obliquely: Felipe Muñiz Delgado makes the occasion and the topic intrude in the final quatrain by making a rather lame reference to the set metre he has been using: "Perdóneme Laura si / su beldad dejo agraviada, / que salí de pie quebrado / esta mañana." See *Ciudad Real*, fol. 32v. As here, it was common practice to make an explicit reference to the fact that a poem was written in a verse-form "de pie quebrado" within the poem; see, for example, the verse attributed to Góngora in *Nuevos poemas atribuidos a Góngora*, ed. by Antonio Carreira (Barcelona: Quaderns Crema, 1994), p. 395.

the challenge posed by the inherent difficulties of simply adopting a standard poetic persona in an academy context. In looking in detail at a poem which is thus representative of all that is distinctive about academy poetry I propose to consider the cumulative effects of the metatextual features so far catalogued. The subject of the poem by Gaspar Penarroia was given as "A un palillo, que arrojándole una dama a su galán, le dio en los ojos", and the topic stipulated that the subject be dealt with in a *romance* of fifteen stanzas:

> A un asunto sin sustancia
> me han mandado componer,
> y, aunque tan seco, me han dado
> muy buen hueso que roer.
> Icaro feliz, pretende
> un cierto amante beber
> las luces del sol, que adora,
> los nectares de un clavel.
> Mira celoso en la boca
> de su dueño humedecer
> con dulcísimos cristales
> de un palillo la enjutez.
> Y atrevido de invidioso
> se le pide, para que
> cayendo de tanto cielo,
> sea segundo Luzbel.
> Indecisa esta hermosura,
> entre piadosa o cruel,
> le arrojó, mas no nos dicen
> si era amor, o fue desdén.
> Diole en los ojos, y dudan
> porque pudo acontecer,
> y aunque es duda de palillos,
> me ha dado bien que entender.
> Si le arrojó fina amante,
> harto patente se ve,
> que entonces da más en ojos
> cuando alarga una mujer.
> Sino es que al revés desea
> darle con esto a saber,
> que aun de las damas, la ofensa
> sabor en los hombres es.
> Si le vibró desdeñosa,
> discurso ingenioso fue,
> que sólo le hierre en ellos,
> porque no la pueda ver.
> Diole en los ojos, que quiere
> mostrarle a mi parecer
> que para ser tan Cupido,

más ciego había de ser.
  Si ya no es que la dama
de las demás al revés,
porque no fuese ella vista
quiso que cegase él.
  Cayó de la boca, y busca
dar en los ojos, porque
quien no se halló en cosas grandes
no sale de la niñez.
  Y puede ser que lo ofenda,
porque le hizo perder
tanta perla, que hasta un palo
siente mucho el no tener.
  Y cuando todo lo dicho
no fue la causa, creeré
que sólo para cansar
mi cholla debió de ser.
  Y así, porque con su intento
no salga, sólo diré
me han dado con el palillo
más que mondar que morder.[49]

The poem has a distant antecedent in a sonnet by Lope de Vega, "En un arco de perlas una flecha", included in his *Rimas de Tomé de Burguillos* (Madrid, 1634). Although similarly addressed to "un palillo que tenía una dama en la boca", Lope's poem bears no relation to Penarroia's beyond the thematic, since it develops an elaborate conceit based around Love protecting the precious pearls which are the woman's teeth, her lips being a bow and the toothpick an arrow.[50] Although there is a clear thematic parallel with a non-academy poem, in its structure, language, attitude and personae, Penarroia's poem reveals itself to be a typical academy composition. Both the first and the last two stanzas posit the topic as a distinct challenge precisely because it is of such consummate triviality ("un asunto sin sustancia"). These three stanzas effectively frame the body of the poem, establishing a kind of *mise-en-abîme* structure in which the amatory poem proper is bracketed by its academic context. This distinction between composition and context is furthered by the disjunction the frame also creates between the two personae employed in the poem: the lover conveyed by the neutral third-person singular and the academy poet by the first person.[51] As a consequence of this, the amatory distance

---

[49] See *Sol de academias*, p. 34.

[50] See *Obras poéticas*, p. 1351. Salazar y Torres also composed some *endechas* on a willow toothpick in the woman's mouth: see *Cítara de Apolo*, pp. 134–37. For a *romance* which similarly employs the opening and conclusion but for humorous self-deflation, see *Señoras*, pp. 147–49.

[51] The poem thereby offers a contrast to the poem by Gaspar de Medina, "Herida al

established by the detachment of the third person is undercut by the poetic proximity fostered by the first person. The poem is at once impersonal and personal, but importantly the personal presence projected belongs to the poet commenting tongue-in-cheek on his poem's banality. When the poet's voice intrudes into the body of the poem it does so to destroy once again the credibility of the subject matter ("aunque es duda de palillos / me ha dado bien que entender"), and to draw our attention thereby away from the amatory topic and back to the interpretative wit of the poet in dealing with it ("diole en los ojos, que quiere / mostrarle a mi parecer . . ."). Consequently, as well as destroying the amatory proximity, the intrusion of the poet both here and in the framing stanzas makes his performance as academy poet more credible, since his own disparagement of the poem's content is patently justified: the topic is inconsequential. Cleverly the very object which is the basis for the poem's amatory content, the toothpick, also becomes part of the closing stanza's metatextual derision of that content ("me han dado con el palillo / más que mondar que morder"), with the wordplay around the "palillo" ("morder", "mondar", with "mondadientes" being the operative noun left unstated) underscoring the subject's insubstantiality and hence expressing the essential futility of the entire poem. In a way typical of academy verse, as we have seen, Penarroia both undermines the poem as a love poem whilst using this very act of subversion as a means of foregrounding his own skill, since the clear implication is that the poem's very completion is testimony to poetic skill and invention in meeting the academy challenge ("Y cuando todo lo dicho / no fue la causa, creeré / que sólo para cansar / mi cholla debió de ser"). Playing with the subject matter in this way makes the role of the poet as creator transparent, and transforms poetry into a type of performance-art, an act. The academy frame narrative, then, by dramatizing and repeatedly emphasizing the challenge to the poet contributes to the performative aspect of the entire poem whose subject proper is itself already an overtly dramatic amatory scenario.

The poetic treatment of the "palillo" is itself typical of the academic procedure with such topics. The object is envied by the lover because of its close and intimate contact with the woman's mouth (lines 9–12), this envy giving rise to the lover's conceit that the toothpick once ejected would be a second Lucifer falling from his beloved's heavenly presence (lines 13–16). Once the pick has been spat out the poet intrudes into the narrative to proclaim that he is capable of explaining why this action was performed (lines 21–24). This he does in the normal format of a series of paired distiches, the first suggesting a hypothesis from which the second will extrapolate a witty explanation or interpretation (lines 25–52). The final explanation brings the subject back to the academy context which gave rise to it when the poet

---

mortal veneno", cited earlier, which opens with the purely descriptive third person and switches to the first in the body of the poem.

suggests that the actual reason for this action was simply to test his powers of poetic invention (lines 53–56). The tone of the entire poem is thus playful as well as performative, the only possible strategy to adopt when confronted with such unpromising material. The result is an amusing and enjoyable composition which, as the poet makes clear within the poem, does not aim to be great love poetry but rather a successful academy piece. To achieve this Penarroia has done what the majority of academy poets choose to do when confronted with challenging academy topics: he has abandoned the Petrarchan persona and employed instead an ironic authorial stance to inject an element of performative self-referentiality into the poem which, among other things, gives the piece a degree of coherency and structure to compensate for the loss of the normal unifying factor, the lyrical "yo". It is this element which radically deviates from the Petrarchan discourse, unbalancing its finely nuanced emotional psychology and replacing its illusion of sincerity with knowing references to artificiality, to the poem as a poetic, rather than an amatory, construct. In contrast to Petrarch and his followers, poetic dexterity is seen as something totally distinct from amatory experience. With such an approach the poet signals his awareness of, and draws his audience's attention to, the relative status of amatory discourse: this is mere language whose signifiers have no inherent or vital link with emotion. He thereby reconfigures the relationship between text and audience, drawing the latter into the same dismissive attitude he adopts. It is precisely this attitude of dismissal and disdain which makes such flippant academy poems distinct from humorous love poetry which had long ridiculed Petrarchan language. Academy poetry is more truly detrimental to the dominant amatory discourses because its approach is not part of a wider rhetorical strategy to dismantle such discourses only to reaffirm their definitional validity. In other words, unlike such poems as Lope's "No ser, Lucinda, tus bellas / niñas formalmente estrellas" or Shakespeare's "My mistress' eyes are nothing like the sun", poems which deny both the utility and validity of Petrarchan language as an adequate descriptive *lexis* only thereby to reaffirm its definitional hegemony and value, Penarroia's poem simply exposes the provisional status of such language as clichéd rhetoric produced to order and devoid of any personal sentiment or sincerity of expression.[52] The poem is thus indicative of the exhaustion and bankruptcy of the Petrarchan discourse in the second half of the seventeenth century, and by openly accepting this emotional and conceptual bankruptcy the poet exploits the terms of the discourse whilst simultaneously dismissing it. The academy has taken poetry a long way from the "rhetoric of presence" which had defined theory and practice for so long: here we see poets refusing to play the game and in so doing revealing it to be a game.

The paradox of academy poetry is that it recast the terms and language of

---

[52] See Lope de Vega, *Poesía selecta*, pp. 538–39; and Shakespeare, *The Sonnets and A Lover's Complaint*, ed. by John Kerrigan (Harmondsworth: Penguin, 1986), p. 141.

the most intimate and ostensibly private of contemporary discourses, the Petrarchan, making it public and impersonal. It exploits, parodies and subverts the intimacy which Petrarchism normally engenders rather than deploying it to unfold the fiction of an autonomous, authentic self. Of course, Petrarchism is itself paradoxical in so far as it cultivates intimacy in public: to state the obvious, love poems addressed by the poet-lover to the lady are actually read by an eavesdropping public. However academy poets create a polyvocal discourse in which amatory and academy personae, sincerity and irony, the personal and the impersonal, all jostle for attention. Aspects of parody and burlesque thus become integral components both of individual poems and, more damagingly, of the general atmosphere or tone in which all poems, regardless of their own individual genres, are received. Consequently the academy's thematic heterogeneity obscures the rigid demarcations which it is the purpose of genre distinctions to establish and which serve to encourage us to employ different aesthetic expectations and evaluative criteria. The result is an atmosphere of reception premised on discontinuity and disassociation rather than on the sustained empathetic engagement which poetic theory and amatory practice had long taken as the corner stone of the Petrarchan enterprise. The metatextuality which predominates in academies is a clear sign that love poetry no longer posits a listener/reader interested in a poem's love message but rather one who is primarily concerned with the poem as a rhetorical construct or exercise, that is to say, with the critical evaluation of its successful completion of the topic in hand. Ironic deprecation and derogation of the subject matter help highlight poetic expertise in a seemingly nonchalant way. In its exploitation of detachment, amatory aloofness, implausibility and insincerity both serious and humorous academy verse comes to constitute a distinct poetic mode in Golden Age love poetry, a form of anti-Petrarchism, which partly depends for its impact on an awareness of the extent to which a poet has diverged from the Petrarchan norm. By refusing to take Petrarchan poetry's long-established procedures as canonical, academies helped contribute to the decline of Petrarchan poetry. Furthermore, because academy poets are no longer interested in invigorating the images and concepts integral to Petrarchism as a discourse – because, fundamentally, they are not seeking to establish themselves as inheritors and continuers of that discourse – these loose their linguistic and psychological force and hence their poetic and lyrical impact.[53] The metatextual element poets constantly build into their

---

[53] With regard to the questions of the academy as a polyphonic discourse and poets' lack of desire to join the "line of tradition", compare Roberto González Echevarría's perceptive comment on the Baroque: "The Baroque does not suffer from an anxiety of influence so much as from an anxiety of confluence and affluence, an excess in which the new is merely one more oddity." See "Poetics and Modernity in Juan de Espinosa Medrano, Known as *Lunarejo*", in *Celestina's Brood: Continuities of the Baroque in Spanish and Latin American Literature* (Durham and London: Duke University Press, 1993), pp. 149–69 (p. 164).

verse, both serious and humorous, also serves to highlight the patent absurdity and triviality not only of academy poetry but also of the trend towards dramatic particularity which is such a dominant aspect of all seventeenth-century love poetry. In this way, such metapoetic elements offer a sharp critique of Baroque poetry in general, and as such often echo modern-day critical evaluations of the period's pursuit of subject matter which is innately inconsequential and ephemeral.

If it is impossible to regard academy poetry as Petrarchan, it is also often difficult to regard it as love poetry at all, other than in a very narrow sense. In part this is because of our expectations; we still require the air of sincerity, of an emotional confession, in "genuine" love poetry. Primarily, though, the academies problematize our expectations of love poetry – either consciously or unconsciously, explicitly or implicitly, and more often the former than the latter – because whatever the tone, subject or sincerity of an individual poem it is always inevitably subordinate to the occasion, and to the requirements made by this. Love poetry is no longer about lyric reflection, or the self and its relations with another, or moral and metaphysical dramas; it is about amusement and entertainment, for love becomes a means to an end other than itself. As poets repeat in poem after poem, an academy love poem cannot be divorced from its context, for an academy love poem is always *academy* poetry before it is *love* poetry.

5

UNITY AND DIVERSITY: ACADEMY POETRY AND THE DISINTEGRATION OF FORM

So far we have seen that the format taken by the academy together with its prevailing atmosphere was instrumental in dictating the subject matter and its treatment and in shaping a particular kind of rhetorical relationship between poet, listener and poem, namely one governed by the projection of distinctive and polyphonic personae which in their very diversity of tone differed markedly from the amatory norm. In this chapter I shall consider the style of academy poetry; more particularly, the presentation, elaboration, and organization of material within individual poems. My purpose is to see how, and indeed if, poets dealt with the conflicting demands prompted by the desire to offer the listener a sustained display of conceits whilst also trying to forge from these a coherent and aesthetically satisfying poem.

The poetic problem faced by academy writers was one long familiar from contemporary aesthetic and poetic theory, namely the creation of a unified whole from individual parts. As we shall see, a poetic centred on a prolonged display of epigrammatic wit over an entire poem necessarily tends towards the privileging of individual parts over the whole. Whilst compositional unity or harmonious integration remained an aesthetic goal, however, it was one largely unattained (and unattainable) within the academy. Of course, this balancing of variety and unity, those two antagonistic poles of Golden Age theory, had long challenged poets, but the challenge was more acute for the academy poet since the prevailing academy style further exacerbated the problem for, in largely jettisoning any degree of amatory narrative held together by the strong poetic presence of a poet-lover persona, it jettisoned the very element which could prevent a poem fragmenting and splintering into its constituent elements, be those stanzas or conceits. The disintegration of a poem into its individual parts also exacerbated another problem, the conclusion. This constituted a problem precisely because the preferred way of ending a poem during this period with a terse, pointed conclusion was insufficient in a composition constructed entirely around a series of self-contained epigrammatic-style conceits. However, I shall suggest that these failures are often more acutely and problematically perceived when such poetry is read on the page, and that, in contrast, when heard the performative context can in some cases provide the very synthesis and satisfactory closure which a composition is otherwise apparently lacking. This is not to brush such problems aside, for I shall argue that they constitute academy poetry's greatest weakness, but rather to place them in proper perspective, the perspective of the occasion for which these poems were written and in which they were recited.

Given the academic propensity for wit in all its varied forms, a propensity which as I have said created formal problems which many poets were unable to overcome, the question of the academy's relationship with the poetic of wit needs addressing. This relationship, profoundly shaped by the oral reception of academy poetry, suggests that it is still necessary to draw a distinction between *conceptismo* and *culteranismo*, with the latter being marked by a degree of lexical and, primarily, syntactic complexity and intricacy which found little place in the academies. The academy in fact channels wit towards its apparently more superficial forms – word-play, puns, and the like – and thus away from the direction taken by Góngora, presumably simply because this direction is inappropriate in a context which demands a rapid and immediate impact and which consequently cannot afford the luxury of time necessary for sustained reflection upon, and unravelling of, intricate syntax and complex, recherché and densely allusive conceits. Gracián's failure to respond to the complexities of Góngora's *Soledades* and *Polifemo*, together with his marked preference for poems whose frequently trite conceits barely match our modern-day and essentially gongorine conception of wit as almost exclusively a matter of the far-fetched linkage of strikingly dissimilar objects or concepts into complex, difficult, and revealing image clusters, suggests that his conception of wit is more closely mirrored by pedestrian or mundane academic practice than by the more artistically accomplished works of Góngora or Quevedo. Academy poetry rather than being seen as debasing the poetic of wit, or as failing to rise adequately to its aesthetic demands, would perhaps be better viewed as actually more accurately reflecting contemporary educated taste and thus as more closely embodying how the seventeenth-century itself conceived and practised that poetic.

The publication of Gracián's *Arte de ingenio* in 1642, and of the vastly expanded definitive version of the work, the *Agudeza y arte de ingenio*, in 1648, marks the point in Spain when the concept of wit became the central tenet of, not a mere adjunct to, a theory of literary discourse. This work is best viewed as the end product of the critical debate in Spain over wonder, novelty and difficulty, and over the competing claims of *res* and *verba*, which had preoccupied poetic theory from at least the time of Herrera's *Anotaciones* in 1580. The importance of Gracián's work both in gaining a valuable insight into a Baroque poetic mentality largely alien to our own post-Romantic conception of poetry and, on a more practical level, in helping to elucidate the rhetorical and conceptual intricacies of seventeenth-century verse has long been recognized. Critics, however, have almost exclusively read his work to gain an understanding of the individual poetic conceit, its definition, mechanisms, and effects, and have then applied their findings to examples drawn mainly from the sonnets of Góngora and Quevedo, poets valued precisely because they are far from typical of seventeenth-century poetic practice.[1] What is entirely ignored is the close affinity between many of Gracián's categories of individual conceits and the style and format of the major and influential strand of contemporary verse which is the subject of this study. Furthermore, just like academy poems the examples choosen by Gracián tend to be neither lyrical nor sentimental, but reveal instead his penchant for verbal acuity. The bulk of his treatise establishes types of conceit seemingly tailor made to describe academy poetry, and such categories can be readily exemplified by the argumentative procedures and thematic content of academy poems. After the opening chapters, the *Agudeza* on the whole blithely ignores the problem of defining the conceit as a distinct form of trope and sets about categorizing types of wit, a significant number of which are based around varieties of witty arguments, the standard topics of the academies. Chapters 20–26, 35–41, and 44–45, for example, discuss types of wit which reach an unusual, unexpected or seemingly impossible conclusion, after first parading a series of problems, paradoxes and difficulties as potential obstacles to finding a satisfactory solution. This is what I shall refer to as the "epigrammatic" conception of wit, for the essence of this argumentative process is to draw a witty, though fallacious, concluding statement from the elements carefully delineated in the body of the poem.[2] Tesauro's conception of wit is similar to Gracián's, though the emphasis he places on argument is more explicit. For Tesauro the scale of wit moves from the "metafora simplice", through "proposition metaforica" to "argomento metaforico", and his description of the latter as an "entimema urbano" indicates how wit appropriates the forms of dialectic for its own ends.[3] Aside from this epigrammatic formulation of wit, many of Gracián's descriptive comments on argumentative wit echo prevailing academy practice. For example, in his discussion of conceits based on "una invención fabulosa de algún suceso o algún dicho ajeno", to which category most academy scenario topics clearly correspond, Gracián notes that

---

[1] The major exception here is Parker's application of Gracián's theory to the *Polifemo*, although even Parker tends to consider more the individual conceits than the structural unity forged from them. See A. A. Parker, *Luis de Góngora: Polyphemus and Galatea. A Study in the Interpretation of a Baroque Poem*, verse trans. by Gilbert F. Cunningham (Edinburgh: Edinburgh University Press, 1977).

[2] It is worth stressing that whilst Gracián never defines wit as epigrammatic, both his categories and the majority of the examples cited throughout the treatise reveal the formative influence of the epigram. As I shall discuss below, the epigram radically transformed poetic practice and theory in seventeenth-century Spain.

[3] See Emmanuele Tesauro, *Il cannocchiale aristotelico* (Bad Homburg: Gehlen, 1968; facsimile of 1670 Turin edn), pp. 279, 492. The "entimema urbano" is defined as "una Cavillatione Ingegnosa, in Materia civile: scherzevolmente persuasiva: senza intera forma di Sillogismo: fondata sopra una Metafora" (p. 495). For a detailed comparison of Gracián and Tesauro, see Smith, *Quevedo on Parnassus*, pp. 37–44.

two of their features are exaggeration and rhetorical questions, which he says greatly facilitate wit both of this and other kinds (*Agudeza*, II, pp. 70, 77). Both of these stylistic traits are common in academy poetry where they are used not only to heighten expectation, as Gracián comments, but to string out the composition, to include the audience in the performance, and to prepare the ground for its conceits. Similarly, regarding "problemas conceptuosos y cuestiones ingeniosas", which clearly correspond to the academy's debate poems, Gracián states that wit increases when the writer offers various possible answers and solutions before giving the definitive one (II, p. 99), and that, as with all these types of argument, the more unexpected or contradictory the solution given the better (II, p. 103; compare II, p. 93 and I, p. 236). Such a process of constant interpretation and recapitulation is the hall-mark of an academy poem. In the *Agudeza* considerable attention is also devoted to verbal wit, which encompasses puns, wordplay, *double entendres*, paronomasia and the like. Verbal wit is one of the most popular forms of wit in the academy, and Gracián indirectly accounts for its widespread and indiscriminate use when he says of word play that it is one of the commonest types of wit and as such is more often "fácil" than "sutil" (II, p. 45). Although such parallels can be extended many times over it is not my purpose here to read academy verse through the filter of Gracián's treatise, but rather to draw attention to the fact that both share a common poetic. I would suggest though that the fact that so much of the *Agudeza* seems better able to describe the structural and logical format of hackneyed academy verse than works such as the *Soledades* or the *Polifemo* should give us pause for thought. I would also suggest that Gracián's theory, coming in the mid-century when the academies had been flourishing for some forty years, owes as much to the distinctive topics and procedures of academy verse shaping and promulgating across the Peninsula a certain type of *conceptista* wit as to the poetic innovations of the century's major poets. Consequently academy poetry, whilst appearing to us to be generally aesthetically unaccomplished, should more accurately be seen as both the product and the promulgator of wit.

Gracián, although barely addressing the formal problems with which a poet is faced in longer poems written in a conceit-laden style, does mention aesthetic criteria, based on Renaissance precepts, with which to evaluate works of wit. Before turning to academy poetry, therefore, I propose to consider the *Agudeza* in the light of the issues with which I shall be concerned in the rest of the chapter, namely the elaboration and organization of material within a poem of unrestricted length (verse-forms such as the *quintilla*, *romance* or *redondilla*). My purpose in doing so is to attempt to foreground the nature of the problems confronting theoretician and poet alike, and thereby to contextualize academic failure. In this way I wish to suggest that the weaknesses of academy poetry are largely weaknesses inherent in the poetic of wit.

In the third chapter of his treatise Gracián considers various possible classifications of wit, and establishes a major distinction pertinent to my discussion of academy poetry between "agudeza incompleja" and "agudeza compuesta". Of the former, "agudeza incompleja" (or "agudeza de artificio menor", as he also calls it), Gracián writes that "es un acto solo, pero con pluralidad de formalidades y de extremos, que terminan el artificio, que fundan la correlación" (I, p. 62); whilst "agudeza compuesta" (or "de artificio mayor") "consta de muchos actos y partes principales, si bien se unen en la moral y artificiosa trabazón de un discurso" (I, p. 63). As his further discussion in the *Agudeza* clarifies, the basic distinction is between a type of wit whose constituent conceits are not interconnected and whose only common link is their connection to the subject in hand ("agudeza incompleja"), and one whose parts connect both with one another and with the subject to form "un todo artificioso mental" ("agudeza compuesta").[4] Gracián devotes the first and longest section of the work to a consideration of the former (chapters 4–50). To this category belong the majority of academy poems in which the only thread tenuously connecting their stanzas is provided by the topic which acts as the unifying concept around which any number of conceits are created.[5] Such poems lack any sustained narrative or argument to bind together their conceits and stanzas and consequently fail to exhibit any sense of "[agudeza] ajustada a un discurso", as Gracián alternatively calls "agudeza compuesta" (II, p. 167). The more fragmented and looser form of composition which results is the primary subject of this chapter. Gracián states that "agudeza compuesta" is the noblest and most satisfying type of wit, precisely because it draws unity from diversity and thereby conforms to the Classical conception of beauty as the harmonious union of parts to form a whole.[6] Similarly when Gracián initially describes "agudeza compuesta" at the start of the treatise he does so via analogies which emphasize not only its greater aesthetic impact but also the fundamental part played by structure in that impact:

---

4 See *Agudeza*, II, p. 168. Here Gracián is discussing "agudeza compuesta" and reformulates his two fundamental types by asking a rhetorical question: "¿Cuál sea más perfecto empleo del ingenio, la agudeza libre o la ajustada a un discurso?" (II, p. 167). "Agudeza libre" (or "suelta" as it is also called) and "incompleja" are thus synonymous. See also T. E. May, "An Interpretation of Gracián's *Agudeza y arte de ingenio*", in *Wit of the Golden Age: Articles on Spanish Literature* (Kassel: Reichenberger, 1986), pp. 3–28 (p. 5).

5 They thus conform to Gracián's description of this style: "La suelta es aquélla en la cual, aunque se levantan tres y cuatro y muchos asuntos de un sujeto, ya en encomio, ya en ponderación, pero no se unen unos con otros, sino que libremente se levantan y sin correlación se discurren. Sea ejemplo la ingeniosa panegiri del segundo Plinio a Trajano, que es un agregado de asuntos y de agudezas, sin unirse entre sí, sino en el material sujeto de la alabanza" (II, p. 167).

6 He writes: "Siempre un todo, así en la composición física, como en la artificial, es lo más noble, el último objeto y el fin adecuado de las artes; y si bien su perfección resulta de la de las partes, pero añade él la mayor de la primorosa unión" (II, p. 170).

> cada piedra de las preciosas, tomada de por sí, pudiera oponerse a estrella, pero muchas juntas en un joyel, parece que pueden emular el firmamento; composición artificiosa del ingenio, en que se erige máquina sublime, no de columnas ni arquitrabes, sino de asuntos y de conceptos. (I, p. 63)

Indeed, whilst in this type of wit unity arises from the narrative or logical thread provided by the subject matter, the key difficulty to be overcome by a writer is one of integrating a work's conceits into a satisfying whole (II, pp. 185–86). (This is not to argue, of course, that "agudeza incompleja" is without structure, only that in "agudeza compuesta" such structure is both aesthetically more necessary and more pronounced.) Despite such comments as these, this overt valorization is constantly undercut in the *Agudeza*, primarily because the supposedly "lesser" form of wit, "agudeza incompleja", is given far more extensive treatment than "agudeza compuesta", a consideration of which only occupies seven chapters (51–57) out of the total of sixty-three.[7] Moreover, even in the chapter which introduces the discussion of this composite form of wit Gracián spends several pages praising the virtues of its inferior counterpart, mentioning:

> la variedad plausible que reina en este modo de conceptuar libre, con su gran tropa de perfecciones, de hermosura, ornato, agrado, fecundidad, que pican el gusto y no le enfadan. (II, p. 170)

Gracián indirectly accounts for the imbalance in his treatise by his suggestion that Spaniards have always favoured a certain "libertad de ingenio", citing the examples of Seneca and Martial to support this view and stating that these writers perfectly exemplify the less structured form of "agudeza libre" (II, pp. 168–69).[8]

I raise the status of "agudeza compuesta" within the *Agudeza*, and the distinction between it and "incompleja", because Gracián's attitude is indicative of the sharp variance between Renaissance poetics, and indeed aesthetics, and Baroque practice. What interests me here is his preference for a type of wit which he consistently labels and describes as inferior. I would suggest that the reason "agudeza compuesta" receives such short shrift in his treatise is not simply a matter of personal preference or of national inclination; rather, as we shall see time and again in academy examples, the poetic of wit as conceived and practised in the seventeenth century severely compromises any attempt to achieve the much praised unity-in-diversity, and this is especially true in longer verse-forms. Gracián's dilemma is this: the type of laconic and pointed wit which he is advocating – essentially epigrammatic wit –

---

[7] Hence although Gracián refuses to pronounce in favour of either type (II, p. 172), the bias of his treatise leans heavily towards "agudeza incompleja".

[8] In contrast Gracián says that the Italians prize "agudeza compuesta" most (II, p. 172).

problematizes Classical aesthetic precepts (those he praises so highly in "agudeza compuesta") almost to the point of making them unattainable in extended verse-forms. Theory and practice favour "agudeza incompleja", in part because the impact of individual pointed conceits tends to be so forceful as to draw attention away from the poem as a whole, and in part because, as a result of this, narrative and logical direction become very much of secondary concern: the impact of a conceit matters more than the fiction (or "discurso", to use Gracián's term) in which it is embedded. Contemporary wit consistently fails to conform to the Classical and Renaissance precepts which Gracián, like most seventeenth-century writers, still propounds as definitive. It is worth emphasizing that "agudeza incompleja" is not a prerogative of shorter verse-forms, nor "agudeza compuesta" of longer ones. However, the fact that the latter is principally defined in terms of its architectural structure, and that the absence of this is normally more evident and thus is arguably more important in longer verse-forms, possibly explains Gracián's preference both for "agudeza incompleja" and for forms such as the sonnet to illustrate both categories of wit in his treatise, since the sonnet is structurally more suited to the presentation of epigrammatic wit, the forceful conceits not detracting from a sense of formal coherency or unity as I shall argue they do in longer poems. Gracián prefers shorter verse-forms, more suited to his conception of wit, and "agudeza incompleja", despite describing "compuesta" as the more accomplished of the two types.[9] Consequently he does not address the very real problem of the conflict between wit and compositional structure in more lengthy verse-forms. It is precisely this tension in longer verse-forms between an epigrammatic conception of wit, which tends to lay greater emphasis on the part rather than the whole, and the need to create some kind of structural coherency with which I shall be concerned throughout this chapter. Gracián's treatise thus sidesteps a major problem which the new conceited style aggravated. Whilst some poets do indeed attempt and achieve a unified poem in which one is struck by "lo selecto de sus partes y lo primoroso de su unión" (II, p. 172), the majority prefer instead to do the opposite, that is to create a poem in which each part stands alone, related only to the initial topic.

Of course, if the Renaissance values underpinning "agudeza compuesta" are rarely achieved, this would perhaps imply that poets are not trying to achieve them, and that contemporary practice is not struggling with theoretical precepts, but has rather moved on from them.[10] Be this as it may, I am

---

[9] Gracián does cite individual conceits from *romances* etc. but rarely the whole poem, in contrast to his practice of citing complete sonnets. Whilst this is in part attributable to ease of citation, it is also due to the fact that a limited and compressed verse-form like the sonnet with its essentially binary presentation of material (octet/sestet) lends itself structurally, unlike more prolix forms, to the form of wit based on argument/solution, statement/restatement, which was popular in the seventeenth century.

[10] Riley's discussion of variety and unity reminds us of the difficulties faced by

suggesting that what I see as the aesthetic shortcomings of academy verse are attributable to the type of wit favoured by the institution, since a style which requires its individual figures to be as novel, brilliant and striking as possible necessarily moves from a conception of the poem as a unified entity to one of the poem as an essentially fragmented form, a structure which simply provides a framework in which to set a dazzling array of conceits.

Verse-forms which are restricted in length, like the sonnet or *décima*, or indeed topics which set a *glosa* and thereby implicitly limit the possible stanzaic extent, have none of the organizational problems associated with longer compositions. Unlike the latter, their very forms require lyric concentration and intensity. Such verse-forms are thus ideally suited to a pointed style precisely because their brevity, as was long recognized by Golden Age theorists, matches the conceptual concision of the conceit. The laconic style of contemporary wit fits perfectly into such succinct and compact verse-forms. Academy sonnets in particular differ little either from their non-academy counterparts or from the many cited in the *Agudeza*, for, like them, they tend to be structured on a binary pattern which establishes a contrast not so much between octet and sestet, but between the final tercet and the preceding eleven lines. This stanzaic division brings Spanish seventeenth-century sonnet practice closer to contemporary English practice, although unlike the English sonnet the Spanish never broke with the Petrarchan model to divide the fourteen lines into three quatrains rounded off with a final distich. The binary partition establishes a clear division between problem and solution, exposition and conclusion, laying the compositional ground therefore for a particular kind of argumentative wit. Such a schematic presentation can be seen in Manuel de Flores' sonnet on the perennially popular topic of the woman who loves the poet in his absence and disdains him when he is present:

> Ausente lloro mi gustosa suerte,
> haciéndome dichoso mi tristeza;
> lloro infeliz, si miro tu belleza,
> pues pierdo tu favor por no perderte.
>   Si en no mirarte, Nise, hallo mi muerte,
> ¿de qué sirve a mi ausencia tu fineza?
> Y si en verte me aflige tu tibieza,
> ¿de qué le servirá a mi amor el verte?
>   A cada dicha sigue un sentimiento,
> pues la ausencia al favor turba la gloria,

Cervantes in his attempted adaptation of these precepts from epic theory to novelistic practice. See *Cervantes's Theory of the Novel*, pp. 116–31. Just as Cervantes wrestles with the concepts despite their apparently tenuous applicability to the novel, so I would argue that academy poets were still confronted with the ubiquitous notion of subordinating parts to the whole despite the fact that it is largely inimical to a style whose form and content are essentially epigrammatic.

> y el desdén en tu vista es mi tormento.
> No permitas que trágica mi historia
> diga que confundió mi entendimiento
> la duda en que le pone tu memoria.[11]

Flores here takes the favoured binary pattern as the template for the entire poem, something suggested no doubt by the antithetical terms of the topic itself. Thus not only is the octet divided into four distiches which state and restate the poet's dilemma as if the problem is being turned over in the mind, but the contrast which a seventeenth-century audience would have been expecting between the final tercet and the preceding lines is reinforced precisely because the last three lines abandon the explicit absence/presence dualism of the rest of the composition. In other words the binary structure of the sonnet is enforced via the very abandonment of binary terms and structures. In its use of both a binary format and an argument presented in terms of the statement and restatement of the set topic, the sonnet adopts two of the stylistic traits of academy verse. However the shorter verse-forms present few structural problems for the poet to resolve; as here, such verse-forms are more readily adapted to embody these pervasive traits. In contrast, with longer and less restricted forms a poet is required to address two problems which result from this epigrammatic presentation of wit, namely the structural coherence and effective closure of a poem. Of course such formal and aesthetic problems are not peculiar to the academy since they are a consequence of the *conceptista* style, but the academy's pursuit of wit at the expense of narrative, emotion and amatory persona brings such problems into sharp focus. My purpose in concentrating on the longer verse-forms is primarily to see how poets surmount the type of compositional and formal difficulties which the style of wit favoured both by the academies and the seventeenth century aggravated and in part caused. It is in such compositions that we see poets struggling to overcome the inherent problems of an institutional style and a frivolous poetic.

Regardless of the type of topic, an academy poem in verse-forms such as the *romance, quintilla, seguidilla,* or *letrilla,* whose number of possible lines is not prescribed, is usually structured into a series of self-contained stanzas, each of which presents developments within or interpretations of the topic, which is itself normally succinctly and clearly summarized in the opening lines. If the poem organizes its material around the presentation or delineation of a narrative, however tenuous, an automatic sequential structure of sorts can be used to coalesce its stanzas. In contrast, those poems which repeatedly interpret and expound the implications and ramifications of the subject matter within each successive stanza emphasize the wit and ingenuity of each individual unit at the expense of the unity or coherency which a linear narrative or

---

[11] See *Real Aduana*, p. 83.

an argumentative progression lends to the whole. Consequently it is in such compositions that the individual stanzas, rather than being subordinated to the effect and impact of the whole, come to predominate and hence to upset the relationship between part and whole which was central to Golden Age poetics and aesthetics. Moreover the highly-polished style of each stanza, and the fact that each one normally amounts to a self-contained conceit unconnected to the others and only related to the initial topic, means that it is in this type of composition which relegates narrative to emphasize interpretative wit that the problem of closure becomes acute.

There are of course academy poems which are still governed more overtly by narrative progression and structure. As a general rule, those poems which foreground a linear narrative are both humorous and exceptionally trivial. Poets tend to adopt this structural and organizational format when the set topic itself gives a clearly delineated scenario of obvious comic or erotic potential. In such poems therefore it is the events themselves as they unfold, and the protagonists' reactions and responses to them, that are the poem's primary focus of attention. This distinct emphasis is apparent in Francisco Morales' *quintillas* on a young lover unable to unsheathe his sword in front of his lady:

> En la ciudad de Valencia
> un milagro sucedió,
> y fue que en una pendencia
> de un hombre que no riñó
> se probó una resistencia.
>   Fue el caso que hablaba un día
> con su dama enamorado,
> y otro, que en celos ardía,
> le provocó, y provocado,
> el hombre no se movía.
>   Sacó la espada a brillar,
> empeñándole a reñir;
> y nuestro amante al quitar,
> aunque la supo ceñir,
> no la pudo desatar.
>   Forcejo dando a entender
> que obraba en él el coraje,
> mas luego se echó de ver
> que era su espada de encaje,
> pues no la pudo correr.
>   La dama, que lo miraba,
> no tuvo ningún recelo
> en el daño que esperaba,
> pues sin rogárselo al cielo,
> ya su galán se guardaba.
>   El viendo la sinrazón

>   de su espada singular,
>   aunque la dio un apretón,
>   no la pudo reventar,
>   por ser hoja de intención.
>   El contrario, en este aprieto,
>   no culpó su cobardía,
>   antes juzgó muy discreto,
>   que el no sacarla sería
>   por no romper un secreto.
>   Sudó la gota mortal
>   el triste galán corrido,
>   y en lance tan desigual
>   porfió de aborrecido
>   sobre hacerlo siempre mal.
>   Alzó los ojos por ver
>   si su dama enternecida
>   le podría socorrer,
>   y ella le dijo advertida
>   que el reñir no era coser.
>   A una pared le arrimó,
>   y de puntillas se puso
>   y por más que trabajó
>   no pudo alcanzar el uso
>   de aquello que ejercitó.
>   Su reputación valida
>   con descréditos andaba,
>   y estando ya departida,
>   vio el pobre que en lo que obraba
>   no daba buena salida.
>   Cansado de porfiar,
>   la arrojó por advertir,
>   que no sabría rodar
>   hoja que no osó salir,
>   en queriéndola sacar.[12]

The poem unfolds the misfortunes of the aspiring gallant as he attempts to draw his sword to defend himself from a rival's provocation. The "action" is very specifically located in Valencia, a degree of specificity which, despite the increased emphasis on the particular and the circumstantial in contemporary verse, is very unusual. The clear phallic potential of the topic, one presumably intended by the secretary setting the subjects, is here fully realized, with the desperate lover grasping, pulling and manipulating his sword in vain. The situation becomes an extended metaphor for impotence: the fighting scenario itself, together with specific nouns such as "encaje", were common means of

---

[12] See *Repetida carrera*, pp. 39–40.

referring to sexual intercourse, whilst the notion of the woman's inability to remedy the situation (stanzas 9–10) had long been a part of erotic poems dealing with impotence.[13] The hapless lover, publicly humiliated and metaphorically emasculated in front of both his rival (who has no problem in brandishing his weapon) and his lady, is left to reject his "espada de encaje" in despair. Thus whilst the poem is almost entirely devoid of wit – of what we would view as conceits – it pursues the comic potential of the topic's *double entendres* to great effect. In a similar, if less sexually suggestive, fashion Cristóbal de Alva's *liras* combine a narrative broadly tracing the steps in a lover's disillusionment when his lady gives birth to a black child with a degree of wit which interprets her infidelity through a series of conceits:

> Lisardo, tus finezas
> fueron de Celia mal correspondidas;
> que es propio de bellezas
> hacer desprecios, viéndose queridas;
> mas el que ciego adora
> de los mismos desprecios se enamora.
>   Pensaste que guardaba
> reliquias de tu amor en sus entrañas;
> mas de que te engañaba,
> engañado tú, a ti te desengañas,
> viendo recién nacido
> de azabache en tu Venus un Cupido.
>   El incendio en que ardía
> de un cautivo tizón se alimentaba;
> mas no se consumía,
> sólo humor entre llamas destilaba,
> formando por lo activo,
> si con alma la pez, el carbón vivo.
>   Prendada de una S
> gustó que su amor fuese señalado,
> y porque más lo fuese,
> hizo de sus facciones un traslado
> siendo el vientre Etiopia,
> pues que de él arrojó la negra copia.
>   Hacer esclava quiso
> toda su voluntad de esclavo objeto,
> con gusto tan preciso,
> que aun no le ha tenido por defecto,
> pues dicen sus antojos

---

[13] For such poems, see Alzieu (ed.), *Poesía erótica del siglo de oro*, pp. 240–43. The phrase "espada de encaje", presumably a fancy ornamental sword worn for show rather than use ("encaje" in the sense of inlay), also picks up on the sexual connotations of "encaje" ("insertion" – *Poesía erótica*, p. 89), thereby ironically describing the weapon in terms which serve to highlight the martial/sexual qualities it actually lacks.

>que ella quiso un galán con sus ojos.
>   Mientras estuvo encinta
>la acción a ti, Lisardo, atribuías,
>y en dibujos de tinta
>mostró que parte en ella no tenías,
>cuando, para tu daño,
>leíste en un borrón tu desengaño.[14]

Here the subject is made to yield a sense of implicit progression through a series of temporal events (the affair and the nine months of the pregnancy) towards the terminus of the topic itself, the disillusionment at the time of the baby's birth. The poet's decision to limit the number of *liras* to six – a decision not dictated by the terms of the topic itself as occasionally happens – curtails the prolixity typical of academy poetry. The poet, in other words, refuses to push his ingenuity and our tolerance to the limit and, at least to a reader often faced with an otiose accumulation of conceits, the resulting brevity is beneficial to the finished poem. This said, the fact that this very brevity in a verse-form with the potential for expansion is atypical in the academy could well have meant the poem was given a more ambivalent reception by a contemporary audience, its brevity taken as a sign of the poet's paucity of imagination and inventive skill rather than of his artistic judgement.

Poems which resort to a narrative progression as an organizational, unifying principle are in the minority in academies. This in itself seems somewhat paradoxical given the overtly dramatic slant and obvious narrative potential of many set topics. Again, it would appear that two factors militated against a more discursive treatment: first, the element of narrative foreknowledge excludes any possibility of surprise or indeed imaginative innovation on the level of "plot" since the audience already knows the direction the poem is to take as well as its narrative outcome; second, the conceited style consequently tends to curtail the delineation of action in so far as it is more concerned with ingenious interpretation than descriptive exposition. Consequently the standard way in which the academy poet develops his composition is by a process of constant redefinition of the subject in hand. That is to say, the poem continually returns to the initial topic and by restating the subject either in new terms, often employing periphrasis to do so, or from a different perspective lays the ground for each successive witticism. This standard structural procedure can be seen in the following *romance* by Sebastiana Cruzate which addresses the following topic, "Pide una dama confites, y danla azar confitado":[15]

---

[14] See *Ciudad Real*, fols 12v–13r.
[15] Cruzate plays throughout the poem with the double meaning of the contracted form of "azahar", "azar".

Con sus voces de clavel
graciosa pidiendo Filis
confites, la dan azar
confitado a sus jazmines.

El dulce pulido embozo,
florido agraciado chiste,
solfa en almíbar te dieran,
si pidieras alfeñique.

Cuanto recata el embozo,
exterior afecto dice,
porque la voz del buen aire
el aire sin voz la explique.

Juguete de la fortuna,
que dulcemente predice,
transformados a influencias
en azares los anises.

Venus golosa, si quieres
candecidamente a Chipre
pide flores, y verás
confitados tus jardines.

Si buscas de azúcar piedra
los Escilas y Caribdis,
en almíbar surcarás
los piélagos de Anfitrite.[16]

Por pérsigos candecidos,
equivocando melindres,
sospecho te dé tu amante,
cubiertas monas matrices.[17]

A fragancias del buen gusto
el embozo, que te asiste,
deshojado en los primores,
explica más tus abriles.

En tiestos en tus ventanas,
reparte el florido chisme,
que lindos naranjos chinos
tendrás en barros de Chile.

Agraciado fue el impulso
del movimiento apacible,
siendo tu mano azucena
reciba el que recibe.

---

[16] Amphitrite was the wife of Poseidon.

[17] The exact meaning of this final line eludes me, but I take it that Cruzate is referring to the tarts known as "monas", mentioned in the *Diccionario de autoridades*, which were baked in Valencia and Murcia, especially during "Pascua de flores", or Easter. If so, the noun incorporates oblique allusions both to flowers and to the occasion of the academy itself, Pascua de Reyes. The fact that such tarts were savoury continues the poem's theme of asking for something sweet, only to be surprised by being given something different.

> Quejosas quedas las flores,
> y dicen los alelíes,
> que a Genova por tu mano
> irán porque las confiten.
>   Si fuera sal confitada,
> fuera una cosa terrible,
> que el azar con el cristal
> se enciende y no con salitre.
>   ¡O tú, florida señora,
> con tu dulzura me asiste,
> o con tu nombre, porque
> digan que acabo con Filis![18]

Here the individual stanzas extrapolate various facets of the set topic, but the disparate nature of the conceits means that whilst interpretative wit is much in evidence the overall impression is of stanzas being little connected causally with each other. Of course poets did try to overcome the tendency of such a poetic style to create a poem lacking any intrinsic sense of progression and any discernible structural unity. One way of doing this is to endow the poem with an explicit and rigid sense of rhetorical structure, as Gaspar Rodríguez Carrión Ponce de León does in employing anaphora in a poem on a lover apologizing for sending a clock and a rose to his lady on her birthday (inappropriate presents as they are symbols of life's brevity) in which he uses each of the stanzas to switch unimaginatively between the two offending presents, praising the lady by her association with each:

> Ya que el número de tus años
> las perfecciones celebra
> de tu hermosura, pues cumple
> años, Lisi, que no empiezas,
>   en esa rosa que rompe
> verde prisión de belleza,
> por diligenciar su ocaso
> los orientes a tu esfera;
>   en ese reloj que el tiempo
> fino amante te presenta,
> que también el tiempo sabe
> no perderle en las finezas;
>   en esa rosa que al aire
> de olores respira néctar,
> porque bebido en tus labios,
> mas en su aurora se alienta;

---

[18] See *Pascua de Reyes*, fols 40r–41r (corrected foliation). For poems exhibiting a similar loose structure, compare "A un asunto sin sustancia" (Chapter 4), and "Si [de] tu aire he de pintar" (Chapter 3).

>   en ese reloj que al sol
> le va cursando las sendas,
> porque el alba de tus luces
> engendre sus influencias;
>   en esa rosa que amante
> hace de siglos cosecha,
> convirtiendo en brevedades
> porque aspira a ser tu estrella;
>   en ese reloj que mide
> tus perfecciones inmensas,
> dando edades al amor
> de hermosa correspondencia;
>   en esa rosa que en ave,
> alas, y hojas purpurea,
> porque al ponerse en tu mano,
> duración y pompa eleva;
>   en ese reloj que edades
> a la admiración sustenta,
> porque siempre te amanece
> con la distancia suspensa,
>   te consagra mi respeto,
> con adoración secreta,
> sobre cuyas blancas aras
> mi atención arde y no humea.
>   Unos años que me debes
> a mis rendidas ternezas,
> de un amor, que todo es rayos;
> de un dolor, que todo es flechas.
>   En rosa y reloj, de quien
> simbolizan en la ofrenda
> milagroso, adorno al culto
> del templo de tus bellezas.[19]

As with many overtly rhetorical pieces the repetitive and unvaried organizational format tends to attract more attention than the poem's clear explicative and persuasive objective. The structure via conceits is here rigidly formalized and unity arises from both the use of anaphora and the fact that the continual oscillation between the rose and the clock all constitute a single apostrophized clause which hinges on line 37, the poet thereby deflecting potential offence not by apologizing for the ineptitude of the presents but rather by making them all hinge on the poem's key word – and excuse, his "respeto".

Academy poems are thus distinguished by their marked tendency to present their material in relatively discrete stanzas, each offering their own witty formulation of the subject set. Whilst such stanzas may form part of an

---

[19] See *Real Aduana*, pp. 25–27.

argument, as in the poem just cited, this rarely takes the form of a genuinely ratiocinative process in which a given stanza plays an integral role in the development of the whole: the most obvious proof of this is that, by and large, stanzas are interchangeable and hence arbitrarily arranged. One reason for this more piece-meal structure is, as already mentioned, the fact that unlike non-academy verse the subject, its protagonists and their vicissitudes are known beforehand. A further, and perhaps more fundamental, reason for the development of the self-contained stanza, or rather, of the stanza as a single unit embodying a conceit, is the gradual transformation of all seventeenth-century poetry by the epigram. The epigram was the major influence behind the rise of the *conceptista* style in Spain, altering the style and structure of virtually all verse-forms. In Renaissance theory the epigram was a compressed short poem, embodying a single idea or concept in which a decisive, witty and sententious conclusion was paramount.[20] Its essential features – concision, the unexpected and surprising light thrown on its subject matter, and a preponderance, particularly in the concluding lines, of puns, word-play, antithesis, balanced periods and alliterated repetitions – exercised a profound effect on seventeenth-century poetry. By the end of the sixteenth century the epigram's structure, as much as its witty content, had already transformed sonnet theory and practice and its influence was beginning to be apparent in the formal disposition of other verse-forms too, with ever greater emphasis being placed on the conclusion of both the overall poem and, more importantly, the individual stanzas.[21] The German Jesuit Matthäeus Rader, whose introduction to his edition of Martial became and remained an authoritative influence on epigram theory, even declared that the epigram's *dispositio*, its characteristic strong conclusion or sting-in-the-tail, was its defining feature.[22] In a very real sense, the epigram provided the perfect formal and thematic model for wit, a poetic which essentially theorized and propagated its characteristics: as I have already mentioned, Gracián's view of wit as revealed by both his taxonomy and his examples is fundamentally epigrammatic.[23] In the academy the epi-

[20] See, for example, Julius Caesar Scaliger, *Poetices libri septem* (Stuttgart: Friedrich Frommann, 1964; facsimile of 1561 Lyons edn), pp. 169–71; and Herrera, *Anotaciones*, in Garcilaso, *Garcilaso y sus comentaristas*, pp. 308–15.

[21] For the links between sonnet and epigram, see Gary J. Brown, "Fernando de Herrera and Lorenzo de' Medici: The Sonnet as Epigram", *RF*, 87 (1975), 226–38; and "Lope de Vega's Epigrammatic Poetic for the Sonnet", *MLN*, 93 (1978), 218–32.

[22] Rader writes: "argutia vel maxime propria est epigrammati, unde nervum, vim & acrimoniam, geniumque. [. . .] tota vis argutiae plerumque est in extremo versu, aut disticho, velut in teli mucrone, quod omnia epigrammata ostendunt, aut si hac careant, epigrammatis nomen relinquant". See *M. Valerii Martialis epigrammaton libri omnes, novis commentariis . . . a Matthaeo Radero* (Ingolstadt: Adam Sartorius, 1602), p. 10.

[23] The close affinity between wit and the epigram is even more explicit in the treatise by the Polish Jesuit, Maciej Kazimierz Sarbiewski, *De acuto et arguto* (1626–27). See Sarbiewski, *Wykłady Poetyki (Praecepta Poetica)*, ed. by Stanislaw Skimina (Cracow: Biblioteka Pisarzów Polskich, 1958), pp. 1–20.

gram's transformation of the lyric was almost total, giving rise to the style of poetry I am here concerned with, namely one based on an endless series of epigrammatic stanzas whose final twists become their whole rationale. A good example of such epigrammatic presentation of stanzas are the *quintillas* by José Navarro which deal with a woman whose face has been slashed for her irreligiosity, the topic itself suggesting the word-play around which most of the poem centres: "A una mujer que nunca se santiguaba y la cruzaron la cara." Here each stanza progressively and cumulatively interprets and reinterprets both the causes and effects of the topic and draws broader conclusions regarding its significance as a means of disclosing facets of the lover's character and identity. However the poet has attempted to formalize more systematically the poem's structure by organizing the stanzas into a standard epigrammatic pattern in which the element of closure is paramount. Thus most stanzas are bipartite: expository material in the opening lines laying the basis for the witty statement or conclusion usually in the final two, the causal link between the two frequently marked by the use of conjunctions:

> A la ley que no estimabas
> ya Clarinda te reduces,
> pues antes con penas bravas
> de que no te santiguabas
> me estaba yo haciendo cruces.
>   Pero ya tu desatino
> se enmendó (acción peregrina)
> y por extraño camino
> una navaja se vino
> a enseñarte la doctrina.
>   Asunto tuvo civil
> tu hermosura soberana,
> porque entre beldades mil
> bien pudiera ser gentil
> sin dejar de ser cristiana.
>   El color, que al gusto brinda,
> con tal acción se desdora
> en una cara tan linda,
> pues siendo como una guinda,
> estaba como una mora.
>   Ya de costumbre has mudado,
> y no pareces la misma;
> y al que de tu fe ha dudado
> muestras que te han bautizado
> con enseñarle la crisma.
>   Por ella necias porfías
> dejaste avergonzada
> Clarinda, y en breves días,
> si un mal hábito tenías

> ya llevas cruz colorada.
>   El que en tu daño trabaja
> con menos alma que un perro,
> viéndose en acción tan baja,
> ensangrentó la navaja,
> por dar color a su hierro.
>   Si imagino tu pesar
> los cabellos se espeluzan;
> mas no me dejo de holgar
> de ver que hay en el lugar
> tantas caras que se cruzan.
>   Ya, pues, que no se remedia
> lloremos Clarinda juntos,
> y guarda en esta tragedia,
> pues te hacen la cara media,
> no te se sueltan los puntos.
>   Al mostrarse tu porfía
> en el santiguarse avara,
> cuantas veces te decía,
> "Advierte, Clorinda mía,
> que ha de salirte a la cara".
>   Y quien pudiera dudar
> cuando todos reparaban
> en vicio tan singular,
> que se había de cortar
> pues tantos la murmuraban.[24]

The dominant influence of the epigram created formal problems of lack of cohesion and momentum, for the epigram, an essentially short verse-form, was not an ideal or obvious structural model for longer verse-forms, even if these were ordered into stanzas. In most epigrammatic poems (which constitute the major part of academy output), the result – aesthetically unsatisfactory on one level – is the fragmentation of a long poem into its individual pointed stanzas through the lack of any cohesive force, be that narrative or, as I argued in the last chapter, a "binding" fictional persona. This fragmentation, as we shall see, also means that the stanzas are very much static units rather than part of a sequential dynamic. This said, the fact that such poems are structured according to an essentially epigrammatic mode of presentation presumably created a degree of genre expectation which militated against them being evaluated negatively according to essentially lyric criteria. Nevertheless, poems often exhibit a peculiar tension between the concision and intensity of the short statements contained within their stanzas and the potential for endlessly and indiscriminately continuing the process of redefinition

---

[24] See *Poesías varias*, pp. 176–78. The poem's title states that this was an academy piece.

and restatement over an indefinite number of stanzas. In other words, the brevity of expression and the economy of the octosyllabic line which characterize the stanzas used in *romances, seguidillas* etc. are undercut by the potential prolixity of the poem itself. Consequently the impression left by the majority of academy poems is that they could be extended *ad infinitum*. Such an impression arises precisely because there is an absence of narrative rationale or control (there is no need to convey sequential information or events) and of argumentative or persuasive purpose (there is no need to make the stanzas justify their inclusion as necessary elements in a logical process). It is the tension thus created between concision and amplification which often leads to an academy poem simply petering out, leaving the reader with the impression that the poet's wit is exhausted.

Basing a long verse-form on the model of a short one also provoked another compositional problem, the conclusion. In poems largely lacking narrative impetus the poet is confronted with the predicament of when and how to conclude suitably and impressively a composition whose academy style is, as I have been arguing, marked by a restless drive for the ultimate witty definitional precision. Interestingly a proliferation of witty conclusions, inferences or solutions to the topic proposed was taken by Gracián to be a prime means of heightening our aesthetic pleasure: writing about "problemas conceptuosos y cuestiones ingeniosas" he states that enjoyment increases in proportion to the number of possible answers proposed by the poem.[25] This was the theory. In practice such a compositional format raised the problem of finding a conclusion to a poem which is itself a series of conclusions, for the mobility and interchangeability of the stanzas in most poems means that the conclusion needs to be as forceful as possible to effect closure and stasis. At a time when it was standard practice to conclude a poem on a piquant and witty note, usually embodied in a rhetorically decisive manner using figures of speech such as compar and antithesis whose structure expresses a degree of contrastive balance and order, and hence of finality, an academy poet was confronted with having to end his piece with, as it were, double the standard force, since the body of the poem itself was structured epigrammatically, both in terms of its rhetorical and conceptual content.[26] Many poets simply fail to find a satisfactory solution to this compositional difficulty. Indeed, it is the relative weakness and arbitrariness of the closing stanzas or lines of many

---

[25] "Cuando el problema tiene tres o cuatro términos que compiten la verdad, es más ingenioso y más gustoso, porque aquella competencia aumenta la suspensión y hace más reñida la dificultad." See *Agudeza*, II, p. 99.

[26] As Barbara Hernstein Smith notes, "what we usually mean by *epigrammatic* closure is something like 'having maximal closure' ". See *Poetic Closure. A Study of How Poems End* (Chicago and London: University of Chicago, 1968), p. 197. Smith also discusses in general terms the non-determinacy of a concluding point and the use of frame stanzas in paratactic structures (pp. 96–109, 148–50). However she does not consider the effects on the whole poem of the strong closures of its constituent stanzas.

academy pieces which is their greatest failing. In the following poem by Jaime Pons, for example, on a lover whose carefully kept love letters have been gnawed by mice, the composition simply stops with a stanza whose unassuming platitude fails to mark a decisive conceptual or rhetorical break with the body of the poem; the impression the reader is left with is of a poem which ends when and where it does for no discernible reason:

>   Amante corito,
> que guardas papeles,
> que sin ser torneos
> ratones mantienen.
>   No los saques más,
> porque si los vieron
> tan pobres y rotos
> justo es les desprecien.
>   Mas salgan a luz,
> porque me parece,
> por ser de la rota,
> respetarse deben.
>   Como allí el amor
> y corazón tienes,
> comen tus entrañas
> cuando en ellos muerden.
>   Cuando así los miras,
> yo sé que lo sientes,
> pues hallas pasados
> favores presentes.
>   Y en verdad que temo
> que rateros fuesen
> conceptos, en que
> cebaron el diente.
>   No valió cerrarlos,
> pues es evidente
> que falsea guardas
> ganzúa tan fuerte.
>   Ya en esos ratones
> amigos previenes,
> que de tus cuidados
> archivos son fieles.
>   Hallas, cuando buscas,
> que guardados queden,
> quien los guarda en parte
> do no se parecen.
>   Ratones de invidia
> a morder se atreven
> el cándido amor,
> que en papel posees.

> Mas yo no me espanto
> que en ruines siempre
> se hallara la invidia
> ejercer sus veces.
> Dísteles al cargo
> de que respondiesen
> a aquellos favores
> que rumian billetes.
> Mas como son rancios
> disculparse pueden,
> tragando por queso
> conceptos de leche.
> Bien sé que a tu amor
> mil cuidados deben,
> pues que así ha gustado
> de provecho serles.
> Amante de viejo,
> quédate y advierte,
> que al más firme amor
> el tiempo le vence.[27]

In such a poem, then, both the disposition of stanzas and the moment of conclusion are entirely arbitrary. Of course it could be argued that the concluding stanza is more effective than I allow since it is possible to take the final reference to time conquering all as obliquely applicable to the poem. To my mind such a reading of the final stanza is simply too oblique to be effective, particularly given the absence of any other rhetorical markers of closure, and especially since obliquity is not particularly a virtue in a context which regularly exploited metatextuality and self-referentiality.[28] Thus when academy poets do signal their compositions' close, they do so in an overt and obtrusive manner, as can be seen in the concluding lines of the following two poems, the first of which offers a "vejamen a las flores a vista de los lucimientos de lo hermoso", and the second, more appositely, a description of the effect on an academy audience once a poet has finished reading a bad academy poem to them:

> ¿Cómo queréis de lo hermoso
> experimentar la altura,
> si el ser asombro a su planta
> os sobra la fortuna?

---

[27] See *Sol de academias*, pp. 39–40.

[28] Smith discusses poems in English which effect closure via references to time etc., but such references in the majority of her examples seem, like Pons' poem here, too weak or oblique to be effective when the dominant poetic is essentially epigrammatic. See *Poetic Closure*, pp. 172–82.

> ¿Cómo...?, pero no. Callemos.
> El romance se concluya,
> que más que a las flores, veja
> a lo hermoso que le escucha.
>
> Nada lo hermoso le atiende,
> y él, leyendo que leyendo,
> concluye el papel y empieza
> su aplauso con el silencio;
> aunque interrumpirse suele
> con lo de ¡gracias al cielo!,
> ¡Jesús, qué cansado ha sido!,
> ¡creí no acabase tan presto!
> Dije hasta aquí lo que pasa
> al oír malas coplas, pero
> mejor lo dirá lo que
> pasó leyendo mis versos.[29]

Both these examples indicate how the element of metatextuality can be an effective means not only of opening a poem and of drawing attention to the poet's skill, but of actually closing it too. Metatextual commentary is thus one solution to the problem of closure created by the style favoured in the academy.

Even in those deliberative topics which set the poet the task of resolving a paradox or dilemma which we might expect him to do by reaching a firm and definitive conclusion, the conclusions lose something of their very finality since their position at the end of a series of other alternative conclusions and definitive statements somewhat inevitably makes them appear arbitrary. This is one of the central paradoxes of this style, for if we take the epigram as being, by its nature, a definitive statement – the last word on its subject – then in academy poems the serial format actually undermines one of the essential characteristics of the epigram: the composition of the whole runs the risk of devaluing the validity of its parts. A good poet can overcome the difficulty of concluding a composition which contains within itself a whole series of decisive conclusions by ending on a note of conceptual and rhetorical contrast, usually via oxymoron and/or antithesis. Such endings are effective since they combine the two standard forms of epigram closure, thereby doubling the force of the final lines by effecting closure on the level of both *res* and *verba*. The conclusions to the following two poems are representative of this pursuit of a strong or decisive ending: the first comes from a poem dealing with a lover who feigns indifference, since he only offends the lady by loving her; the second from one in which the lover faints on seeing his lady's house

---

[29] See *Señoras*, pp. 127, 148–49. Both poems also begin with metatextual references to their compositional context.

in flames, only to awake to the sight of her being rescued in the arms of another man:

> Entre las flores el áspid
> se esconde tan contrapuesto,
> que es, si se mira, hermosura,
> y si se encuentra, escarmiento.
>   Escarcha y humo respira
> el volcán a un mismo tiempo,
> y sólo avisa el peligro
> a aquel que conoce el riesgo.
>   Pues viva yo en mi cuidado,
> a dos razones atento,
> nieve y flor en lo aparente,
> volcán y áspid encubierto.[30]
>
>   Libróte, en fin, un dichoso,
> yedra que al irte ciñendo,
> ascendió por la fortuna
> más allá del pensamiento.
>   Emulo altivo de Atlante,
> otro feliz Prometeo,
> arrebató de las llamas
> el móvil de tus luceros.
>   Déjame callar mi ultraje,
> pues vinculando al ejemplo
> halló materia caduca
> para impresionarse eterno.
>   El caso fue, bella Irene,
> influjo de airado aspeto:
> yo lidiaba con un astro,
> y tú con un elemento.[31]

Similarly by resolving a paradox with a further witty and paradoxical statement Antonio de Solís manages to lend the concluding lines of a piece on "¿Por qué llaman entendidas a las feas, si no hay mayor necedad que ser feas?" a suitable degree of force and finality:

>   Y así yo a la pregunta
> de la academia
> brevemente respondo
> con esta letra:
>   Socorrer a las feas

---

[30] See *Pascua de Reyes*, fol. 37r (corrected foliation). The poem establishes a final double contrast which thereby revivifies two long-standing Petrarchan clichés.

[31] See *Real Aduana*, p. 44.

> con lo entendido
> es taparse los ojos
> con los oídos.[32]

As in these two stanzas which offer a "double" closure, the final paradox being preceded by a metatextual gesture towards the academy, some poets, especially those writing poems organized around a narrative proper, overcompensate for the academy's inclination towards random and arbitrary poetic closure by offering several concluding stanzas, each of which finalizes a different strand or aspect of the poem. Cáncer y Velasco's poem on a groom who forgets to sleep with his bride on their wedding night is a good example of such pieces which overcorrect, with humorous effect and intent, a general fault of academy verse. The body of the poem follows a sequential narrative, starting with a mock opening invocation to any of the muses devoted to "Apolillo" and a brief description of the wedding – this section achieving its own degree of sequentiality and stanzaic integration via the use of enjambement (between stanzas 1 and 2, and 5 and 6) and the development of a conceit based on gambling ("jugar", "perder", "pagar") between stanzas 3 and 4:

> Musa mía de mi guarda
> cualquiera que de las nueve
> por mandado de Apolillo
> me amparas y me defiendes,
>   asísteme a este romance,
> y líbrame como puedes
> de la vil cacofanía,
> y el bajo simul cadente.
>   Fuese a casar, sobre tantos,
> sobre su palabra fuese
> a ennoviar Fabio con Clori,
> no es bobo si halla quien juegue.
>   Perdió como todos hacen,
> y lo que a la novia debe
> no pagó, que para hacerlo
> horas veinticuatro tiene.
>   Apenas los maniató
> el párroco competente
> con el nudo indisoluble,
> que sólo corta la muerte,
>   cuando a acostarse fue Clori,
> y Fabio a su casa fuese,
> sin acordarse que había
> nacido para que engendre.

---

[32] See *Varias poesías*, p. 247.

The next section gives us the bride Clori's lament in her bed over her absent husband and her unsatisfied sexual desires, a lament which occupies the bulk of the poem. This part of the poem broadly follows the normal format of discrete quatrains each of which offers an interpretation of her situation. The poet here uses the types of conceits much favoured in the academy, such as the coining of appropriate nouns ("solinovios"):

> Viéndose novia ermitaña.
> más sola mucho que el Fénix,
> solinovios hizo al aire,
> quejándose de esa suerte.

Or the use of repetition for dramatic effect:

> "Si eres flaco de memoria
> ¿qué más tiene, qué más tiene,
> acordarte que te vayas,
> que acordarte que te quedes?"

Most in evidence, however, are a string of *double entendres* used to convey Clori's sexual frustration, such as in the following stanza:

> "Bien pensé yo aquesta noche
> ser de las novias alegres
> que por la mañana buscan
> entre lo rojo lo verde".

Here Cáncer quotes a line from Góngora, "entre lo rojo lo verde", but in doing so shifts it from its original martial context in the ballad "Entre los sueltos caballos" into a marital one where it becomes an overtly sexual reference to the loss of virginity on the wedding night.[33] Once Clori's lament to her absent husband is over, Cáncer y Velasco offers what effectively amounts to two concluding stanzas:

> "Como el casarse y morirse
> todo es de una misma especie,
> dicho el responso del sí,
> dejas el cuerpo, y te vuelvas."
> Dijo; y vencida del sueño,
> porque a cualquiera la vence,

---

[33] See Góngora, *Romances*, ed. by Antonio Carreño, 3rd edn (Madrid: Cátedra, 1988), pp. 143–48 (p. 143). Lines 49–52 are typical of academy wit, and are a good example of what Gracián calls "ingeniosas equívocas" (*Agudeza*, II, p. 53), a type of *double entendre* which is always strongly in evidence in more risqué and satirical/burlesque academy poems.

> soñó que Fabio venía,
> y soñaba lo que quiere.
>   Pardiez que él anduvo bien
> (y digan lo que dijeren)
> en irse, porque las cosas
> no han de durar para siempre.[34]

In the first of these concluding stanzas, the amatory narrative proper – Clori's complaint against her absent groom – is concluded by allowing her the sexual fulfilment in a dream which she has been denied in reality.[35] Cáncer, like other seventeenth-century poets, thus sexualizes the long-familiar dream topos, with the difference that it is the woman who finds sexual release in her sleep and the man who is unresponsive; in his reversal of protagonists, the poet follows the precedent of overtly sexual poetry rather than the restrained eroticism of more decorous amatory verse.[36] The final stanza proper returns us both to the groom and, beyond the subject itself, back to the poem's academy context with which the piece began. The unexpected closing comment that nothing good can last forever, hence the groom acted correctly in forgetting his bride, can obviously be neatly applied to the poem itself. In this way Cáncer offers a conclusion to both the amatory drama and his oral presentation or performance of the poem. This double conclusion – double in terms of the two stanzas and the final stanza's dual reference to the topic and the poem – recalls the many examples of self-reflexive conclusions mentioned in the previous chapter, as well as the close of Sebastiana Cruzate's poem cited in full above which ends on a note of ambiguous self-commentary thereby achieving the very finish it is discussing:

> ¡O tú, florida señora,
> con tu dulzura me asiste,
> o con tu nombre, porque
> digan que acabo con Filis!

As I commented above, self-referentiality is therefore an effective means of concluding a series of conceits by providing a switch in register, discourse and generic context to mark the end of the amatory content of a poem, thereby side-stepping the problem of concluding like with like.[37] In Cáncer's poem,

---

[34] See *Obras*, pp. 116–19.

[35] Compare Francisco de Avellaneda's poem on a groom losing his way back to bed after getting up for a drink which is equally sexually suggestive and similarly combines narrative thrust, humour and wit. See *Real Aduana*, pp. 34–38.

[36] For an example of the latter, the man dreaming, see Quevedo's "¡Ay, Floralba! Soñé que te . . . ¿Dirélo?", *Poesía original completa*, pp. 365–66, no. 337; and for various examples of women having sexual dreams, see Alzieu (ed.), *Poesía erótica del siglo de oro*, pp. 243–45.

[37] The difference between the close of Cáncer's poem and that of Jaime Pons'

then, the potential problem of a how to conclude a poem is avoided by closing the piece with more than one stanza and on more than one level. Furthermore such a closure has the potential to gain in impact during delivery, since what reads as a rather lame conclusion on the page – "porque las cosas / no han de durar para siempre" – can be given a more incisive edge when declaimed, if a certain flourish and dramatic emphasis are employed to lend the conclusion a greater air of finality. Consequently, as well as bearing in mind the generic expectations created by what I term the epigrammatic mode of construction in longer verse-forms as a mitigating factor when evaluating the formal presentation and reception of a poem's subject, we must also recognize the importance of performance as a means of supplementing the elements of finality and closure otherwise absent or ineffective on a purely textual level.[38]

If metatextual reference is an effective means of concluding a poem and of giving it a degree of coherence by placing it as a composition in its performative context, then intertextual reference can serve the same function in so far as it fosters an appreciation of the poem as a whole within the context of the models incorporated. Golden Age Petrarchism was of course essentially a discourse of imitation; success in this enterprise was largely a question of the way in which several models were shuffled and consequently reassembled into a poetic whole. As I commented in the previous chapter, academy poetry was fundamentally similar, working along lines comparable to the contemporary theatrical practice of *refundiciones*: the same dramatic scenarios, paradoxical questions and mundane objects reoccur with endless variations and twists. By the second half of the century the academy style and, more importantly, academy thematics had established themselves to the extent of becoming intertextual models. The academy began gradually and in an unsystematic way to use its own distinctive poetry as an imitable model. Importantly, though, specific, and therefore presumably intentional, direct references, such as Cáncer's incorporation of the line from Góngora's ballad ("entre lo rojo lo verde"), are minimal. Imitation tends to be of topics and the clichés associated with them, rather than of individual poems.[39] This is all part of the

("Amante corito", cited above) is precisely the overdetermined nature of the former. This type of academy closure is usually explicit, direct and thematically gratuitous, and often connected to a poetic persona disassociated from the amatory one.

[38] Smith makes a similar point regarding poems on the printed page having their closing lines enhanced unconsciously when they are read or recited due to the fact that we know them to be terminal. See *Poetic Closure*, pp. 211–12. What I am suggesting is that academy poets, aware that their poems are primarily performative and that consequently their listeners are unable to know when the poem is to close, signal that closure with suitable performative gestures and vocal emphases which in turn can reinforce strong, explicit textual references to closure. In this way they can supplement what is formally absent, and even, perhaps, what is therefore strictly formally unnecessary.

[39] Direct imitation and indeed plagiarism do of course occur. For example, in a poem on a woman fainting after pricking her finger on a rose Felipe Muñiz Delgado incorporates unacknowledged, and with only minor alterations, the entire second *décima* from a poem

academy being primarily a collective style, marked more by the wit of its topics than the individuality of its poets and their poems, and arises largely because academy poets are little concerned with inserting themselves into a line of tradition. The use of such non-specific thematic references can be illustrated with the following *décimas* by Mateo Freire de Andrade on a lady pecked on the lips by a goldfinch whilst feeding it from her mouth:

> Herida Clori te vi,
> y tan rendido quedé,
> que al punto que te miré,
> no el menos herido fui,
> con tal perfección en ti
> se vio entonces la beldad,
> que ya de su libertad
> duda el alma mal segura
> si herida vio la hermosura,
> si hermosa la crueldad.
>   Deslustrarte quiso aleve
> el jilguerillo cruel,
> que al más vividor clavel
> funesta opresión se atreve,
> sienta tu achaque la nieve,
> y llore el cristal su abril,
> quéjese el marfil sutil,
> que si Clori tiene mal,
> ya el cristal no es cristal,
> y ya el marfil no es marfil.
>   Si bien mucho se atrevió
> el sutil pico o lanceta,
> cuando la aguda saeta
> de amor cultos te rindió,
> disculpa en su culpa halló
> el jilguerillo fatal,
> descubriendo el mineral
> del más precioso rubí,
> para esmaltar carmesí
> en márgenes de cristal.
>   Bien conoció su locura,
> o su ambición cruel
> ser deidad y no clavel,
> labios con tanta hermosura,
> mas librando su ventura
> en el grillo cristalino,

on a different subject by Bocángel, itself considered an academy composition by Trevor Dadson. See *Ciudad Real*, fols 32v–33r, and Bocángel, *Lira*, p. 203 (p. 75 for Dadson's comments on the probable academy origin of Bocángel's piece).

> no se valió peregrino
> en la prisión celestial
> de sustento material,
> mas de alimento divino.
>   Viéndose morir de amores
> filósofo dio la herida,
> para eternizar la vida
> con tu sangre y tus favores;
> de este susto resplandores
> fulminaste bella diosa,
> con que afrentaste la rosa
> en el carmín de tu labio,
> y con el purpurio agravio
> te ostentaste más hermosa.
>   Mas, ¡ay! que acrecentaría
> jilguerillo mi codicia,
> la sangre que desperdicia
> esa pequeña sangría,
> una gota bastaría
> de ese licor que derrama,
> para mitigar la llama,
> y mi corazón que estima
> morir sólo en lo que anima
> para vivir en lo que ama.[40]

One of the aspects that is most striking about this very effective poem is the poet's incorporation of motifs drawn from one of the century's most popular and enduring subjects, blood-letting. Our attention is obviously explicitly drawn to the subject in the third and sixth stanzas in which the bird's bill is referred to as a "lanceta" and the peck itself as a "pequeña sangría". This should alert us, if we have not already noticed them, to other motifs drawn directly from the same topic: the notion of the lover suffering more than the woman undergoing the treatment (lines 1–4);[41] the linking of the "lanceta" with Love's arrows (lines 21–24);[42] the description of the blood itself (lines 27–30);[43] and the life-giving power of her blood (lines 41–44, 51–60).[44]

---

[40] See *Fonseca Feb 1663*, fols 19r–20r.

[41] Compare Lope de Vega, *Obras poéticas*, pp. 97–98; and Soto de Rojas, *Obras*, pp. 61–62.

[42] See Carmen Riera Guilera, "Un poeta inédito del siglo XVII: Don Gabriel de Henao y Monjaraz", *BBMP*, 50 (1974), 137–76 (pp. 166–67).

[43] Though standard amatory terms are used, compare Lope, *Obras poéticas*, pp. 97–98.

[44] See Faria y Sousa: "En ansiosos deseos el alma ardía, / viendo la breve y saludable herida, / por bañarse en la fuente que corría. / Porque, como la sangre es cierta vida, / para animar en ella la alma mía, / en ella se intentaba ver tendida." (*Fuente de Aganipe*, Part 2, fol. 49v; compare fol. 41r).

These intertextual conceits transposed from one contemporary amatory topic to another serve to situate the poem as actively engaged with the kaleidoscopic nature of academy poetry, and, more directly, to unify the composition by providing a conceptual means of linking together its various conceits. The blood-letting references show a poet alert to academy practice and provide a running motif which creates a good example of what Gracián terms "agudeza compuesta".

Throughout this chapter I have been concerned with the effects of wit on the structure and closure of academy poems. In the final poem I shall consider I propose to bring together these different strands to see how the essentially dramatic rather than lyric nature of academy poetry can be deployed to supplement apparent formal deficiencies. The poem in question, written in 1669 by Juan de la Torre on the subject of a man who, passing beneath a lady at a balcony, is struck simultaneously both by her beauty and a laurel branch she throws down at him, adroitly confronts the compositional issues of coherency and closure which I have been addressing but in two ways which are so distinct that they create a sense of structural and thematic dissonance:

> De hacia ti, ¡o Fili bella!,
> un ramo descendió, que fue mi estrella;
> que con hojas felices
> de mi amor en la esfera echó raíces,
> para que fuese ya sin extrañeza
> mi constancia raíz, flor tu belleza.
> De tu esfera cayó, Fili divina,
> ¡o novedad!, que en lluvia repentina
> caen del cielo ya menos crueles
> así como los rayos, los laureles.
> Dafne en laurel se cae de tu cielo,
> huye otra vez del sol su ingrato vuelo,
> pero en más bello paso,
> en ti se queda el sol. ¡O feliz caso!;
> pues en ti (para anuncio a mi ventura)
> cae el desdén y queda la hermosura.
> Ese rayo, ese triunfo, es quien me abona,
> que ya de emperadores fue corona,
> y, que imperios mayores,
> al venirse a mi frente tus favores
> ya pueden los trofeos aclamarme,
> pues el favorecerme es coronarme.
> Pero, ¡ay!, como dichoso me computo,
> si ese verde esplendor rayo es sin fruto.
> Mas ¿qué digo? Gran logro Amor alcanza,
> pues ¿qué premio mayor que la esperanza?
> Tu condición ya cesa rigurosa,
> pues el laurel me das como piadosa,

porque, excusando enojos,
me libre de los rayos de tus ojos,
mas el laurel no intente esos ensayos
porque en tus ojos quiero yo mis rayos.
Planta del sol se arguya
el laurel, y por eso planta tuya,
admíteme a tus pies, será grandeza
que al coronar tu lauro mi cabeza
en postrada atención, en gloria tanta,
dos veces mi cabeza esté en tu planta.
Estudiando respuesta en su ruido,
el gentilismo vano y presumido
ponía, para anuncios de amor ciego,
las hojas del laurel dentro del fuego;
así yo que en el mismo ardor me copio
porque hable afectos dentro el ruego propio
en los anuncios de mi amor deshecho,
este laurel pondré dentro de mi pecho.
Pues sereno y lucido hace que viva,
ya es para mí el laurel más que la oliva;
pues altos triunfos le conduce al alma
ya es para mí más que la palma,
pero no mal he dicho, mal arguyo,
más la palma será que el laurel tuyo;
premio la palma es más soberano
si la palma es la palma de tu mano.
Cuando el laurel despides y le arrojas,
escribiré mil libros en sus hojas,
papel siendo el candor de tu hermosura,
en donde se encuaderna mi ventura;
prólogo el que en tu aurora fiel alabo;
título el de tu esclavo;
aprobación si asiste tu presencia;
tu luz asumpto, tu piedad licencia;
línea la que dilata mi deseo;
punto las breves horas que te veo;
letra la voz con que muriendo canto;
admiración la gloria de tu encanto;
registro tus luceros vencedores;
plana tu frente, márgenes las flores;
rasgo la dulce herida en que me pierdes;
y en fin en estas hojas, aunque verdes,
blanco ya de tu acierto,
será mi corazón el libro abierto,
y sin salir de amor será en mi suerte
el principio el amarte, el fin quererte.[45]

[45] See *Real academia*, pp. 64–66. Lines 4, 12 and 20 have been slightly emended.

Three things are immediately apparent about this poem: the insistent emphasis on the addressee, Fili, and the consequent foregrounding of the speaker; the repeated use of conjunctions ("para que", "pues", "mas", "porque") as markers of its conceits; and the sheer diversity and accretion of these conceits which pile up one upon another until the final extended conceit of the last twenty lines. The last two features are, as we have seen, normal in academy poetry: given the length of this particular poem and its constant restatements and reframings of the subject, the use of explicit signals to mark the turns and conclusions of its various conceits forestalls a feeling of stasis, of an argument going nowhere, and introduces an element of conceptual dynamism. The poet may be trying to argue or prove no one thing, but he shows himself capable of formulating and concluding endless minor witty arguments.

At first reading the poem appears to amount to little more than a series of discrete or self-contained conceits, an example of what Gracián terms "agudeza incompleja". This impression is reinforced by the fact that it divides into two distinct sections: the first 54 lines, which postulate a succession of interpretations of the lady's action and their amatory significance for the poet-lover, and the final 20 lines which offer an extended conceit which enumerates in an exhaustive manner the various facets of an initial pun on "hojas" (line 56). The switch in stylistic procedure from a string of conceits lacking any ratiocinative links between themselves to the spinning out of all the possible ramifications of one particular conceit is dramatic. The first section, as we shall see, conveys a sense of moving out through a series of concentric circles, each circle a conceit generated by the initial topic but tenuously linked lexically and conceptually both to proceeding and subsequent conceits; whilst the closing metaphor, with its systematic linkage of all aspects of a book – from prologue to official licence, from opening eulogistic verse to its censor's statement – to various aspects of the poet's love, provides an immediately clear conceptual unity which extends into the structure of the section itself in so far as each extension of the original metaphor occupies a series of single paratactic lines (lines 59–69). Such procedural disparity suggests that the poet simply got carried away with the potential of the final book metaphor and developed this without regard for the stylistic format or content of the rest of the poem.

The structure and conceptual unity of the closing section is so forcefully evident that it initially makes the body of the poem seem fragmentary. However both lexical and conceptual links between its various constituent conceits belie the initial impression of random conceits arbitrarily strung together. The first unifying element stems from the repeated use of the possessive adjective "tu" and the object pronoun "te" (together, of course, with the second-person verbs which are used, if more sparingly). These link the poem, its conceits and the poet to the lady and hence to the academy topic. The structural linkage which results from this foregounding of the relationship between the poet and his lady is reinforced by the use of repetition and synonyms, both within and between conceits. The most obvious example is the use of "rayo". Its first explicit occurrence in the conceit contained in lines 7–10 establishes a conceptual cluster linking laurel/sunbeam and Fili/heaven/sun (the "esfera" of line 7 is itself an echo of line 4 and, in turn, an extension of the laurel/star conceit of the opening lines). This conceit leads in turn to that of lines 11–16 which, whilst not mentioning "rayo", picks up on and develops the preceding conceptual cluster around Fili/heaven/sun, and furthers it by linking the laurel branch with Daphne, turned into a laurel whilst pursued by Apollo, the sun. These six lines in fact neatly invert the Dafne/Apollo myth; indeed the inversion is explicitly signalled in line 13: Fili, the woman, as the dazzling Petrarchan lady who surpasses the sun, is equated with Apollo. The next pair of conceits (lines 17–22, 23–26) both employ the metaphorical epithet "rayo" to describe the laurel and thus they too are linked with the previous conceits. (These two conceits also forge their own degree of integration via their use of parallel synonyms: the "triunfo" and "trofeos" of the first conceit are paralleled by the "gran logro" and "premio mayor" of the second.) "Rayo" finally reappears in lines 27–32 where it shifts from being a metaphor for the laurel branch to its standard Petrarchan use as a metaphor for amorous eye contact. The next conceptual unit, lines 33–38, is in turn linked to earlier sections via both direct repetition (the verb "coronar" recalls lines 17–22) and its word-play on elements employed in earlier conceits (the pun on "planta", which arises from labelling the laurel the "planta del sol", picks up on the earlier Fili/sun and Apollo/Dafne conceits of lines 7–10 and 11–16 respectively). Finally the "hojas"-leaves of lines 39–46 become the "hojas"-pages of lines 55–74, thereby providing a specific link of sorts between the two otherwise procedurally distinct sections of the poem.

The first section of the poem is, then, a tightly-worked series of interconnected conceits. This said it certainly lacks the ingenuity, intricacy and, above all, the concision and compression of the conceits used by poets such as Quevedo and Góngora. This relative slackness is itself typical of the *conceptista* style of the second half of the century. Even so, the poem is at times exceptionally heavy-handed and, perhaps worst of all, lacks any degree of subtlety. To take one example, the pun on "palma" in lines 47–54 looses its wit precisely because it is so laboriously and explicitly spelt out; like a joke explained, it consequently looses its force and impact, unlike the more successful pun on "planta" in lines 33–38 which gains by a relative lack of explicitness. This lack of subtlety places the listener in an entirely passive exegetical role. This is not simply a question of the conceits never aspiring to metaphysical or indeed amatory insight, but of the mind's satisfaction and pleasure in active engagement with a poem, whether that engagement is caused by empathy or provoked by syntactic or conceptual difficulty, and whether it leads to a lasting truth or not. This is a primary reason why the poem, like so many academy poems, disappoints: its relative lack of subtlety means that the mind is never actively engaged in any way with its numerous conceits.

If the two sections of the poem reveal individually careful construction via the development of conceptual and lexical patterning, albeit in distinct ways, this raises the question of whether the poem achieves an overall sense of unity from the diversity and variety of its parts. Like the majority of academy compositions, the poem proceeds not so much by logical steps whose rationale consists in their contribution to an overall argument within the poem's avowed sentimental context, as by conceits, stanzas and indeed whole sections whose position within the poem is fundamentally arbitrary and whose primary purpose is simply to impress the listener with their ingenuity and inventiveness rather than to involve him or her on either an emotional or an intellectual level with the textual scenario as prescribed. Consequently the disparity between the two sections in particular can easily be seen as a failure of integration. However I would argue that the change from relatively discrete conceits typical of academy poetry to the more unusual extended metaphor is effective for a variety of reasons. Primarily it brings about a change of tempo, moving us from the perpetual *conceptista* flux of the first section to the rapid, concise and forceful lines of the second, and thereby avoids the sense of monotony and redundancy which the technique of considering a topic from potentially endless perspectives can easily generate. The performance of such a poem would potentially further emphasize the transition in style, with the poet's declamation accentuating the shift to the rapid accumulation of short incisive statements which constitute the final conceit. If viewed as a type of dramatic soliloquy delivered by the poet to the academy audience, the move from a more leisurely and reflective, because reasoned, exposition of the situation to the crescendo of the final metaphor is less abrupt because mediated by the poet's delivery. Of course, the mere fact of reading a poem aloud is not in itself sufficient to create unity: a "performance" can only supplement a poem's rhetoric, not act as a substitute for it. My suggestion that the performance of the poem is a potential means of creating cohesion is purely speculative and presupposes that the poet, when delivering the poem, performs like an actor "in character". However in Juan de la Torre's poem the lack of regular stanzas and the use of rhyming couplets, both very unusual in academy poetry, convey a sense of unrestricted, because seemingly more natural and spontaneous, engagement with the subject which supports a more theatrical delivery. The performative dimension of a poem reminds us that the academy poet had potential recourse to other means beyond the purely formal to achieve a satisfying, coherent and dynamic poem. The combination of a change in tempo underlined by performance together with the switch in rhetorical procedure also creates a successful sense of closure as the point-by-point comparison culminates in the definitive statement of absolute love neatly presented in the rhetorical and conceptual balance of the final line ("el principio el amarte, el fin quererte") in a way typical of an epigrammatic ending. With the provisos outlined above regarding the lack of sophistication and acuity of its conceits, therefore, this poem is an impressive example of what can be achieved by a poet working within the distinctive restraints of the academy and using them to a poem's advantage.

In this chapter I have focused on what I see as the principal formal problems confronting poets writing for academies. Structural coherency and closure are aesthetic problems in longer verse-forms in part because of the style which poets adopt: the epigrammatic structure which poets favour unbalances the Classical and Renaissance notion of harmony and proportional unity since, depending on striking singularity, it promotes ceaseless diversity. The antagonism between Renaissance theory and the Baroque conception and, more importantly, practice of wit is more acute in the academies due to several of its distinctive features. The poet's studied detachment from, and indifference to, the amatory content of a poem; the relegation of narrative; and the light-hearted and strictly non-serious atmosphere: each of these aspects of academy verse removes a potential means of endowing a poem with purpose, direction and organization, if only because they encourage an ethos in which the poem becomes primarily an ephemeral vehicle for immediate entertainment rather than a lasting aesthetic artefact. What we see in academy poetry, then, is the disintegration of both Renaissance form and content. Behind this process which is at its most evident in academies lies the poetic of wit, in which the necessity for ingenuity of insight and force of expression combine to decentre structural harmony and thematic decorum.

After looking at the format of the academy, its atmosphere, subject matter, projection of poetic presence and stylistic difficulties, we are now in a position to summarize the features of academy verse discussed over the course of the preceding chapters. The hallmark of any academy poem is variety; within a single academy the listener/reader encounters both a wide array of subject matter and, within individual poems, an impressive diversity of conceits. The type of conceits favoured are what might be termed interpretative or elucidatory rather than descriptive or lyrical. Such interpretative wit is used to draw endless novel conclusions and to cast the subject repeatedly in a new and unexpected light, rarely to provide a genuine, or lasting, insight. There is a corresponding preference for verbal wit, with wordplay tending towards the trivial rather than the profound, such that style matches content. Indeed all conceits lack the concision and finesse which characterize the best seventeenth-century poetry. Instead they are all too often trite, unsubtle and heavy-handed. Consequently the conceits encountered in an academy poem are of the type critics have called "ornamental" rather than "organic" or "metaphysical"; they are "constructs" rather than "insights".[46] They also

---

[46] See Arthur Terry, "Quevedo and the Metaphysical Conceit", *BHS*, 35 (1958), 211–22 (p. 213); and Robert Pring-Mill, " 'Porque yo cerca muriese': An Occasional Meditation on a *conceptista* Theme", *BHS*, 61 (1984), 369–78 (p. 370).

consistently take an epigrammatic form (the broadly binary division of material into statement and conclusion), and are distributed within self-contained stanzas. Stanzaic units which are each self-contained formulations and reinterpretations of the set topic create a poem which embodies both concision and prolixity, for each stanza amounts to a pithy statement which nevertheless looses its force since its definitive format is seen to be both random and provisional in the wider context of a poem. Such a structural format in which stanzas are connected only with the topic, and rarely in any causal manner with one another, is a consequence of the premium set on entertainment via light-hearted and inconsequential subject matter, for this prompted the abandonment of both logical argument and rhetorical purpose as organizational principles. In terms of the reader's active intellectual or emotional involvement, then, the academy creates a situation of diminishing returns: as the particularity of the topics increases and conceits become ever more self-contained, leading to a poem's increased fragmentation, so the irrelevance of its conceits to anything beyond their own extravagant formulation becomes more pronounced and our complete detachment from them more inevitable. Significantly, as the style, structure and content of poems moved in the direction of non-engagement so academy poets developed the metatextual elements of their compositions, drawing the audience into the performance and receptive context of the poem, if not into its actual amatory content.

Academy poems are truly inconsequential exercises in wit rather than genuine attempts to convince the listener/reader of the veracity and immediacy of the emotions, situations and protagonists which they convey. In many ways this is why such poetry ultimately had a deleterious effect on seventeenth-century verse, acting as an important catalyst in its rapid decline. Although working towards different ends from non-academy poetry, and therefore employing distinct strategies to do so, poets still retained the topics, clichés and linguistic formulations of love poetry proper, essentially Petrarchan poetry. This meant that over the course of the century as academies became and remained a permanent fixture in the literary life of the country love poetry was inadvertently subverted from within, since academy poets in taking the trappings of love poetry helped finally to empty it of all sentiment, purpose and gravity. Such a debasement or devaluation helped to destroy Petrarchism as a viable, serious and effective discourse, and the academies were at the centre of this process precisely because their institutionalized style and format took so much further the broader trend of the Baroque lyric towards realism, understood as the presentation of love in a non-idealized way. The literary academies thus played a central part in the history of love poetry in Spain. Indeed, the love lyric's trajectory which begins with Garcilaso and Boscán ends with the literary academies at the close of the seventeenth century, for, whilst they might ultimately have travestied the original tradition, academies did continue to develop and shape it. To see Golden Age poetry as culminating in Góngora and Quevedo is to ignore the final stages in the process of adaptation of a discourse originating with Petrarch and to disregard the developments wrought by the confluence of a distinctive and formative occasion, the academy, and a ubiquitous and striking style, wit. In the academies, therefore, we see the final flourishing of a lyric tradition, but in ways which spelt the end for that tradition.

WORKS CONSULTED

ACCOUNTS OF ACADEMIES

Manuscripts

Segundo día de ejercicios . . . Academia de Valencia . . . día de los años de S.M. Carlos II (1683) (NLS: G.24c.1)
Manuscritos de diversas prosas y versos (Biblioteca Lázaro Galdiano, MS 407). This contains a variety of *vejámenes* and academy pieces from the mid-seventeenth century, mainly from Aragon.

Printed accounts
(Ordered chronologically, preceded where appropriate by the abbreviated title employed if the account is cited in the text.)

1591–94   *Academia de los Nocturnos*:   *Actas de la Academia de los Nocturnos*, ed. by José Luis Canet, Evangelina Rodríguez and Josep Lluís Sirera, 2 vols to date (Valencia: Institució Valenciana d'Estudis i Investigació, 1988–90)
1637   *Academia burlesca*:   *Academia burlesca en Buen Retiro a la majestad de Felipe Cuarto el Grande*, in *L'Espagne au XVIe et au XVIIe siècle. Documents historiques et littéraires*, ed. by Alfred Morel-Fatio (Paris: Heilbronn, 1878), pp. 603–80
1655   *Jardín*:   Melchor de Fonseca y Almeida (ed.), *Jardín de Apolo. Academia celebrada por diferentes ingenios* (Madrid: Julián de Paredes, 1655)
1658   *Sol de academias*:   *Sol de academias o academia de soles. En los lucidos ingenios de Valencia que la celebraron y en la hermosura y nobleza que la asistieron. Su mecenas. El ilustrí[simo] señor don Basilio de Castelví y Ponce [. . .] Su Presidente, el ilustre señor don Juan Andrés Coloma Peréz Calvillo, Conde de Elda [. . .] Su secretario para el vejamen, don Antonio de Cardona [. . .] Su poeta para la introducción, don Francisco de la Torre [. . .]* (Valencia: Juan Lorenzo Cabrera, 1658)
1659   *Repetida carrera*:   *Repetida carrera del sol de academias, o de la academia de soles. Su zodiaco, la casa del ilustre señor Don Basilio de Castelví y Ponce [. . .] Su presidente, el ilustre señor Don Felipe Folch de Cardona, Aragón y Borja, Conde de Buñol, y primogénito del Almirante de Aragón. Su secretario para la introducción, Don José de Borja Lansol*

[. . .]. *Su fiscal para el vejamen, Don Juan de Valda [. . .]* (Valencia: Juan Lorenzo Cabrera, 1659)

1661 *Granada*: *Academia que se celebró en la ciudad de Granada en ocho de diciembre al nacimiento del Príncipe Don Carlos, que Dios guarde. Presidente Don Pedro Alfonso de la Cueva Benavides [. . .] Secretario Don Nicolás de Cervantes y Ervías Calderón. Celebróse en casa de Don Pedro de Córdoba y Valencia* (Granada: Francisco Sánchez, 1661)

1661 *Fonseca Jan 1661*: *Academia que se celebró en seis de Enero en casa de Don Melchor de Fonseca de Almeida, siendo Presidente D. Juan Alfonso Guillén de la Carrera [. . .] Secretario Don Fernando de Monleón y Cortés [. . .] y Fiscal Don Alonso de Zárate y la Hoz* (Madrid: n.pub., 1661)

1661 *Fonseca Feb 1661*: *Academia que se celebró en casa de D. Melchor de Fonseca de Almeida en trece de Febrero, siendo Presidente Don Francisco Pinel y Monroy, Secretario Don Juan Alfonso Guillén de la Carrera, y Fiscal Don Bernardo de Monleón y Cortés. Año M.DCL.XI* (n.p., n.pub., n.d.)

1662 *Fonseca Jan 1662*: *Academia que se celebró en siete de enero al feliz nacimiento del serenísimo Príncipe D. Carlos, N. S.. Presidióla en su casa Don Melchor de Fonseca de Almeida. Fue Secretario Don Luis Nieto y Fiscal D. Alonso de Zárate y la Hoz [. . .]* (Madrid: n.pub., 1652 [1662])

1662 *Fonseca April 1662*: *Academia que se celebró en veinte y tres de abril, en casa de Don Melchor de Fonseca de Almeida. Siendo Presidente Don Luis Antonio de Oviedo y Herrera. Secretario Don Fermín de Sarasa. Y Fiscal Don Luis Nieto* (Madrid: n.pub., 1662)

1663 *Fonseca Feb 1663*: *Academia que se celebró en casa de Don Melchor de Fonseca de Almeida, en cuatro de Febrero, siendo Presidente él mismo, Secretario Don Juan de Montenegro y Neira, y Fiscal Don José Berné de la Fuente, Aposentador de su Majestad, en la Real Junta de Aposento* (Madrid: Francisco Nieto, 1663)

1664 *Festiva academia, celebridad poética, en que fue presidente Don Juan de Trillo y Figueroa. Secretario Don Francisco Velázquez de Carvajal [. . .] Aplaudióse en casa de Don Rodrigo Velázquez de Carvajal [. . .] en 12 de febrero de 1664* (Granada: Baltasar de Bolibar, 1664)

1667 *Seville*: *Academia que se celebró en Sevilla, jueves diecisiete de febrero de 1667 años, en festejo de las Carnestolendas. Presidióla Don Cristóbal Bañes de Salcedo. Siendo Secretario Don Fernando de la Torre Farfán. En casa de D. Jerónimo de Texada y Aldrete, y de Don Nicolás Riser Barba de la Cueva* (Seville: Lucas Antonio de Bedmar, n.d.)

1669 *Real academia*: *Real academia, celebrada en el Real de Valencia, palacio de las S.S. C.C. M.M. de los S.S. Reyes de Aragón (de gloriosa memoria) y hoy participada habitación a los virreyes de su nobilísimo reino. Siéndolo el excelentísimo señor don Vespasiano Gonzaga, Conde de Paredes [. . .] A los años de Carlos Segundo [. . .] en el día 6 de noviembre, venturosísimo por cumplirse en él. Siendo presidentes y protectores las S.S. C.C. R.R. y A.A. M.M. de los S.S. R.R. Carlos y Mariana, en las asistentes luces de su sombra, en la venerada asistencia de sus retratos. Secretarios para la introducción, Don Onofre Vicente de Híjar,*

&c. Conde de la Alcudia y Gestalgar, &c. Y para el vejamen Don Francisco de la Torre, Caballero del hábito de Calatrava [. . .] (Valencia: Jerónimo Vilagrasa, 1669)

1672 *Jamaica*: *Academia con que el Exmo. Señor Marqués de Jamaica celebró los felices años de su Maj. la Reina N. Señora D. María Ana de Austria, el día 22 de diciembre de 1672. Que presidió Don Diego de Contreras [. . .], siendo fiscal D. José de Montoro, y secretario D. José de Trejo* (Cadiz: Juan Vejarano, 1673)

1674 *Pascua de Reyes*: *Academia que se celebró en día de Pascua de Reyes, siendo presidente Don Melchor Fernández de León. Secretario Don Francisco de Barrio, y Fiscal Don Manuel García de Bustamente. Año M.DC.LXX.IIII* (n.p., n.pub., n.d.)

1675 *Carnestolendas*: *Academia que se celebró por Carnestolendas, jueves 21 de febrero de este año de 1675 en casa del licenciado D. Gabriel de Campos, abogado de los Reales Consejos, que fue presidente de ella. Secretario Don Francisco Bueno; y fiscal el Lic. D. Manuel de Flores Vélez [. . .]* (Madrid: Lucas Antonio de Bedmar, n.d.)

1678 *Real Aduana*: *Academia que se celebró en la Real Aduana desta Corte. Siendo Presidente Don Melchor Fernández de León, Secretario Don Manuel Ochoa, y Fiscal Don Antonio Saravia. Año de 1678* (Madrid: Imp. del Reino, n.d.)

1678 *Ciudad Real*: *Academia que se celebró en la ciudad de Ciudad Real; siendo Presidente el licenciado Don Martín de la Vera Cimbrón, Corregidor de dicha Ciudad, Secretario Don Juan Manuel Ruiz Pardo, Fiscal el licenciado Don Andrés Romo de Ontova, día primero de mayo de 1678* (n.p., n.pub., n.d.)

———, *Academia que se celebró en la ciudad de Ciudad Real en 1678*, ed. by Juan Manuel Rozas (Ciudad Real: Instituto de Estudios Manchegos, 1965)

1679 *Academia, que se celebró en esta Corte, en amante jubilo, y vasalla demonstración de los desposorios de sus Majestades (que Dios guarde) el Rey nuestro Señor Don Carlos Segundo con la Reina nuestra Señora Doña María Luisa de Borbón, el mes de noviembre de mil seiscientos y setenta y nueve* (Madrid: Andrés García de la Iglesia, n.d.)

1681 *Academia que se celebró a los años de la Reina madre nuestra señora el día 22 de Diciembre de mil seiscientos y ochenta y uno, en casa de Don Agustín de Campo, Sumiller de S.M., por sus criados* (n.p., n.pub., 1681)

1684 *Badajoz*: *Academia que se celebró en Badajoz, en casa de Don Manuel de Meneses y Moscoso, Caballero de la Orden de Calatrava, siendo Presidente D. Gómez de la Rocha y Figueroa [. . .] Secretario Don Manuel Zavala [. . .] Fiscal [. . .] Don Francisco Féliz de Vega y Cruzat* (Madrid: Julián de Paredes, 1684)

1685 *Católica acción*: *Academia, a que dio asunto la religiosa y católica acción que el Rey nuestro señor (Dios le guarde) ejecutó el día 20 de enero deste año de 1685, encontrando un sacerdote en el campo, que llevaba el Viático a un enfermo a quien acompañó a pie, haciéndole entrar en su coche hasta la iglesia de San Marcos. Celebróse el día 3 de febrero en casa de Don Pedro de Arce [. . .] Fue Presidente D. Andrés Sánchez de Villamayor [. . .] Secretario Don Manuel de Ochoa. Fiscal*

Don Marcos de Lanuza Mendoza y Arellano [. . .]. Segunda impresión, añadida y enmendada por sus autores de los yerros de la primera (n.p., n.pub., n.d.)

1685 *Valencia, Real Palacio: Academia que se celebró en la ciudad de Valencia, en la Alcaidía del Real Palacio, casa de don Luis Juan de Torres y Centellas, Conde de Peñalba [. . .] Siendo Secretario don Francisco Figuerola. Fiscal don José Ortí. En 5 de Febrero 1685* (Valencia: Vicente Cabrera, 1685)

1691 *Poética festiva: Poética festiva celebridad a los años y nombre de Carlos II Rey de las Españas. Ejecutada en la Casa de la Diputación del Reino de Valencia, el día 4 de Novembre 1691. Presidente Don Antonio Ladrón de Pallas. Fiscal Don José Ortí. Secretario Don Fancisco Figuerola. Conságrala al Rey nuestro señor, que Dios guarde, la Academia de Valencia. Por manos del exc. señor Marqués de Castel-Rodrigo [. . .]* (Valencia: Francisco Mestre, 1691)

1698 *Señoras:* José Ortí y Morales, *Academia de las señoras (1698)*, ed. by Pasqual Mas i Usó (Kassel: Reichenberger, 1994)

OTHER PRIMARY SOURCES

Acuña, Hernando de, *Varias poesías*, ed. by Luis F. Díaz Larios (Madrid: Cátedra, 1982)

Aguilar, Gaspar, *Rimas humanas y divinas*, ed. by Francisco de A. Carreras de Calatayud (Valencia: Diputación Provincial de Valencia, 1951)

Alfay, Josef (ed.), *Poesías varias de grandes ingenios españoles recogidas por Josef Alfay*, ed. by José Manuel Blecua (Zaragoza: CSIC, 1946)

Alonso, Alvaro (ed.), *Poesía de Cancionero*, 2nd edn (Madrid: Cátedra, 1991)

Alvares Soares, Antonio, *Rimas varias* (Lisbon: Mattheus Pinheiro, 1628)

Alzieu, Pierre, Robert Jammes, and Yvan Lissorgues, *Poesía erótica del siglo de oro*, 2nd edn (Barcelona: Editorial Crítica, 1984)

Avilés, Miguel (ed.), *Sueños ficticios y lucha ideológica en el siglo de oro* (Madrid: Editora Nacional, 1981)

Baena, Juan Alfonso de, *Cancionero de Juan Alfonso de Baena*, ed. by José María Azaceta, 3 vols (Madrid: CSIC, 1966)

Bances Candamo, Francisco, *Theatro de los theatros de los passados y presentes siglos*, ed. by Duncan W. Moir (London: Tamesis, 1970)

Blecua, José Manuel (ed.), *Cancionero de 1628* (Madrid: CSIC, 1945)

——, *La poesía aragonesa del barroco*, ed. by José Manuel Blecua (Zaragoza: Nueva Biblioteca de Autores Aragoneses, 1980)

—— (ed.), *Poesía de la edad de oro, II, Barroco* (Madrid: Castalia, 1985)

Bocángel y Unzueta, Gabriel, *Obras*, ed. by Rafael Benítez Claros, 2 vols (Madrid: CSIC, 1946)

——, *La lira de las musas*, ed. by Trevor J. Dadson (Madrid: Cátedra, 1985)

Boccaccio, Giovanni, *Filocolo*, ed. by Mario Marti (Milan: Rizzoli Editore, 1969)

Bonilla, Alonso de, *Nuevo jardín de flores divinas, en que se hallará variedad de pensamientos peregrinos* (Baeza: Pedro de la Cuesta, 1617)

Borja y Aragón, Francisco de, Prince of Esquilache, *Obras en verso* (Antwerp: Baltasar Moreto, 1663)
Boscán de Almogáver, Juan, *Obras*, ed. by Carlos Clavería (Barcelona: PPU, 1991)
Calderón de la Barca, Pedro, *Obras completas*, ed. by A. Valbuena Briones, 3 vols, vol. 1, *Dramas*, 5th edn (Madrid: Aguilar, 1966)
Camerino, José, *La dama beata* (Madrid: Pablo de Val, 1655)
Cáncer y Velasco, Jerónimo, *Obras varias poéticas* (Madrid: Manuel Martín, 1761)
Carreira, Antonio (ed.), *Nuevos poemas atribuidos a Góngora* (Barcelona: Quaderns Crema, 1994)
Carrillo y Sotomayor, Luis de, *Obras*, ed. by Rosa Navarro Durán (Madrid: Castalia, 1990)
Casas, Elena (ed.), *La retórica en España* (Madrid: Editora Nacional, 1980)
Castillo Solórzano, Alonso de, *"Las harpías en Madrid" y "Tiempo de regocijo"*, ed. by Emilio Cotarelo y Mori (Madrid: Librería de los Bibliófilos Españoles, 1907)
——, *Las harpías en Madrid*, ed. by Pablo Jauralde Pou (Madrid: Castalia, 1985)
Castro, Adolfo de (ed.), *Poetas líricos de los siglos XVI y XVII*, 2 vols, vols 32 and 42 of the Biblioteca de Autores Españoles (Madrid: Ediciones Atlas, 1951)
Cervantes, Miguel de, *El ingenioso hidalgo don Quijote de la Mancha*, ed. by Luis Andrés Murillo, 2 vols, 5th edn (Madrid: Castalia, 1987)
Cetina, Gutierre de, *Sonetos y madrigales completos*, ed. by Begoña López Bueno (Madrid: Cátedra, 1981)
Colodrero de Villalobos, Miguel, *Varias rimas* (Córdoba: Salvador de Cea Tesa, 1629)
——, *El Alpheo, y otros asuntos en verso, ejemplares algunos* (Barcelona: Sebastián y Jaime Matevad, 1639)
Corral, Gabriel de, *La Cintia de Aranjuez*, ed. by Joaquín de Entrambasaguas (Madrid: CSIC, 1945)
Covarrubias, Sebastián de, *Tesoro de la lengua castellana o española*, ed. by Martín de Riquer, 2nd edn (Barcelona: Editorial Alta Fulla, 1989)
Covarrubias y Leyva, Diego de (ed.), *Elogios al Palacio Real del Buen Retiro. Escritos por algunos ingenios de España. Recogidos por Don Diego de Covarrubias y Leyva* (Madrid: Imprenta del Reino, 1635)
Cubillo de Aragón, Alvaro, *El enano de las Musas* (Madrid: María de Quiñones, 1654)
Dadson, Trevor J. (ed.), *"Avisos a un cortesano": An Anthology of Spanish Seventeenth-Century Moral-Political Poetry* (Exeter: University of Exeter, 1985)
Díez y Foncalda, Alberto, *Poesías varias* (Zaragoza: Juan de Ibar, 1653)
Duque de Estrada, Diego, *Comentarios del desengañado de sí mismo. Vida del mismo autor*, ed. by Henry Ettinghausen (Madrid: Castalia, 1982)
Enríquez Gómez, Antonio, *Academias morales de las musas* (Bordeaux: Pedro de la Court, 1642)

———, *El siglo pitagórico y Vida de don Gregorio Guadaña*, ed. by Teresa de Santos (Madrid: Cátedra, 1991)

Faria y Sousa, Manuel de, *Fuente de Aganipe, o rimas varias* (Madrid: Carlos Sánchez Bravo, 1646)

———, *Noches claras, divinas y humanas flores* (Lisbon: Antonio Craesbeeck de Mello, 1674)

Ferrero, Giuseppe Guido (ed.), *Marino e i Marinisti* (Milan and Naples: Riccardo Ricciardi, 1954)

Francia y Acosta, Francisco de, *Jardín de Apolo* (Madrid: Juan González, 1624)

Garcilaso de la Vega, *Garcilaso y sus comentaristas*, ed. by Antonio Gallego Morell, 2nd edn (Madrid: Gredos, 1972)

———, *Obras completas*, ed. by Elias L. Rivers (Madrid: Castalia, 1974)

Góngora y Argote, Luis de, *Obras completas*, ed. by Juan and Isabel Millé y Giménez, 3rd edn (Madrid: Aguilar, 1951)

———, *Romances*, ed. by Antonio Carreño, 3rd edn (Madrid: Cátedra, 1988)

———, *Sonetos completos*, ed. by Biruté Ciplijauskaité, 6th edn (Madrid: Castalia, 1990)

Gracián, Baltasar, *Agudeza y arte de ingenio*, ed. by Evaristo Correa Calderón, 2 vols (Madrid: Castalia, 1969)

Herrera, Fernando de, *Poesía castellana original completa*, ed. by Cristóbal Cuevas (Madrid: Cátedra, 1985)

Hurtado de Mendoza y Larrea, Antonio, *Obras poéticas*, ed. by Rafael Benítez Claros, 3 vols (Madrid: RAE, 1947–48)

Lazarraga, Fray Cristóbal de, *Fiestas de la Universidad de Salamanca al nacimiento del Príncipe Don Baltasar Carlos Domingo, Felipe V Nuestro Señor . . . Refiérelas por orden de la Universidad . . . el maestro Fray Cristóbal de Lazarraga* (Salamanca: Jacinto Tabernier, 1630)

Leonardo de Argensola, Lupercio and Bartolomé, *Rimas*, ed. by José Manuel Blecua, 2 vols (Zaragoza: CSIC, 1950–51)

López de Zárate, Francisco, *Obras varias*, ed. by José Simón Díaz, 2 vols (Madrid: CSIC, 1947)

———, *Sesenta y seis poemas inéditos*, ed. by José Simón Díaz (Logroño: Editorial Gonzalo de Berceo, 1976)

Marino, Giambattista, *Poesie varie*, ed. by Benedetto Croce (Bari: Gius. Laterza, 1913)

Martial, M. *Valerii Martialis epigrammaton libri omnes, novis commentariis . . . a Matthaeo Radero* (Ingolstadt: Adam Sartorius, 1602)

Medrano, Sebastián Francisco de, *Favores de las musas* (Milan: Juan Baptista Malatesta, 1631)

Moncayo y Gurrea, Juan de, *Rimas*, ed. by Aurora Egido (Madrid: Espasa-Calpe, 1976)

Montoro, Antón de, *Cancionero*, ed. by Emilio Cotarelo y Mori (Madrid: José Perales y Martínez, 1900)

Navarro, Ana (ed.), *Antología poética de escritoras de los siglos XVI y XVII* (Madrid: Castalia, 1989)

Navarro, José, *Poesías varias* (Zaragoza: Miguel de Luna, 1654)

Ovando y Santarén, Juan de, *Ocios de Castalia en diversos poemas*, ed. by Cristóbal Cuevas García (Málaga: Diputación Provincial de Málaga, 1987)

Pantaleón de Ribera, Anastasio, *Obras*, ed. by Rafael de Balbín Lucas, 2 vols (Madrid: CSIC, 1944)
Paravicino y Arteaga, Hortensio Félix, *Obras póstumas, divinas y humanas* (Madrid: María Fernández, 1650)
Paz y Melia, Antonio (ed.), *Sales españoles, o Agudezas del ingenio nacional*, 2nd edn, ed. by Ramón Pez, vol. 176 of the Biblioteca de Autores Españoles (Madrid: Ediciones Atlas, 1964)
Pellicer de Tovar, José (ed.), *Anfiteatro de Felipe el Grande, Rey Católico de las Españas . . . Contiene los elogios que han celebrado la suerte que hizo en el toro en la fiesta agonal de trece de octubre, deste año de M.DC.XXXI* (Madrid: Juan González, 1631)
——— (ed.), *Anfiteatro de Felipe el Grande*, ed. by Antonio Pérez Gómez (Cieza: Ediciones de la Fonte que mana y corre, 1974)
Pérez de Montalbán, Juan, *Para todos. Ejemplos morales, humanos y divinos. En que se tratan diversas ciencias, materias y facultades. Repartidos en los siete días de la semana, y dirigidos a diferentes personas, y con algunas adiciones nuevas en esta sexta impresión* (Madrid: Antonio Duplastre, 1640)
Petrarca, Francesco, *Rime*, ed. by Guido Bezzola, 2nd edn (Milan: Rizzoli Editore, 1985)
Polo de Medina, Salvador Jacinto, *Obras escogidas*, ed. by José María de Cossío (Madrid: Clásicos Olvidados, 1931)
———, *Poesía. Hospital de incurables*, ed. by Francisco J. Díez de Revenga (Madrid: Cátedra, 1987)
Quevedo y Villegas, Francisco de, *Obra poética*, ed. by José Manuel Blecua, 4 vols (Madrid: Castalia, 1969–81)
———, *Poesía original completa*, ed. by José Manuel Blecua, 2nd edn (Barcelona: Planeta, 1983)
———, *Poems to Lisi*, ed. by D. Gareth Walters (Exeter: University of Exeter, 1988)
———, *Sueños*, ed. by Ignacio Arellano (Madrid: Cátedra, 1991)
Quirós, Pedro de, *Poesías divinas y humanas*, ed. by M. Menéndez Pidal (Seville: Sociedad del Archivo Hispalense, 1887)
Relación de las exequias que en la muerte del rey nuestro señor don Felipe Cuarto el Grande, rey de Españas, y emperador de las Indias hizo la Universidad de Oviedo en el Principado de Asturias. Ofrécela en la real mano de la reina nuestra señora doña María Ana de Austria (Madrid: Pablo de Val, 1666)
Rioja, Francisco de, *Poesía*, ed. by Begoña López Bueno (Madrid: Cátedra, 1984)
Rodríguez-Moñino, Antonio (ed.), *Segunda parte del cancionero general. Agora nuevamente copilado de la mas gracioso y discreto de muchos afamados trovadores* (Oxford: The Dolphin Book Co., 1956; facsimile of Zaragoza 1552 edn)
Rodríguez Puértolas, Julio (ed.), *Poesía crítica y satírica del siglo XV* (Madrid: Castalia, 1981)
Rodríguez de Monforte, Pedro, *Descripción de las honras que se hicieron a la católica majestad de don Felipe cuarto, rey de las Españas y del nuevo mundo en el Real Convento de la Encarnación, que de orden de la reina nuestra señora como superintendente de las Reales Obras dispuso D. Baltasar Barroso de Ribera, Marqués de Malpica* (Madrid: Francisco Nieto, 1666)

Roys, Francisco de, *Pira real, que erigió la mayor Atenas a la mayor majestad; la Universidad de Salamanca, a las inmortales cenizas, a la gloriosa memoria de su rey y señor don Felipe el Grande* (Salamanca: Melchor Estevez, 1666)

Saavedra y Guzmán, Martín, *Ocios de Aganipe, divididos en diferentes poesías* (Trani: Lorenzo Valerii, 1634)

Salas Barbadillo, Alonso Jerónimo de, *Rimas castellanas* (Madrid: Viuda de Alonso Martín, 1618)

Salazar y Torres, Agustín de, *Cítara de Apolo, varias poesías divinas y humanas. Primera parte* (Madrid: Antonio González de Reyes, 1694)

Salcedo Coronel, García de, *Cristales de Helicona* (Madrid: Diego Díaz de la Carrera, 1650)

Salinas, Juan de, *Poesías humanas*, ed. by Henry Bonneville (Madrid: Castalia, 1987)

Sarbiewski, Maciej Kazimierz, *Wyklady Poetyki (Praecepta Poetica)*, ed. by Stanislaw Skimina (Cracow: Biblioteka Pisarzów Polskich, 1958)

Scaliger, Julius Caesar, *Poetices libri septem* (Stuttgart: Friedrich Frommann, 1964; facsimile of 1561 Lyons edn)

Shakespeare, William, *The Sonnets and A Lover's Complaint*, ed. by John Kerrigan (Harmondsworth: Penguin, 1986)

Silva y Mendoza, Diego de, Count of Salinas, *Antología poética 1564–1630*, ed. by T. J. Dadson (Madrid: Visor, 1985)

Simón Díaz, José (ed.), *Textos dispersos de autores españoles. 1: Impresos del Siglo de Oro* (Madrid: CSIC, 1978)

Solís y Ribadeneyra, Antonio de, *Varias poesías sagradas y profanas*, ed. by Manuela Sánchez Regueira (Madrid: CSIC, 1968)

Soto de Rojas, Pedro, *Obras*, ed. by Antonio Gallego Morell (Madrid: CSIC, 1950)

Suárez de Figueroa, Cristóbal, *El pasajero*, ed. by María Isabel López Bascuñana, 2 vols (Barcelona: PPU, 1988)

Tassis y Peralta, Juan de, Count of Villamediana, *Poesía impresa completa*, ed. by José Francisco Ruiz Casanova (Madrid: Cátedra, 1990)

———, *Poesía inédita completa*, ed. by José Francisco Ruiz Casanova (Madrid: Cátedra, 1994)

Tasso, Torquato, *Poesie*, ed. by Francesco Flora (Milan and Naples: Riccardo Ricciardi, 1952)

Tesauro, Emmanuele, *Il cannocchiale aristotelico* (Bad Homburg: Gehlen, 1968; facsimile of 1670 Turin edn)

Tirso de Molina, *Comedias*, ed. by Emilio Cotarelo y Mori, vol. 1 (Madrid: Bailly-Baillière e Hijos, 1906)

Torre y Sevil, Francisco de la, *Entretenimiento de las musas en esta baraja nueva de versos. Dividida en cuatro manjares, de asuntos sacros, heroicos, líricos y burlescos* (Zaragoza: Juan de Ibar, 1654)

———, *Entretenimiento de las musas*, ed. by Manuel Alvar (Valencia: Universitat de València, 1987)

Trillo y Figueroa, Francisco de, *Obras*, ed. by Antonio Gallego Morell (Madrid: CSIC, 1951)

Ulloa Pereira, Luis de, *Obras*, ed. by Juan Antonio de Ulloa Pereira (Madrid: Francisco Sanz, 1674)

Valeria, Gaspar Alonso de, *Engaños desengañados a la luz de la verdad. Poesías sacras, místicas, morales y fúnebres, escritas con la clara tinta del santo desengaño. Añádense también algunas obras, que estándose imprimiendo las sobredichas, llegaron a manos del impresor y ha sabido que son de don Manuel García Bustamente* (Naples: Carlos Porfile, 1681)

Vega Carpio, Lope de, *Justa poética y alabanzas justas que hizo la insigne villa de Madrid al bienaventurado San Isidro en las fiestas de su beatificación* (Madrid: Viuda de A. Martín, 1620)

———, *Relación de las fiestas que la insigne villa de Madrid hizo en la canonización de su bienaventurado hijo y patrón, con las comedias que se representaron y los versos que en la justa poética se escribieron* (Madrid: Viuda de A. Martín, 1622)

———, *Obras escogidas*, 2 vols, ed. by Federico Carlos Sainz de Robles (Madrid: Aguilar, 1946)

———, *Obras poéticas*, ed. by José Manuel Blecua (Barcelona: Planeta, 1983)

———, *Poesía selecta*, ed. by Antonio Carreño (Madrid: Cátedra, 1984)

———, *Cartas*, ed. by Nicolás Marín (Madrid: Castalia, 1985)

Vélez de Guevara, Juan, *Los celos hacen estrellas*, ed. by J. E. Varey and N. D. Shergold (London: Tamesis, 1970)

Vélez de Guevara, Luis, *El diablo cojuelo*, ed. by Adolfo Bonilla y San Martín (Vigo: Eugenio Krapf, 1902)

———, *El diablo cojuelo*, ed. by Angel R. Fernández and Ignacio Arellano (Madrid: Castalia, 1988)

Vergara Salcedo, Sebastián Ventura de, *Ideas de Apolo y dignas tareas del ocio cortesano* (Madrid: Andrés García, 1663)

Zabaleta, Juan de, *El día de fiesta por la mañana y por la tarde*, ed. by Cristóbal Cuevas García (Madrid: Castalia, 1983)

SECONDARY SOURCES

Alvar, Manuel, "Dos notas sobre don Francisco de la Torre y Sevil", in *Teatro del Siglo de Oro. Homenaje a Alberto Navarro González* (Kassel: Reichenberger, 1990), pp. 1–3

Amadei-Pulice, María Alicia, *Calderón y el barroco. Exaltación y engaño de los sentidos* (Amsterdam, Philadelphia: John Benjamins Publishing Company, 1990)

Arco y Garay, Ricardo del, *La erudición española en el siglo XVII y el cronista de Aragón Andrés de Uztarroz*, 2 vols (Madrid: CSIC, 1950)

Bacon, George W., "The *comedias* of Doctor Juan Pérez de Montalbán", *RH*, 17 (1907), 46–65

———, "The Life and Dramatic Works of Doctor Juan Pérez de Montalbán (1602–1638)", *RH*, 26 (1912), 1–320, 321–474

Barella, Julia, "Bibliografía: Academias literarias", *Edad de Oro*, 7 (1988), 189–95

Barnard, Mary E., "Garcilaso's Poetics of Subversion and the Orphean Tapestry", *PMLA*, 102 (1987), 316–23

Barrera y Leirado, Cayetano Alberto de la, *Catálogo bibliográfico y biográfico del teatro antiguo español desde sus orígenes hasta mediados del siglo XVIII* (London: Tamesis, 1968; facsimile of Madrid 1860 edn)

Bergman, Hannah E., "A Court Entertainment of 1638", *HR*, 42 (1974), 67–81

———, "El «Juicio final de todos los poetas españoles muertos y vivos» (MS inédito) y el Certamen poético de 1638", *BRAE*, 55 (1975), 551–610

Blanco, Mercedes, "La oralidad en las justas poéticas", *Edad de Oro*, 7 (1988), 33–47

Blecua, José Manuel, *Sobre la poesía de la Edad de Oro. (Ensayos y notas eruditas)* (Madrid: Gredos, 1970)

———, "El vejamen segundo de Anastasio Pantaleón de Ribera", in *The Two Hesperias. Literary Studies in Honour of Joseph G. Fucilla on the Occasion of his 80th Birthday*, ed. by Américo Bugliani (Madrid: José Porrúa Turanzas, 1977), pp. 55–67

Brand, C. P., *Torquato Tasso: A Study of the Poet and his Contribution to English Literature* (Cambridge: Cambridge University Press, 1965)

Brown, Gary J., "Fernando de Herrera and Lorenzo de' Medici: The Sonnet as Epigram", *RF*, 87 (1975), 226–38

———, "Lope de Vega's Epigrammatic Poetic for the Sonnet", *MLN*, 93 (1978), 218–32

Brown, Jonathan, *Images and Ideas in Seventeenth-Century Spanish Painting* (Princeton: Princeton University Press, 1978)

———, and J. H. Elliott, *A Palace for a King. The Buen Retiro and the Court of Philip IV* (New Haven and London: Yale University Press, 1980)

———, *Velázquez. Painter and Courtier* (New Haven and London: Yale University Press, 1986)

Brown, Kenneth, *Anastasio Pantaleón de Ribera (1600–1629). Ingenioso miembro de la república literaria española* (Madrid: José Porrúa Turanzas, 1980)

———, "Gabriel de Corral: sus contertulios y un MS poético de academia inédito", *Castilla*, 4 (1982), 9–56

———, "El cancionero erótico de Pedro Méndez de Loyola: parte segunda del «Gabriel de Corral: sus contertulios y un MS poético de academia inédito»", *Castilla*, 11 (1986), 57–80

Caro Baroja, Julio, *Ensayo sobre la literatura de cordel* (Madrid: Ediciones Istmo, 1990)

Carrasco Urgoiti, María Soledad, "Notas sobre el vejamen de academia en la segunda mitad del siglo XVII", *RHM*, 31 (1965), 97–111

———, "La oralidad del vejamen de academia", *Edad de Oro*, 7 (1988), 49–57

Carreño, Antonio, "Amor 'regalado' / amor 'ofendido': las ficciones del yo lírico en las *Rimas* (1609) de Lope de Vega", in *Hispanic Studies in Honour of Geoffrey Ribbans*, ed. by Ann L. Mackenzie and Dorothy S. Severin (Liverpool: Liverpool University Press, 1992), pp. 73–82

Carrete Parrondo, Juan, "Estampas fantásticas: Imágenes y descripciones de monstruos", in *Art and Literature in Spain: 1600–1800. Studies in Honour of Nigel Glendinning*, ed. by Charles Davis and Paul Julian Smith (London: Tamesis, 1993), pp. 55–67

Casalduero, Joaquín, "Parodia de una cuestión de amor y queja de las fregonas", *RFE*, 19 (1932), 181–87

Casey, James, *The Kingdom of Valencia in the Seventeenth Century* (Cambridge: Cambridge University Press, 1979)
Chicharro Chamorro, Antonio, "En torno a una oración académica de Soto de Rojas: el 'Discurso sobre la poética' ", in *Al Ave el Vuelo. Estudios sobre la obra de Soto de Rojas* (Granada: Universidad de Granada, 1984), pp. 13–31
Cochrane, Eric, *Tradition and Enlightenment in the Tuscan Academies 1690–1800* (Rome: Edizioni di Storia e Letteratura, 1961)
———, "The Renaissance Academies in their Italian and European Setting", in *The Fairest Flower: The Emergence of Linguistic National Consciousness in Renaissance Europe* (Florence: Presso l'Accademia, 1985), pp. 21–39
Cotarelo y Mori, Emilio, "Luis Vélez de Guevara y sus obras dramáticas", *BRAE*, 3 (1916), 621–52
———, "Don Antonio Coello y Ochoa", *BRAE*, 5 (1918), 550–600
———, "Los hermanos Figueroa y Córdoba", *BRAE*, 6 (1919), 149–91
Crawford Volk, Mary, "New Light on a Seventeenth-Century Collector: The Marquis of Leganés", *AB*, 62 (1980), 256–68
Cruickshank, D. W., "A Contemporary of Calderón", *MLR*, 63 (1968), 864–68
———, " 'Literature' and the Book Trade in Golden Age Spain", *MLR*, 73 (1978), 799–824
Cruz, Anne J., *Imitación y transformación. El petrarquismo en la poesía de Boscán y Garcilaso de la Vega* (Amsterdam, Philadelphia: John Benjamins Publishing Company, 1988)
Cummins, John G., "Methods and Conventions in the 15th-Century Poetic Debate", *HR*, 31 (1963), 307–23
———, "The Survival in the Spanish *cancioneros* of the Form and Themes of Provençal and Old French Poetic Debates", *BHS*, 42 (1965), 9–17
Dadson, Trevor J., *The Genoese in Spain: Gabriel Bocángel y Unzueta (1603–1658), A Biography* (London: Tamesis, 1983)
———, "Dos autógrafos desconocidos de Gabriel Bocángel", *El Crotalón. Anuario de filología española*, 2 (1985), 275–98
———, "El Conde de Salinas y la poesía cancioneril", in *Actas del Congreso Internacional sobre literatura hispánica en la época de los Reyes Católicos y el descubrimiento* (Barcelona: PPU, 1989), pp. 270–78
———, "La psicología del amor en los sonetos a Filis de Bocángel", in *Actas del X Congreso de la Asociación Internacional de Hispanistas*, ed. by Antonio Vilanova, 4 vols (Barcelona: PPU, 1992), I, pp. 863–71
———, "Trayectoría de la poesía barroca", in *Historia y crítica de la literatura española. 3/1 Siglos de oro: Barroco. Primer suplemento*, ed. by Aurora Egido et al (Barcelona: Editorial Crítica, 1992), pp. 345–63
———, "La poesía amorosa de los Condes de Salinas y Villamediana: ¿un diálogo subtextual?", in *Estado actual de los estudios sobre el Siglo de Oro. Actas del II Congreso Internacional de Hispanistas del Siglo de Oro*, ed. by Manuel García Martín, et al. (Salamanca: Ediciones Universidad de Salamanca, 1993), pp. 269–77
Davies, Gareth A., *A Poet at Court. Antonio Hurtado de Mendoza (1586–1644)* (Oxford: The Dolphin Book Co., 1971)
———, " 'Pintura': Background and Sketch of a Spanish Seventeenth-Century Court Genre", *JWCI*, 38 (1975), 288–313

Delgado, Juan, "Bibliografía sobre justas poéticas", *Edad de Oro*, 7 (1988), 197–207

Dixon, Victor, "Juan Pérez de Montalbán's *Segundo tomo de las comedias*", *HR*, 29 (1961), 91–109

———, "Juan Pérez de Montalbán's *Para todos*", *HR*, 32 (1964), 36–59

Domínguez de Paz, Elisa, "Problemas documentales para el estudio de la vida y de la obra de Juan de la Hoz y Mota", in *Teatro y vida teatral en el Siglo de Oro a través de las fuentes documentales*, ed. by Luciano García Lorenzo y J. E. Varey (London: Tamesis, 1991), pp. 317–26

Dowling, John, "La farsa al servicio del naciente siglo de las luces: *El hechizado por fuerza* (1697), de Antonio de Zamora", in *El teatro español a fines del siglo XVII. Historia, cultura y teatro en la España de Carlos II*, 3 vols, vol. 2, *Dramaturgos y géneros de las postrimerías*, ed. by Javier Huerta Calvo, Harm den Boer, Fermín Sierra Martínez (Amsterdam, Atlanta: Rodopi, 1989), pp. 275–86

Dunn, Peter N., *Castillo Solórzano and the Decline of the Spanish Novel* (Oxford: Blackwell, 1952)

Egido, Aurora, "Los modelos en las justas poéticas aragonesas del siglo XVII", *RFE*, 60 (1978–80), 159–71

———, *"Retratos de los reyes de Aragón" de Andrés Uztarroz y otros poemas de academia* (Zaragoza: Institución Fernando el Católico, 1983)

———, "Certámenes poéticas y arte efímero en la Universidad de Zaragoza (Siglos XVI y XVII)", in *Cinco estudios humanísticos para la Universidad de Zaragoza en su centenario IV*, ed. by Aurora Egido *et al* (Zaragoza: Caja de Ahorros de la Inmaculada, 1983), pp. 9–78

———, "Las academias literarias de Zaragoza en el siglo XVII", in *La literatura en Aragón*, ed. by M. Alvar (Zaragoza: Caja de Ahorros y Monte de Piedad de Zaragoza, Aragón y Rioja, 1984), pp. 101–28

———, "La enfermedad de amor en el *Desengaño* de Soto de Rojas", in *Al Ave el Vuelo. Estudios sobre la obra de Soto de Rojas* (Granada: Universidad de Granada, 1984), pp. 32–52

———, "De las academias a la Academia", in *The Fairest Flower: The Emergence of Linguistic National Consciousness in Renaissance Europe* (Florence: Presso l'Accademia, 1985), pp. 85–94

———, *Fronteras de la poesía en el barroco* (Barcelona: Editorial Crítica, 1990)

———, "Floresta de vejámenes universitarios granadinos", *BH*, 92 (1990), 309–32

———, "Descubrimientos y humanismo: el almirante aragonés don Pedro Porter y Casanate", *Edad de Oro*, 10 (1991), 71–86

Elliott, J. H., *The Count-Duke of Olivares. The Statesman in an Age of Decline*, 2nd edn (New Haven and London: Yale University Press, 1988)

———, "Una sociedad no revolucionaria: Castilla en la década de 1640", in *1640: La monarquía hispánica en crisis* (Barcelona: Editorial Crítica, 1992), pp. 102–22.

Entrambasaguas, Joaquín de, "Lope de Vega en las justas poéticas toledanas de 1605 y de 1608", *RL*, 32 (1967), 5–104, and 33 (1968), 5–52

Ettinghausen, Henry, "The News in Spain: *Relaciones de sucesos* in the Reigns of Philip III and IV", *EHQ*, 14 (1984), 1–20

———, "Sexo y violencia: noticias sensacionalistas en la prensa española del siglo XVII", *Edad de Oro*, 12 (1993), 95–107

———, "Prensa comparada: relaciones hispano-francesas en el siglo XVII", in *Estado actual de los estudios sobre el Siglo de Oro. Actas del II Congreso Internacional de Hispanistas del Siglo de Oro*, ed. by Manuel García Martín, et al (Salamanca: Ediciones Universidad de Salamanca, 1993), pp. 339–45

———, "The Illustrated Spanish News. Text and Image in the Seventeenth-Century Press", in *Art and Literature in Spain: 1600–1800. Studies in Honour of Nigel Glendinning*, ed. by Charles Davis and Paul Julian Smith (London: Tamesis, 1993), pp. 117–33

Ferrer Valls, Teresa, *La práctica escénica cortesana: de la época del Emperador a la de Felipe III* (London: Tamesis, 1991)

Forster, Leonard, *The Icy Fire. Five Studies in European Petrarchism* (Cambridge: Cambridge University Press, 1969)

Frenk, Margit, " 'Lectores y oidores'. La difusión oral de la literatura en el siglo de oro", in *Actas del séptimo congreso de la Asociación Internacional de Hispanistas*, ed. by Giuseppe Bellini, 2 vols (Rome: Bulzoni Editore, 1981), I, pp. 101–23

———, "La ortografía elocuente. (Testimonios de lectura oral en el Siglo de Oro)", in *Actas del VIII congreso de la Asociación Internacional de Hispanistas*, ed. by A. David Kossoff, José Amor y Vázquez, Ruth H. Kossoff and Geoffrey W. Ribbans, 3 vols (Madrid: Ediciones Istmo, 1986), I, pp. 549–56

Fucilla, Joseph G., *Relaciones hispanoitalianas* (Madrid: CSIC, 1953)

———, *Estudios sobre el petrarquismo en España* (Madrid: CSIC, 1969)

Gallego Morell, Antonio, *Francisco y Juan de Trillo y Figueroa* (Granada: Universidad de Granada, 1950)

Gil, Xavier, " 'Conservación' y 'defensa' como factores de estabilidad en tiempos de crisis: Aragón y Valencia en la década de 1640", in *1640: La monarquía hispánica en crisis* (Barcelona: Editorial Crítica, 1992), pp. 44–101

Giménez Fernández, Clara, "Poesía de academias (MSS. 1–4000)", *Manuscrt.Cao.*, 2 (1989), 47–55

González de Garay Fernández, María Teresa, *Introducción a la obra poética de Francisco López de Zárate* (Logroño: CSIC, 1981)

González Echevarría, Roberto, *Celestina's Brood: Continuities of the Baroque in Spanish and Latin American Literature* (Durham and London: Duke University Press, 1993)

Graf, E. C., "Forcing the Poetic Voice: Garcilaso de la Vega's Sonnet XXIX as a Deconstruction of the Idea of Harmony", *MLN*, 109 (1994), 163–85

Green, Otis, "The Literary Court of the Conde de Lemos at Naples, 1610–1616", *HR*, 1 (1933), 290–308

Greene, Thomas M., *The Light in Troy. Imitation and Discovery in Renaissance Poetry* (New Haven and London: Yale University Press, 1982)

———, "*Il Cortegiano* and the Choice of a Game", in *Castiglione. The Ideal and the Real in Renaissance Culture*, ed. by Robert W. Hannard and David Rosand (New Haven and London: Yale University Press, 1983), pp. 1–15

Griffin, Nigel, Review of *El día de fiesta por la mañana y por la tarde*, ed. by Cuevas García, *MLR*, 82 (1987), 1003–06

Hankins, James, "The Myth of the Platonic Academy of Florence", *RQ*, 44 (1991), 429–75

Hazañas y la Rúa, Joaquín, *Noticias de las academias literarias, artísticas y científicas de Sevilla en los siglos XVII y XVIII* (Seville: C. de Torre, 1888)

Heiple, Daniel L., *Garcilaso de la Vega and the Italian Renaissance* (University Park, Pennsylvania: Pennsylvania State University Press, 1994)

Howatson, M. C. (ed.), *The Oxford Companion to Classical Literature*, 2nd edn (Oxford: Oxford University Press, 1993)

Jammes, Robert, *Etudes sur l'oeuvre poétique de Don Luis de Góngora y Argote* (Bordeaux: Institut d'Etudes Ibériques et Ibéro-américaines de l'Université de Bordeaux, 1967)

Javitch, Daniel, *Poetry and Courtliness in Renaissance England* (Princeton: Princeton University Press, 1978)

Johnson, Caroll B., "Personal Involvement and Poetic Tradition in the Spanish Renaissance: Some Thoughts on Reading Garcilaso", *RR*, 90 (1989), 288–304

Jones, Harold G., " 'El hortelano del Prado': Tirso or Don Antonio Sigler de Huerta", *BCom*, 29 (1977), 25–27

Kagan, Richard L., *Students and Society in Early Modern Spain* (Baltimore: The Johns Hopkins University Press, 1974)

Kennedy, Ruth L., "*Escarramán* and Glimpses of the Spanish Court in 1637–38", *HR*, 9 (1941), 110–36

———, "Pantaleón de Ribera, 'Sirene', Castillo Solórzano, and the Academia de Madrid in Early 1625", in *Homage to John M. Hill. In Memoriam*, ed. by Walter Poesse (Bloomington: Indiana University Press, 1968), pp. 189–200

Kincaid, William A., "Life and Works of Luis de Belmonte Bermúdez (1587?–1650?)", *RH*, 74 (1928), 1–260

King, Willard, "The Academies and Seventeenth-Century Spanish Literature", *PMLA*, 75 (1960), 367–76

———, *Prosa novelística y academias literarias del Siglo de Oro español* (Madrid: RAE, 1963)

Lacadena y Calero, Esther, "El discurso oral en las academias del Siglo de Oro", *Criticón*, 41 (1988), 87–102

Lawrance, J. N. H., "On Fifteenth-Century Spanish Vernacular Humanism", in *Medieval and Renaissance Studies in Honour of Robert Brian Tate*, ed. by Ian Michael and Richard A. Cardwell (Oxford: Dolphin, 1986), pp. 63–79

le Gentil, Pierre, *La Poésie lyrique espagnole et portugaise à la fin du moyen âge*, 2 vols (Rennes: Plihon, 1949)

Lorch, Jennifer, "Petrarch and Petrarchism in Italy", *JIRS*, 2 (1992), 87–99

Lowry, Martin, "The Proving Ground: Venetian Academies of the Fifteenth and Sixteenth Centuries", in *The Fairest Flower: The Emergence of Linguistic National Consciousness in Renaissance Europe* (Florence: Presso l'Accademia, 1985), pp. 41–51

MacKay, Angus, *Spain in the Middle Ages. From Frontier to Empire, 1000–1500* (London: Macmillan, 1977)

Mackenzie, Ann L., *La escuela de Calderón. Estudio e investigación* (Liverpool: Liverpool University Press, 1993)

Madroñal Durán, Abraham, and Luciano López Gutiérrez, "Nuevos datos acerca de la personalidad y la obra del dramaturgo don Antonio Martínez de Meneses", *BRAE*, 67 (1987), 271–86

Márquez Villanueva, Francisco, "El retorno del Parnaso", *NRFH*, 38 (1990), 693–732

Mas i Usó, Pasqual, "El certamen valenciano a San Vicente Ferrer (1600) y la polémica entre Jaime Orts y Melchor Orta", *Rilce*, 7 (1991), 69–93

——, "Poetas bajo nombres de pastores en *El Prado de Valencia* de Gaspar Mercader", *RL*, 197 (1992), 283–334

——, "Academias ficticias valencianas durante el Barroco", *Criticón*, 61 (1994), 47–56

Maurer, Christopher, " 'Soñé que te ... ¿Dirélo?': El soneto del sueño erótico en los siglos XVI y XVII", *Edad de Oro*, 9 (1990), 149–67

May, T. E., *Wit of the Golden Age: Articles on Spanish Literature* (Kassel: Reichenberger, 1986)

Mazzotta, Giuseppe, *The Worlds of Petrarch* (Durham and London: Duke University Press, 1993)

Mirollo, James V., *The Poet of the Marvellous. Giambattista Marino* (New York and London: Columbia University Press, 1963)

Molho, Mauricio, "El soplo y la letra: Gabriel Bocángel ante sus escritos", *Edad de Oro*, 6 (1987), 189–99

Moll, Jaime, "Diez años sin licencias para imprimir comedias y novelas en los reinos de Castilla: 1625–1634", *BRAE*, 54 (1974), 97–103

Montañés, José Angel, "Las meninas comían barro", *Babelia* (Literary Supplement), *El País*, 2 May 1992, p. 10

Montesinos, José F., "Una cuestión de amor en comedias antiguas españoles", *RFE*, 13 (1926), 280–83

Navarrete, Ignacio, *Orphans of Petrarch: Poetry and Theory in the Spanish Renaissance* (Berkeley: University of California Press, 1994)

Neumeister, Sebastian, "Los retratos de los Reyes en la última comedia de Calderón (*Hado y divisa de Leonida y Marfisa*, Loa)", in *Hacia Calderón. Cuarto coloquio anglogermano*, ed. by Hans Flasche, Karl-Hermann Körner and Hans Mattauch (Berlin: Walter de Gruyter, 1979), pp. 83–91

O'Connor, Thomas Austin, "A Bibliographical Note on Salazar y Torres' *Cytara de Apolo*", *RN*, 15 (1973), 129–31

——, "Don Agustín de Salazar y Torres: a Bibliography of Primary Sources", *Bulletin of Bibliography and Magazine Notes*, 32 (1975), 158–61, 167–80

——, "On Dating the *comedias* of Agustín de Salazar y Torres: A Provisional Study", *Hispanófila*, 23 (1979), 158–61

Orozco Díaz, Emilio, *Lope y Góngora frente a frente* (Madrid: Gredos, 1973)

——, *Manierismo y barroco*, 4th edn (Madrid: Cátedra, 1988)

Orso, Steven N., *Art and Death at the Spanish Habsburg Court: The Royal Exequies for Philip IV* (Columbia: University of Missouri Press, 1989)

——, *Velázquez, "Los borrachos" and Painting at the Court of Philip IV* (Cambridge: Cambridge University Press, 1993)

Pacheco, Francisco, *El arte de la pintura*, ed. by Bonaventura Bassegoda i Hugas (Madrid: Cátedra, 1990)

Palau Claveras, Agustín, *Addenda & corrigenda o volumen complementario del tomo primero del "Manual del librero hispanoamericano" de Antonio Palau y Dulcet* (Empuries: Palacete Palau y Dulcet, 1990)

Pardo Manuel de Villena, Alfonso, *Un mecenas español del siglo XVII. El Conde de Lemos* (Madrid: J. Ratés Martín, 1911)

Parker, A. A., *Luis de Góngora: Polyphemus and Galatea. A Study in the Interpretation of a Baroque Poem*, verse trans. by Gilbert F. Cunningham (Edinburgh: Edinburgh University Press, 1977)

———, *The Philosophy of Love in Spanish Literature, 1480–1680*, ed. by Terence O'Reilly (Edinburgh: Edinburgh University Press, 1985)

Pedraza Jiménez, Felipe, "La parodia del petrarquismo en las *Rimas de Tomé de Burguillos* de Lope de Vega", in *Homenaje a Gonzalo Torrente Ballester* (Salamanca; n.pub., 1981), pp. 615–38

Pérez Priego, Miguel Angel, "Poetas toledanos del barroco: Baltasar Elisio de Medinilla", *AEF*, 9 (1986), 225–38

Pike, Ruth, "The *converso* Origins of the Sevillian Dramatist Diego Jiménez de Enciso", *BHS*, 67 (1990), 129–35

———, "Adding to the Biography of Diego Jiménez de Enciso", *BCom*, 43 (1991), 233–37

Porqueras Mayo, Antonio, *La teoría poética en el manierismo y barroco españoles* (Barcelona: Puvill Libros, 1989)

Portus Pérez, Javier, "La intervención de Lope de Vega y de Gómez de Mora en las fiestas de canonización de San Isidro", *Villa de Madrid*, 26 (1981), 30–41

Prieto, Antonio, *La poesía española del siglo XVI*, vol. II: *Aquel valor que respetó el olvido* (Madrid: Cátedra, 1987)

———, "El *Desengaño de amor en rimas* de Soto de Rojas como cancionero petrarquista", in *Serta Philologica F. Lázaro Carreter*, 2 vols (Madrid: Cátedra, 1983), II, pp. 403–12

Pring-Mill, Robert, " 'Porque yo cerca muriese': An Occasional Meditation on a *conceptista* Theme", *BHS*, 61 (1984), 369–78

Quiviger, François, "The Italian Academies of the Sixteenth Century", *BSRS*, 12 (1995), 13–19

Ramírez de Arellano y Gutiérrez de Salamanca, Carlos, *Ensayo de un catálogo biográfico-bibliográfico de los escritores que han sido individuos de las cuatro órdenes militares de España*, in *Colección de documentos inéditos para la historia de España*, vol. 109 (Vaduz: Kraus Reprint Ltd, 1966; reprint of Madrid 1898 edn)

Reckert, Stephen, *Beyond Chrysanthemums: Perspectives on Poetry East and West* (Oxford: Clarendon Press, 1993)

Riera Guilera, Carmen, "Un poeta inédito del s.XVII: Don Gabriel de Henao y Monjaraz", *BBMP*, 50 (1974), 137–76

Riley, E. C., *Cervantes's Theory of the Novel* (Oxford: Oxford University Press, 1962)

Rivers, Elias L., "La poesía culta y sus lectores", *Edad de Oro*, 12 (1993), 267–79

Robbins, J. M. W., "The Habsburgs and Hunting: Creating an Image of Philip IV", *JHP*, 17 (1993), 103–28

Rodríguez Cuadros, Evangelina (ed.), *De las academias a la enciclopedia: el discurso del saber en la modernidad* (Valencia: Institució Valenciana d'Estudis i Investigació, 1993)

Rodríguez Marín, Francisco, *Nuevos datos para las biografías de cien escritores de los siglos XVI y XVII* (Madrid: Revista de Archivos, Bibliotecas y Museos, 1923)

Rodríguez Sánchez de León, María José, "La academia literaria como fiesta barroca en tres ejemplos andaluces (1661, 1664 y 1672)", *Diálogos hispánicos de Amsterdam*, 8 (1989), 2 vols, II, 915–26

Romera-Navarro, Miguel, "Querellas y rivalidades en las academias del siglo XVII", *HR*, 9 (1941), 494–99

Rosales, Luis, *El sentimiento de desengaño en la poesía barroca* (Madrid: Ediciones Cultura Hispánica, 1966)

Rossi, Antonio, *Serafino Aquilano e la poesia cortigiana* (Brescia: Morcelliana, 1980).

Rozas, Juan Manuel, "Petrarca y Ausias March en los sonetos-prólogo amorosos del siglo de oro", *Homenajes. Estudios de filología española*, 1 (1964), 57–75

———, *Sobre Marino y España* (Madrid: Editora Nacional, 1978)

Ruano de la Haza, José M., "Dos censores de comedias de mediados del siglo XVII", in *Estudios sobre Calderón y el teatro de la edad de oro: Homenaje a Kurt y Roswitha Reichenberger*, ed. by Franciso Mundi Pedret (Barcelona: PPU, 1989), pp. 201–29

Russell, Peter E., *Temas de "La Celestina" y otros estudios. Del "Cid" al "Quijote"* (Barcelona: Editorial Ariel, 1978)

Sánchez, José, *Academias literarias del Siglo de Oro español* (Madrid: Gredos, 1961)

Sánchez Escribano, Federico, and Alberto Porqueras Mayo, *Preceptiva dramática española del renacimiento y el barroco*, 2nd edn (Madrid: Gredos, 1972)

Santo, Elsa Leonor di, "Noticias sobre la vida de Juan de Matos Fragoso", *Segismundo*, 14 (1978–80), 217–31

Serís, Homero, *Nuevo ensayo de una biblioteca española de libros raros y curiosos* (New York: Hispanic Society of America, 1964), I, pp. 5–30

———, "Un certamen poco conocido del siglo XVII: Remón y López Remón", in *Studies in Honor of M. J. Benardete (Essays in Hispanic and Sephardic Culture)*, ed. by Izaak A. Langnas and Barton Sholod (New York: Las Americas Publishing Company, 1965), pp. 127–41

Serralta, Frédéric, "Román Montero de Espinosa, escritor del XVII: apostillas biográficas", *Criticón*, 28 (1984), 119–35

———, "Nueva biografía de Antonio de Solís y Rivadenyra", *Criticón*, 34 (1986), 51–157.

Shergold, N. D. *A History of the Spanish Stage from Medieval Times until the End of the Seventeenth Century* (Oxford: Clarendon Press, 1967)

Simón Díaz, José, *Bibliografia de la literatura hispánica*, vol. 1– (Madrid: CSIC, 1950–)

———, *Siglos de oro: Indice de justas poéticas* (Madrid: CSIC, 1962)

———, "Las 'Exequias reales' de Gaspar Dávila", *RL*, 25 (1964), 121–23

———, "Primer índice de publicaciones poéticas del siglo XVII", *RL*, 27 (1965), 144–96

———, "Censo de escritores al servicio de los Austrias", in *Censo de escritores al servicio de los Austrias y otros estudios bibliográficos* (Madrid: CSIC, 1983), pp. 7–32.

Smith, A. J., *The Metaphysics of Love. Studies in Renaissance love poetry from Dante to Milton* (Cambridge: Cambridge University Press, 1985)

———, *Metaphysical Wit* (Cambridge: Cambridge University Press, 1991)

Smith, Barbara Hernstein, *Poetic Closure. A Study of How Poems End* (Chicago and London: University of Chicago, 1968)

Smith, Paul Julian, *Quevedo on Parnassus: Allusive Context and Literary Theory in the Love-Lyric* (London: The Modern Humanities Research Association, 1987)

———, *Writing in the Margin. Spanish Literature of the Golden Age* (Oxford: Clarendon Press, 1988)

Soons, Alan, *Alonso de Castillo Solórzano* (Boston, Twayne Publishers, 1978)

Soria Olmedo, Andrés, " 'Fuegos de amor abrasan mis escritos': La conciencia literaria en el 'Desengaño de amor en rimas' ", in *Al Ave el Vuelo. Estudios sobre la obra de Soto de Rojas* (Granada: Universidad de Granada, 1984), pp. 139–57

Stradling, R. A., *Philip IV and the Government of Spain, 1621–1665* (Cambridge: Cambridge University Press, 1988)

Suárez Alvarez, Jaime, "Los inéditos estatutos de 'La Peregrina', academia fundada y presidida por el Doctor Don Sebastián Francisco Medrano", *RBAM*, 16 (1947), 91–110

Terry, Arthur, "Quevedo and the Metaphysical Conceit", *BHS*, 35 (1958), 211–22

———, *Seventeenth-Century Spanish Poetry: The Power of Artifice* (Cambridge: Cambridge University Press, 1993)

Thompson, I. A. A., "The Nobility in Spain, 1600–1800", in *The European Nobilities in the Seventeenth and Eighteenth Centuries*, ed. by H. M. Scott, 2 vols (London: Longman, 1995), I, pp. 174–236

Trueblood, Alan S., *Letter and Spirit in Hispanic Writers: Renaissance to Civil War. Selected Essays* (London: Tamesis, 1986)

Tuve, Rosemund, *Elizabethan and Metaphysical Imagery* (Chicago and London: University of Chicago Press, 1947)

Varey, John E., "Calderón, Cosme Lotti, Velázquez, and the Madrid Festivities of 1636–37", *Renaissance Drama*, New Series I (1968), 253–82.

———, "An Additional Note on Pedro de Arce", *Iberoromania*, 23 (1986), 204–09

———, and N. D. Shergold, "Datos históricos sobre los primeros teatros de Madrid: prohibiciones de autos y comedias y sus consecuencias (1644–1651)", *BH*, 62 (1960), 286–324

Vickers, Brian, *In Defence of Rhetoric* (Oxford: Clarendon Press, 1989)

Waller, Marguerite R., *Petrarch's Poetics and Literary History* (Amherst: University of Massachusetts Press, 1980)

Whinnom, Keith, "The Problem of the 'Best-Seller' in Spanish Golden Age Literature", *BHS*, 57 (1980), 189–98

———, *La poesía amatoria de la época de los Reyes Católicos* (Durham: University of Durham, 1981)

Wickersham Crawford, J. P., "Some Unpublished Verses of Lope de Vega", *RH*, 19 (1908), 455–65

Williamson, Vern G., *The Minor Dramatists of Seventeenth-Century Spain* (Boston: Twayne, 1982)

Wilson, E. M., "Calderón and the Stage-Censor in the Seventeenth-Century. A Provisional Study", *Symposium*, 15 (1961), 165–84

———, "La estética de don García de Salcedo Coronel y la poesía española del s.XVII", *RFE*, 44 (1961), 1–27

———, "Calderón's Enemy: Don Antonio Sigler de Huerta", *MLN*, 81 (1966), 225–31

———, *Entre las jarchas y Cernuda. Constantes y variables en la poesía española* (Barcelona: Editorial Ariel, 1977)

Yates, Frances A., *The French Academies of the Sixteenth Century* (London: Warburg Institute, 1947)

INDEX

Citations are to the main text only, except where a footnote carries important information. In the case of accounts of individual academies, however, I have listed every citation both in the body of the text and in the footnotes so that a comprehensive overview of their output can rapidly be formed. The abbreviated title of each academy is as given in the list of Works Consulted.

Academies 7–17
   Academia burlesca 13n, 28, 34, 36, 39, 51–52, 58, 93n, 121n
   Academia Castellana 25
   Academia de Huesca 15
   Academia de Madrid 8, 15, 16n, 17, 18, 19, 24–29, 32–33, 34, 37, 39–43, 48, 49, 51, 84n, 87, 121n, 122n
   Academia de los Nocturnos 4, 9n, 15, 30n, 32, 55, 74n
   Academia a Nuestra Señora de los Desamparados y San Javier 121; see also *Poética festiva*
   Academia peregrina 8, 9
   Academia del Prado 22
   Academia de Salamanca 19
   Academia Selvaje 25, 33
   Accademia della Crusca 18–19
   Accademia degli Oziosi 29
   Badajoz 64n, 79n, 81n, 118n, 126n
   Buen Retiro Academy (1638) 11, 12–13, 120
   Carnestolendas 74n, 79n
   Católica acción 55–58
   Ciudad Real 11–12, 53–54, 76n, 78n, 81n, 90, 115n, 119n, 128n, 147n, 162n
   Fonseca de Almeida, academies of 33–43, 44, 46, 71
      Fonseca Jan 1661 90n, 93n
      Fonseca Feb 1661 83n
      Fonseca Jan 1662 35n, 42n, 50, 121n
      Fonseca April 1662 16n, 35n, 67n, 70n, 91n, 93n, 94n, 116n
      Fonseca Jan 1663 35n, 71n
      Fonseca Feb 1663 67n, 72n, 110n, 118n, 124n, 164n
      Jardín 40n, 41n, 74n, 83n
      see also Melchor Fonseca de Almeida
   Granada 50
   Jamaica 12–13
   Pascua de Reyes 10n, 16n, 36, 61, 67n, 69n, 79n, 83n, 85, 89n, 91n, 113n, 149n, 158n
   Poética festiva 120–22; see also *Academia a Nuestra Señora de los Desamparados y San Javier*
   Real Academia 54, 61n, 120, 166n
   Real Aduana 2–3, 10n, 36, 67n, 79n, 83n, 84n, 90n, 126n, 127n, 128n, 143n, 150n, 158n, 161n
   Repetida carrera 70n, 71n, 79n, 83n, 93n, 125n, 145n
   Señoras 69–70, 157n
   Seville 78n
   Sol de academias 16, 30n, 32n, 42n, 64n, 67n, 72n, 78n, 79n, 83n, 125n, 130n, 156n
   Valencia, Real Palacio 70n, 79n, 83n, 90n, 93n
   see also *justas poéticas*; patronage; *vejamen*; women
Acuña, Hernando de 106
Aguilar, Gaspar 15
Alva, Cristóbal de 146

Andrade, Count of 29–30
Androsilla Larramendi, Juan de 26n
Aquilano, Serafino 63, 97
Aranda, Count of 30
Arce y Tofiño, Pedro Ignacio de 41
Avellaneda, Francisco de 41
Baena, Juan Alfonso de 93
Balda, Hernando de 15
Baltasar Carlos, Prince, son of Philip IV 47
Bances Candamo, Francisco 40
Batres, Alfonso de 51
Benavente, Luis de 26, 28
Blanquer, Vicente 121
Bocaccio, Giovanni 94–95
Bocángel, Gabriel 4, 15, 26, 27, 40, 41, 91, 93, 105, 106, 162n
Bonifaz, Gaspar 51
Borja y Aragón, Francisco de see under Esquilache
Boscán, Juan 98–99, 102, 105, 106
Buñol, Count of 15
Bustos, Francisco de 55
Calatayud, Francisco de 51
Calderón de la Barca, Pedro 26, 28, 95, 99, 120
Calero, Francisco 52
Camerino, José 14, 15, 91n
Cáncer y Velasco, Jerónimo 25, 159–62
cancionero 59, 61, 73, 86–87, 92, 93–94, 95, 96, 97, 108
Cañizares, Marquis of 30
Carbonel, Alonso de 51
Cardona, Antonio de 31–32
Carillo y Sotomayor, Luis 44
Cariteo, Benedetto 97
Castel Rodrigo, Marquis of 121
Castiglione, Baldassare 98–99
Castillo, Felipe Bernardo del 26n
Castillo, Hernando del 95
Castillo Solórzano, Alonso de 12, 14, 17, 26, 27, 40, 77–78, 84n, 93
Castro y Bellvís, Guillén de 26n, 48
Catalán, Bernardo 15
Cervantes, Miguel de 14n, 29
Cetina, Gutierre de 118
Charles II, King of Spain 35, 38, 42, 47, 50, 54, 55
conceptismo 45n, 85, 96–97, 136, 138, 143, 147, 151–52, 169, 170–71
Corral, Gabriel de 14, 15, 26, 27
Cortizos de Villasante, Manuel de 34

Covarrubias y Leyva, Diego de 51–52
Cruzate, Sebastiana 147, 161
Cubillo de Aragón, Alvaro 41, 101, 111
Cuéllar, Jerónimo de 36, 37, 38
culteranismo 9, 44, 45, 48, 77, 136
Dávila, Gaspar 26n, 28
Díaz Jurado, José 118
Díez y Foncalda, Alberto 30
discreto / vulgo 43–45, 99
Duque de Estrada, Diego 14
Enciso, Diego Jiménez de 26n
Enciso y Velasco, Diego de 35
Enríquez Gómez, Antonio 14
epigram / epigrammatic style 49, 126, 135, 137, 140–41, 143, 151–54, 156n, 157, 162, 169–70, 171
Espinosa, Antonio de 36
Esquilache, Prince of, Francisco de Borja y Aragón 26, 28, 30, 51, 106
Felipe Próspero, Prince, son of Philip IV 38, 47, 50
Ferdinand III, Emperor and King of Hungary 28, 51
Feria, Duke of 25
Ficino, Marsilio 7
Figueroa y Córdoba, Diego de 41
Figueroa y Córdoba, José de 41
Figuerola, Francisco 121
Flores, Manuel de 142
Fonseca de Almeida, Melchor 33, 34–35, 36
Freire de Andrade, Manuel 67
Freire de Andrade, Mateo 38, 163
Garcilaso de la Vega 8, 99, 102
Góngora y Argote, Luis de 4, 26, 29, 44, 48, 102, 108, 136, 137, 160, 162, 168, 171
Gracián, Baltasar 4, 61, 65, 95, 136–42, 151, 154, 165, 167
Guillén de la Carrera, Juan Alonso 35, 36, 38
Haro, Luis Méndez de 51
Herrera, Fernando de 8, 62, 102, 105, 136
Herrera, Rodrigo de 26n
Híjar, Duke of 29, 30
Hurtado de Mendoza, Antonio 4, 12, 23, 25, 26, 28, 51, 97
intertextuality 162–65
justas poéticas 3n, 10, 17, 41, 42, 43, 47–50, 52–54
Ledesma, José de 35

Lemos, Count of   14, 29
Leonardo de Argensola, Lupercio   29
Leonardo de Argensola, Bartolomé   29
Lerma, Duke of, Francisco Gomez de
    Sandoval y Rojas   24, 25, 29
Lezcano, Francisco de   84
López de Aguilar, Francisco   26n
López de Zárate, Francisco   26, 36
Lotti, Cosme   12–13, 120
Mal Lara, Juan de   8
María Margarita Catalina, Princess,
    daughter of Philip IV   49
Marino, Giambattista   63, 73, 97–98
Martínez de Grimaldo, José   52
Matos Fragoso, Juan de   40, 41
Medici, Cosimo de'   7
Medina, Francisco de   8
Medina, Gaspar de   111, 113
Medina-Sidonia, Duke of   38
Medinaceli, Duke of   29
Medrano, Sebastián Francisco de   8, 16,
    25, 26, 29, 48
Méndez de Loyola, Pedro   28, 87, 94
Mendoza, Francisco de   25, 26n, 27, 39
Mesa, Cristóbal de   26n
metatextuality   102, 119–20, 123, 126,
    128, 133–34, 156, 161–62; *see
    also* orality
Mexía, Juan   28
Mira de Amescua, Antonio   26, 48
Miravet del Castillo, José   124
Moncayo y Gurrea, Juan de   30
Monleón y Cortés, Bernardo de   35
Montenegro y Neira, Juan de   35
Montero de Espinosa, Román   35, 36,
    37–38, 39
Monterrey, Count of   25
Montoro, Antón de   73, 92, 95n
Morales, Francisco   144
Muñiz Delgado, Felipe   114–15, 128n,
    162n
Navarro, José   30, 152
Nieto, Luis   16, 35, 36, 37, 126
Olivares, Count-Duke of, Gaspar de
    Guzmán   24, 25, 29, 33
Olivares Vadillo, Sebastián de   36, 37
Olivenza, Juan de   35, 36
orality, and oral performance of poems
    11, 12, 17, 21, 86, 100, 110,
    116, 118, 119, 122, 135–36,
    162, 169–70; *see also*
    metatextuality

Ortí, José   121
Orts, Jaime   15
Ossera, Marquis of   30
Oviedo, Alonso de   15
Oviedo y Herrera, Luis Antonio de   35,
    37, 38, 39
Oviedo y Herrera, Pedro de   36
Pacheco, Francisco (uncle and nephew)   8
Pallás, Antonio   121
Pantaleón de Ribera, Anastasio   15n, 18,
    27–28, 49
Paredes, Count of   54
Pastrana, Duke of   25
patronage, of academies by nobility
    28–33, 41–42
Pellicer y Tovar, José de   9, 15, 17–20,
    21, 24, 26, 27, 28, 40, 42
Pellicer de Tovar, Juan   109
Penarroia, Gaspar   129–32
Pérez de Montalbán, Juan   26
Petrarch   62–63, 64, 66, 75, 104, 105, 106
petrarchism   3, 53, 58, 59, 60, 62, 71,
    72–73, 79–80, 82, 83, 85, 90,
    93, 96–99, 102, 103–10, 113,
    115–16, 132–34, 162, 171–72
Philip III, King of Spain   24
Philip IV, King of Spain   24, 29, 31, 33,
    34, 38, 47, 48, 51, 53, 54–55, 95
Pinel y Monroy, Francisco   35, 36, 38
Polo de Medina, Salvador Jacinto   14,
    81–82, 85, 86, 124
Pons, Jaime   155
Porter y Casanate, Juan José   35, 36, 38
Portocarrero de la Vega, Antonio   51
Quevedo y Villegas, Francisco de   4, 26,
    73, 80, 84n, 102, 105, 108, 136,
    137, 168, 171
Quintana, Francisco de   26n, 48
Rader, Matthäeus   151
refundiciones   99, 162
Reinalte, José   36, 38
relaciones de sucesos   44, 76n
Rioja, Francisco de   51, 107
Roa, Gabriel de   26n
Rodríguez Carrión Ponce de León,
    Gaspar   149
Rojas Zorrilla, Francisco de   11, 51
Ruiz de Alarcón, Juan   26
Salas Barbadillo, Alonso Jerónimo de
    26, 27, 40
Salazar y Torres, Agustín de   40–41, 88
Salcedo Coronel, García de   22

Saldaña, Count of   11, 25, 28, 33, 78
Salinas, Count of, Diego de Silva y Mendoza   4, 29, 62, 97
Salinas, Juan de   84n
Sarasa y Arce, Fermín de   36, 38–39, 125
Serrano de la Paz, Manuel   48
Shakespeare, William   132
Sigler de Huerta, Antonio   28
Silva, Francisco de   25
Silva y Mendoza, Diego de   *see under* Salinas, Count of
Silveira, Miguel de   26n
Solís y Rivadeneira, Antonio de   19, 40, 158
Soto de Rojas, Pedro   11, 25, 105, 106–07
Sotomayor, Diego de   36
Suárez de Deza y Avila, Vicente   35, 37, 38
Súarez de Figueroa, Cristóbal   49
Tassis y Peralta, Juan de   *see under* Villamediana
Tasso, Torquato   66–67, 97
Tebaldeo, Antonio   97
Tesauro, Emmanuele   137
Tirso de Molina   26
Torre y Sevil, Francisco de la   30, 40
Torre, Juan de la   165, 167–70
Torres Granero, Pedro de   123
Torres, Marquis of   30
Trillo y Figueroa, Francisco de   106

Ulloa y Pereira, Luis de   65–66, 69, 91–92
Uztarroz, Andrés de   30
Valdivieso, José de   26
Valterra, Pedro   121
Vargas Machuca, Pedro   26n
Vega Carpio, Lope Félix de   4, 25, 26, 48, 71–72, 78, 102, 105, 130
vejamen   10–11, 13, 16, 25, 27, 31–32, 35, 51, 55, 121, 156
Velada, Marquis of   29
Vélez de Guevara, Juan   40
Vélez de Guevara, Luis   11, 12, 14, 25, 26, 27, 28, 40, 51
Vera y Villarroel, Juan de   127
Vergara Salcedo, Sebastián Ventura de   35, 37, 38, 116
Villaizán, José de   26n
Villamediana, Count of, Juan de Tassis y Peralta   4, 29, 62, 106
Villanueva, Matías Diego de   36
Villatorcas, Marquis of   30
Villegas, Diego de   26n, 48
wit   *see under conceptismo, culteranismo,* epigram, Gracián
women, place of in academies   3n, 12, 16–17, 35
Zabaleta, Juan de   20–22, 76–77, 78
Zamora, Antonio de   40
Zárate y la Hoz, Alonso de   35, 38, 39